THE DRUIDS

THE DRUIDS

Peter Berresford Ellis

WILLIAM B. EERDMANS PUBLISHING COMPANY
GRAND RAPIDS, MICHIGAN

© 1994 Peter Berresford Ellis

First published in Great Britain 1994 by
Constable and Company Limited
3 The Lanchesters, 162 Fulham Palace Road
London W6 9ER

This edition published in the United States of America 1995
through special arrangement with Constable by
Wm. B. Eerdmans Publishing Co.
255 Jefferson Ave. S.E., Grand Rapids, Michigan 49503
All rights reserved

Printed in the United States of America

00 99 98 97 96 95   7 6 5 4 3 2 1

ISBN 0-8028-3798-0

This book would not have been written had it not been for the inspiration caused by a Sunday afternoon's radio broadcast of Vincenzo Bellini's opera 'Norma'. Thank you, Ben, for that happy inspiration.

Contents

I am the Wind that blows across the Sea;
I am the Wave of the Ocean;
I am the Murmur of the Billows;
I am the Bull of the Seven Combats;
I am the Vulture on the Rock:
I am a Ray of the Sun;
I am the Fairest of Flowers:
I am a Wild Boar in Valour;
I am a Salmon in the Pool;
I am a Lake on the Plain;
I am the Skill of the Craftsman;
I am a Word of Science;
I am the Spear-point that gives Battle;
I am the god who creates in the head of man the Fire of Thought.
Who is it that Enlightens the Assembly upon the mountain, if not I?
Who tells the ages of the moon, if not I?
Who shows the place where the sun goes to rest, if not I?
Who calls the cattle from the House of Tethra?
On whom do the cattle of Tethra smile?
Who is the god that fashions enchantments —
— the enchantment of battle and the wind of change?

The Song of Amairgen
Leabhar Gabhála

Illustrations

Introduction

Identifying the Druids

IF this were an academic dissertation, I would probably choose the subtitle 'An introductory argument'. The French anthropologist, Claude Lévi-Strauss, once said: 'There are no final truths. The scientific mind does not so much provide the right answers as ask the right questions.' In no field is it more necessary to ask the right questions than when attempting to discover the Druids. The simple truth is that one person's Druid is another person's fantasy. The Druids have been conjured in a wide variety of perceptions, as to who they were, what they believed and what they taught, since the sixteenth century. The basic problem is that no Druid, nor sympathetic contemporary observer, ever committed to writing the necessary unequivocal information for our latter-day understanding. We have to search diligently among many sources to come up with our answers and, as Lévi-Strauss implies, the result of the search depends on what questions we ask.

In spite of several references to Druids in Greek and Latin writings and in spite of the traditions recorded in the native Celtic literatures, we are still far from being absolutely knowledgeable.

It is true that we possess a few respectful Greek sources; but the bulk of the 'Classical' observations consist of the anti-Celtic propaganda of the Roman Empire. There has been a tendency for scholars to accept these sources as giving us facts writ in stone which are not to be questioned. By the time the Celts themselves came to commit their knowledge to writing, they had become Christianized and, not surprisingly, the Druids continued to get 'a bad Press'. Their portrayal remains an extremely biased one. And when some of the 'gentlemen antiquarians' of the seventeenth and eighteenth centuries felt that they could see the Druids in a more sympathetic light, they romanticized them out of all recognition to what their rôle in Celtic society originally was.

Most people these days would be able to make some response if asked to define a Druid. In fact, the Druids have achieved something of a unique place in the folklore of Western Europe and its New World offshoots. They captured the imagination of the ancient world as no other group of people ever did and they still have a tremendous impact on the esoteric life of the modern world. The Celtic scholar, Nora Chadwick, has commented: 'The fascination of the subject is everlasting.' Apart from a vague acknowledgement that the Druids were the intellectual class of the ancient Celts, they are usually perceived as variations of religious mystics and priests.

Many will remember being taught at school that the Romans saw the Druids as bizarre, barbaric priests who indulged in the most horrendous human sacrifices, searching for auguries in the entrails of their victims. According to others, they were simply ancient patriarchal religious mystics, generally portrayed in white robes and beards, who worshipped nature, particularly trees, and who gathered in stone circles to perform their religious rites at the time of the solstice. To some they were powerful magicians and soothsayers. To others merely bards and prophets. How many would immediately conjure Merlin of Arthurian Saga fame as the archetypal Druid? No doubt a good many modern children would see the Druid through the eyes of Goscinny and Underzo, in *Astérix le Gaulois*, where the character of the Druid is known in the English translations as 'Getafix', originally Panoramix, supplying magic potions from his mystical cauldron.

Those readers who have encountered Celtic mythology, and the early sagas of Ireland and Wales, will know that the Druids are depicted as an all-powerful and essential element in society. By Christian times they had, more or less, been reduced to the status of wizards and soothsayers.

Others will associate the Druids as something to do with the re-creation of the Welsh, Breton and Cornish *Gorseddau* and the romantic movement of the late eighteenth century. The robed figure of the ArchDruid of Wales is now an easily recognizable one, thanks to the press and media coverage of the Gorsedd ceremonies – particularly the Welsh Gorsedd – as part of the National Eisteddfod.

However, in England, people popularly associate Druids with earnest looking, white-robed men and women who continue to hold mystic ceremonies at the time of the summer solstice in stone circles such as Stonehenge and even at such sites as Parliament Hill or Tower

Hill in London. Indeed, there still exist descendant groups of the Ancient Order of Druids formed by enthusiasts in London in 1781. Sir Winston Churchill was initiated into the Albion Lodge of the Order in 1908. These gatherings, of course, have nothing to do with Celtic culture, ancient or modern, and the 'mystic' incantations of these particular Druids, to the sun and pagan deities, are chanted in English.

Indeed, Druids have also been hijacked by the 'New Age' movement and conjured to their philosophies. An offering which has been reprinted several times now, *The Mind of the Druid*, by Dr E. Graham Howe, has a foreword by David Loxley, claiming to be 'Chief Druid of the Druid Order'. Again, this work has absolutely nothing to do with ancient Celtic philosophy, but, sadly, Druids are commercially acceptable in the new wave of esoterica and alternative religious thought. Any half-baked philosophy can have the word 'Druid' or even 'Celtic' attached to it and be assured of an enthusiastic, if somewhat gullible, following.

The first problem, then, is – who is right in their perception of the Druids? The simple answer is rather like the logic found in *Alice in Wonderland*. Everyone is wrong but everyone has glimpsed a tiny part of the reality, so everyone is right and we all get a prize!

Readers will recall the story of the blind men being asked to define an elephant by touch. One, feeling a leg, claimed that the elephant was like a tree; another, feeling its trunk, claimed it was like a snake, yet a third, feeling an ear, thought the elephant was a large winged creature and so on and so forth. This is precisely what has been happening over the last three hundred years in the case of the Druids. Definitions are derived from small items of knowledge and no one seems to have perceived a totality of information to give an accurate picture of who they were and why they have survived into our modern folklore.

This work, which is an attempt to present the Druids to a general readership, sets out to demonstrate the rôle of the Druids in ancient Celtic society; what we know of their teachings, and how they imparted their knowledge without the aid of writing. This oral tradition existed not because they had no knowledge of the art of writing but because they placed a religious prohibition on committing their knowledge to that form, in order that such knowledge should not fall into the wrong hands. It thus took between twelve and twenty years of study to reach the highest level of learning among them.

This prohibition on committing their knowledge and philosophy to writing has been a great stumbling block for modern scholars attempting to understand exactly what they believed and taught; that, combined with the periodic destruction of native Celtic books and manuscripts by conquering forces. Indeed, it is argued that when the Celtic civilization first became known to the Greeks, the Greeks called them the *Keltoi*, which was a Celtic word used to describe themselves meaning 'the hidden people'. Celt is seen by some linguists as being cognate with the Old Irish *ceilid*, used in Modern Irish as *ceilt* – to hide or conceal. It is also argued that the word *kilt*, entering English in about 1730 from Scottish Gaelic, meaning the distinctive short skirt of male Celtic dress, comes from this same root word. However, it should be pointed out that others have contended that the word *kilt* derived from the Scandinavian languages, *kilte* meaning 'to tuck up'. This latter derivation seems a little too plausible.

The Druids were no simple barbaric priests or priestesses. Indeed, nothing in the accounts really suggests a priesthood nor does any Classical writer call them priests or *sacerdotes*. This is not to say that some Druids were not called upon to oversee religious functions. I would suggest, as many other scholars in this area have now done, that the Druids were the parallel caste to the social group which developed in another Indo-European society – the Brahmins of the Hindu culture. They formed the intellectuals, or learned class, of Hindu society and were deemed the highest caste. While they had a priestly function, they were not solely priests. So, too, with the Druids; they were a caste incorporating all the learned professions. The caste not only consisted of those who had a religious function but also comprised philosophers, judges, teachers, historians, poets, musicians, physicians, astronomers, prophets and political advisers or counsellors. Druids could sometimes be kings or chieftains, such as Divitiacus of the Aedui, but not all kings were necessarily Druids.

Our earliest and most extensive sources, as I have pointed out, are from Greek and Roman writers. In other words, from writers alien and often extremely hostile to Celtic culture. Significantly, the Greek sources are generally more respectful to the Druids, particularly the Alexandrian School of writers, while the Latin sources are universally hostile. Yet, as I have said, these sources have, in the main, been accepted without question even by scholars who are usually more critical of source material. Imagine, the culture and history of the American Indians from the perceptions of nineteenth century white American settlers being accepted without question. What a curious, prejudiced view we would have of the Native Americans.

Imagine, too, the commander of a foreign army which has been sent to conquer and destroy a people then writing a book about the culture and customs of those people and it being regarded by subsequent generations as written totally without prejudice. Yet we are asked to accept Julius Caesar's accounts of the Celts and Druids as totally accurate. Had General, Lord Chelmsford, written an account of the culture and philosophies of the Zulu nation, following his conquest of Zululand in 1879, we might have had some reservations in accepting everything he wrote as being without prejudice. Yet many would have us believe that the passage of time makes for unquestioning accuracy. We can accept that Chelmsford would very likely have been prejudiced, but that Julius Caesar's comments on the Celtic civilization and the Druids are beyond reproach. This is not to say that Caesar *was* totally inaccurate to the point where he should be dismissed. Indeed, from native Celtic sources, we can confirm several of his observations. We should question everything, especially if it comes from sources hostile to Celtic civilization. The cultural prejudice of both the Greek and Roman sources must be taken into account when they speak of matters pertaining to a culture they generally deemed as barbaric or inferior.

When Christianity replaced the pre-Christian Celtic religion and the Druidic proscription on writing down the native history and philosophy was ended, the Celts poured out a wealth of literature. Indeed, Irish became Europe's third written language. From early Irish and Welsh sources there are many references to the Druids and, in a few places, they do confirm some of the information found in Greek and Roman sources.

What emerges from a close study of the sources is that the commonly held belief, that the Romans attempted a widespread repression of the Druids because they were horrified by Druidic priestly practices, is no more than a conjecture which has become an accepted historical myth. There is, indeed, evidence that the Romans attempted to abolish the Druidic caste although Nora Chadwick argues that the attempt was not as widespread as later historians would have us believe. Certainly such an attempt was not the result of Roman sensitivities about the religious rites practised by the Celts. As an intellectual class, the repository of Gaulish and British cultural and national resistance to Roman conquest, it would be inevitable that Rome would attempt to suppress them. It is a traditional imperialist maxim that to conquer a nation you must first subvert or remove the class which is most dangerous to your objectives, that is – the intellectuals.

Professor Jean Markle, in his *La Femme Celte* (1972) makes the following argument as to why the Romans attempted to suppress the Druids:

> When Rome spread its empire over the whole Mediterranean and into part of Western Europe, care was taken to eliminate anything that might harm its socio-political organisation. This is very evident in Celtic countries: the Romans pursued the Druids until they disappeared into Gaul and later into Britain. The Druids represented an absolute threat to the Roman State, because their science and philosophy dangerously contradicted Roman orthodoxy. The Romans were materialistic, the Druids spiritual. For the Romans the State was a monolithic structure spread over territories deliberately organised into a hierarchy. With the Druids it was a freely consented moral order with an entirely mythical central idea. The Romans based their law on private ownership of land, with property rights entirely vested in the head of the family, whereas the Druids always considered ownership collective. The Romans looked upon women as bearers of children and objects of pleasure, while the Druids included women in their political and religious life. We can thus understand how seriously the subversive thought of the Celts threatened the Roman order, even though it was never openly expressed. The talent of the Romans in ridding themselves of the Gallic and British élites is always considered astonishing, but this leaves out of account the fact that it was a matter of life or death to Roman society.

Pliny the Elder (AD 23/24–79) seems to be the first to raise questions about the reasons for the decline of the Druids and certainly has no hesitation in attributing it to Roman repression. Yet one cannot really take seriously the claim that this was done because of Roman outrage against a religion they associated with human sacrifice when

Rome itself was so used to mass sacrifices. Eminent men from the nations that Rome had conquered were dragged though the streets, chained to the chariots of her victorious generals, and ritually strangled in the Tullianum at the foot of the Capitol to propitiate Mars, the Roman god of war. Vercingetorix, the famous leader of Celtic resistance to Caesar in Gaul, met his end here. It can hardly be believed that the Romans, especially during the reigns of such emperors as Caligula and Nero, could be shocked by human sacrifice. It is only the Romans, of course, who would have us believe in their sensitivity to human sacrifice. The curious fact is that no Insular Celtic literature, nor traditions, provides evidence for the practice of human sacrifice as a religious rite.

When Augustus excluded the Druids from Roman citizenship by forbidding Roman citizens to practise Druidical rites, when Tiberius banned the Druids by a decree of the Roman Senate and when Claudius attempted to 'wholly abolish' them in AD 54, it was not, I believe, in disapproval of 'inhuman rites' practised by the Druids, but to wipe out an intellectual class who could, and did, organize national revolt against Rome.

Further, my argument is that the Druids were not entirely suppressed in the Celtic lands under Roman rule as is commonly thought. Nor would I accept Nora Chadwick's contention that they perished by slow strangulation from the superimposition 'of a higher culture on a lower'. Mrs Chadwick, for example, claims that when the inhabitants of the chief town of the Aedui in Gaul, that is Bibracte (Mont-Beuvray), were transferred to the new Roman town of Augustodunum (Autun), and their oral Druidical school was replaced by a Romanized university, the Druids were driven into the backwoods where they eventually perished. On the contrary, I believe that the Druids remained and adapted to the new culture.

The great Gaulish intellectual Decimus Magnus Ausonius (c.AD 310–c.393) provides us with some fascinating evidence in this respect. He was the son of a physician of Burdigala (Bordeaux) where he taught for thirty years before being appointed as tutor to Gratian, son of the Emperor Valentinian I. When Gratian succeeded as emperor, Ausonius became prefect of Gaul and finally consul in AD 379. He was nominally Christian, but without any deeply committed feeling. He wrote one discourse on the properties of the number *three*, so closely associated with Druidic teachings. Ausonius came from an educated Celtic family which would have been of the Druidic caste before Roman proscription.

Ausonius himself admits that his contemporary Delphidius, famous for his eloquence, and a likely teacher of his, also descended from a Druidic family. Delphidius' father was Attius Patera, a famous rhetorician, whose own father, Phoebicius, had been an *aedituus* or 'temple guardian' of the Celtic god Belenus at Bordeaux until he had been persuaded to become a teacher in the local Latin university.

Ausonius' own maternal grandfather was banished by Victricius, the Roman bishop of Rouen (*c.*AD 330–*c.*407), with the two local chieftains, to Tabellae (Dax) on the Adour for taking part in an insurrection of the Aedui. In *Parentalia*, Ausonius also tells us that his maternal grandfather practised astrology in secret and implies that he was from a Druidic family. Victricius was an ex-Roman soldier who converted to Christianity while he was still serving and stationed in Gaul. He was an implacable opponent of 'Pelagianism', which Rome claimed to be an attempt to revive the concepts of Druidism. And, most interesting of all, Ausonius had an aunt called Dryadia which means 'Druidess'.

With the arrival of Christianity, the Druids began to merge totally with the new culture, some even becoming priests of the new religion and continuing as an intellectual class in much the same way as their forefathers had done for over a thousand years previously. We find an interesting reference in a *Life of Colmcille* that, when the Irish missionary arrived on the island of Iona, he encountered two Druids who were bishops and who claimed that they had already planted the Christian faith there. Colmcille did not believe that they had been properly ordained and ordered them to depart, which they did. Many early Celtic Christian saints were referred to as 'Druids'. According to the earliest known surviving biography of a British Celtic saint, written about the end of the sixth century AD, *A Life of Samson*, Samson's teacher, the famous Illtyd (*c.*AD 425–505) was 'by descent a most wise Druid'. In the life of the seventh century AD British Celtic saint Beuno (which survives in a manuscript written in 1346) we are told that his last words, as he lay dying, were that he saw the Holy Trinity and the saints *and Druids*. Beuno was the father of St Gwenfrewi, more popularly known as Winifred of Gwytherin in Denbigh.

The late fourth, early fifth century AD, Celtic Christian theologian Pelagius, of whom Victricius so strongly disapproved, was eventually declared a heretic after his conflict with Augustine of Hippo. Pelagius was accused of attempting to revive Druidic philosophy on Nature and Free Will. Pelagius' argument was that human beings had free will, while Augustine believed in predestination. We hear how the Bishops of Rome despaired of the hold Pelagian philosophy had in the Celtic Church during subsequent centuries. This is not so surprising if such a philosophy was simply a centuries old cultural attitude passed down by generations of Druids. The ninth century AD Welsh historian, Nennius, says that when the Celtic king Vortigern was excommunicated by Germanus of Auxerre (c.AD 378–448) for adhering to the teachings of Pelagius, he invited twelve Druids to assist him in his councils. We shall consider the matter of Pelagianism in the discussion on the Druids as philosophers.

The father of St Brigid of Kildare was a Druid named Dubhthach who is often wrongly associated with Dubhthach Maccu Lugir, who taught Patrick about the Irish law system. Significantly, there were no recorded Christian martyrdoms in Ireland and, indeed, scarcely any among the other Celtic peoples. Those few martyrdoms which occurred in Britain, for example that of Alban in c.AD 287, were the result of antagonism among the Roman occupiers and not the native Celts. In Irish ecclesiastical records we have a comment on the extensive land holdings of converted Druids being granted by them to the Church. Adomnán's *Life of St Columba* certainly indicates that the Druids were regarded as belonging to the same class as the leaders of Celtic Christianity.

The adoption of Christianity in Ireland did not lead to the abolition of the Druids but simply to their transformation. Father Joe McVeigh, in his polemic work *Renewing the Irish Church: Towards an Irish Liberation Theology* (1993), points outs:

The first Christian missionaries to Ireland did not attempt a root and branch eradication of the Celtic Druidic tradition and beliefs. Instead, the new religion absorbed the holy mountains and the innumerable holy wells and gave them a Christian name. (It has been estimated that there were approximately 3,000 holy wells some of which, like Doon well in Donegal, remain in use.) This popular or vernacular religion, separate and distinct from the institutional hierarchical Church, has, from the outset, been a vibrant characteristic of Irish Christianity.

I believe that this transformation of the Druids occurred in other Celtic societies as well.

There is no support at all for Caesar's contention that in Celtic society 'the (ordinary) people are treated almost like slaves' and that only the Druids and the warrior class of Celtic society had any rights at all. No other observer goes so far as this, nor do the native sources indicate such a situation. Indeed, native sources demonstrate a contrary state of affairs. Again we encounter the bellicose propaganda of the conqueror attempting to find justification for his conquests. If the people are being treated like slaves by their own ruling class, then the logic is that their conquest is justified.

Druids were recognized by Irish law even after the introduction of Christianity. The civil law of Ireland was first known to have been codified in AD 438 as the *Senchas Mór*. The criminal law, contained in the *Book of Acaill*, was codified shortly afterwards. The Druids still had a place in these codices, which gives authority to the idea that they were not suppressed nor did they disappear with the onset of Christianity. Indeed, a Druid was entitled to a position in society although, so far as any religious practices were concerned, the *Bretha Crólige* puts the Druid on the same social level as a *cáinte* (satirist) or a *díberg* (brigand), and as a religious functionary the Druid was reduced to a sorcerer or prophet. Indeed, the Irish word *Druidecht* came to mean sorcery, magic or necromancy while the Welsh word *Derwydd* meant a prophet. So, with Christianity, the perception of the function of the Druid was already changing within Celtic society.

Under ancient Irish law the provision of sick maintenance, including curative treatment, attendance allowance and nourishing food, was made available to all who needed it. The Druids were 'entitled to sick maintenance (*othrus*) only at the level of the *bóaire* (literally, a cow-chieftain or local magistrate), *no matter how great his rank, privilege or other rights*'. It is obvious from this qualification that a Druid still attained to high rank. Indeed, as both the civil and criminal law code of Ireland survive in their completest form in the *Leabhar na hUidre* (Book of the Dun Cow) dating from the late eleventh or early twelfth centuries, it might be remarked that there had been no amendment of the laws relating to the Druids by that time. Two reasons can be argued: one, that the Druids still existed with a definite, if diminished, rôle in Irish society; two, that the Druids had vanished and so no one bothered to change the laws. A comparison here might be that it was not until 1951 that the English judicial system finally scrapped the medieval laws relating to the prohibition of witchcraft.

This work has been arranged in order to attempt the easiest presentation to the general reader. The initial chapters present the Celtic world to which the Druids belonged, together with their origins in that world. Next, we consider our sources concerning the Druids; firstly, how they were perceived through the foreign eyes of the Greeks and Romans, and secondly, how the Celts themselves, albeit Christianized Celts, perceived these influential figures in their national ancestry. The reader will note a heavy reliance on Irish sources. This is because there is a veritable treasure trove of Irish material which remains near to the original pre-Christian source.

Druids, of course, were both male and female and we shall examine some of the prominent female Druids or Druidesses.

In religious terms, just what did Druids believe, and what were their rituals? What we know from Classical and native sources, together with archaeological evidence, is presented together with an examination of the controversial matter of whether they did, or did not, practise the rite of human sacrifice.

Once again, relying on both Classical and native sources, we discuss the wisdom of the Druids in those areas of knowledge in which Classical sources claim the Druids had especial renown. We examine them, among their other occupations, as philosophers, judges, historians, physicians, seers, astrologers and magicians.

Finally, we examine how the Druids came to be 'revived' and have developed as part of our modern folklore.

This book, as I have stated at the beginning, is no more than a modest attempt at an introductory argument about the reality and the legend of the Druids. As Nora Chadwick has already stated, there can be no doubt that the Druids were the most enlightened and civilizing spiritual influence in prehistoric Europe. Yet in trying to recreate the historical reality of the Druids, myths of white bearded sages, of rites at the summer solstice in megaliths belonging to an earlier culture than the Celts, have developed into wild theories and speculations, to poetic romanticism and mystical dreaming and outright literary forgeries.

If, however, at the end of this work, the reader comes nearer to glimpsing even a little of the reality of what was once 'Druidism', then this book will have served its intended purpose.

[1]

The Celtic World

NORA Chadwick has pointed out that 'The Druids are the most advanced of all intellectual classes among the peoples of ancient Europe beyond the Greek and Roman world.' To what sort of society or world did they belong? What type of people did they represent?

By the time that the first Classical references to the Druids, or rather those which have survived, were being written, the Celts, who were the first European people north of the Alps to emerge into recorded history, were spread across Europe from Ireland and Britain in the west, as far east as the central plains of what is now Turkey; and from what is now Belgium in northern Europe, they were settled southward into the Iberian peninsula as far as Gades (Cadiz) and were also established south of the Alps, in northern Italy, with the Apennines constituting their main southern borders. But the first references to the Celtic people generally began to appear in Greek sources from the sixth and fifth centuries, almost four centuries before the first references to the Druids.

The Celts were a linguistic group, identified as speaking a language descended from the hypothetical common Indo-European from which all languages of Europe, with the exceptions of Finnish and Estonian, Hungarian (Magyar) and Basque, are said to have descended. Numerals provide the easiest way of showing a relationship between these languages. The English *one, two, three,* finds a parallel in the Irish *aon, dó, tri,* the Welsh *un, dau, tri,* the Greek *énas, duo, treis,* the Latin *unus, duo, tres* or the Russian *odin, dva, tri.* There is no relationship between such groups of numerals and the Basque *bat, bi, hirur* or the Finnish *yksi, kaksi, kolme.* Such comparisons of numerals are said to demonstrate that at some historical epoch all the peoples of Europe, with the exceptions already named, and indeed, Mesopotamia and northern India, descended from a common linguistic group. At some time in remote antiquity there is said to have existed an Indo-European parent language but such a language cannot be satisfactorily described nor ascribed to a specific period, though most scholars have argued for the third millennium BC in which to place its origin in the steppes of Southern Russia. Certainly, by the middle of the first millennium BC there was no memory or sense of a common ancestry between the Greeks and the Hindus. The Indo-European hypothesis is important to any study of the Celts and it is one to which we must return as a means of explaining the extraordinary parallels and similarities between the Celtic and Hindu cultures, occurring in the areas of language, law, religious attitudes and mythology, music and caste.

It must be borne in mind that the Celtic peoples are identified solely by their language and cultures, of which, of course, language is the highest form of cultural expression. As with the Indo-European parent, it is hypothesized that at one time, perhaps before the start of the first millennium BC, there existed a Common Celtic which divided into two distinct dialects. Henri Hubert has asserted that the oldest form of Celtic is Goidelic, or Gaelic, which spread to Spain and Portugal and also to the British Isles. Scholars such as Eoin MacNeill, Julius Pokorny, Sir John Rhŷs and Heinrich Wagner have suggested that these 'early Celts' were a minority Aryan (*aryas*, noble) military society who rode into Europe from the Russian steppes and imposed themselves and their language on the farming populations who were not Indo-European. This is by no means a generally accepted theory and scholars such as Myles Dillon propose alternative views which we will be studying later.

It is, however, accepted that Goidelic was the earliest form of Celtic spoken but that the Continental Celts then began to develop the form known as Brythonic from it, simplifying its case endings, losing the neuter gender and dual number, creating differentiations in matters of initial mutation and aspiration. This Brythonic form later spread to Britain where it displaced the earlier Goidelic form. It also remained on the Continent and is known to us as Gaulish, of which several texts and inscriptions have now been found. The main easily recognizable difference between the two forms is the substitution of P for Q in the Brythonic Group which has led scholars to label the groups as P- and Q-Celtic. The sound *qu* (*kw*) in Goidelic was replaced by *p*. An easy example being the word ma*c* (meaning son) in Goidelic, which becomes ma*p* in Brythonic, or *c*eann (meaning head in Goidelic) which becomes *pen* in Brythonic. The modern day survivors of the ancient Celtic languages are Irish, Manx and Scottish Gaelic or Goidelic and Welsh, Cornish and Breton.

The earliest textual evidence of Continental Celtic dates from the third and second centuries BC, from funeral inscriptions, a couple of major texts recently discovered in southern France and northern Spain, and the famous Coligny Calendar. Together with such textual evidence are coupled place-names, and the recording of personal names and individual words by Greek and Latin authorities. Among the Insular Celts, an alphabet called Ogham was devised in Ireland. It survives mainly in inscription form, the main bulk of which, some 369 known inscriptions, date to the fifth and sixth centuries AD when the Irish, with the incoming of Christianity and the final dropping of religious prohibitions on committing their knowledge to writing, adopted the Latin alphabet and Irish then became the vehicle of Europe's third oldest literature. As Professor Máirtín Ó Murchú has pointed out: 'In Ireland there survive in Irish more extensive early records than for any other part of the Celtic world'. So it is to Ireland that we continually refer as a yardstick when judging the comments about the Celts made by non-Celtic observers.

Hecateus of Miletus (*c*.500–476 BC) and Herodotus of Halicarnassus (*c*.490–425 BC) were the first to record the existence of '*Keltoi*'. Their 'place of origin' was identified at the headwaters of the Danube, the Rhine and the Rhône, and archaeology would support this contention. It can be presumed with a fair degree of certainty that the Greeks, through their traders and colonizers, had first encountered the Celts when voyaging in the western Mediterranean. The great age of Greek colonization was from the mid-eighth to mid-sixth centuries BC. Around 600 BC colonizers from Phocaea, an Ionian Greek city, founded a colony called Massilia (Marseilles) within the Celtic territory of southern Gaul, east of the river Rhône. Tradition has it that the Phoenicians had established trading colonies on the Iberian peninsula about the same time as the Celts were flooding into that peninsula from the north, that is at about the start of the first millennium BC. But it is the Greeks again who left the first records of encounters with Iberian Celtic settlements, having colonized the coastal areas of Iberia in the seventh and sixth centuries BC. It was the Greeks of Phocaea again who established their colonies on the coast of what is now Spain.

By this time the Celts had been developing since the start of the first millennium BC. They had highly advanced weaponry, having learnt the art of smelting iron. Formidable axes, billhooks and other tools allowed the Celts to open up roadways through previously impenetrable north European forests. Not only did the new metal-working allow the Celts to become more mobile and to excel in farming techniques, but it provided them with new armaments of swords and spears which rendered them, for a while, militarily superior to most of their neighbours.

With such 'new technology', by the sixth century BC they were spreading in all directions and by the fifth century BC they were in northern Italy and beginning to encounter the Etruscans and Romans. They populated the Po Valley and settled with the Apennine Mountains as their southern border, but established themselves as far south as Ancona. About 474 BC the Celts defeated the Etruscans near the Ticino and were in total control of the plains of northern Italy.

Under their leader, Brennos (the name could mean a title as *brenin* is still the Welsh word for a king), the Celts defeated the Etruscans again and when the Romans came to the aid of the Etruscans the Romans themselves were defeated. This was in about 390/387 BC, when, after their victory at Allia, the Celtic army poured into Rome itself and the Romans were forced to pay a large ransom to persuade the Celts to withdraw.

The Celts were also spreading eastwards. In 366 BC Celtic mercenaries were being employed by Sparta in their war against Thebes and playing a decisive role. Large groups of Celts were following the Danube valley and reached the Carpathians, establishing settlements as they went. Soon the Celts were on the northern borders of Macedonia, and Alexander the Great journeyed north to meet the Celtic leaders on the banks of the Danube in 335/334 BC in order to arrange a peace treaty of equals. With Alexander's death, the Celtic leaders considered the peace treaty null and void. They had, in 298 BC, under Cambaules, conquered and settled Thrace. In 280 BC three Celtic armies were poised on the northern border of Macedonia. The following year one of these armies, under Bolgios, defeated the Macedonians and slew Ptolemy Ceraunos, the heir of Alexander, and his once favourite general, in battle. Another Celtic army, led by Brennos and Acichorios, entered the Greek peninsula, defeated a combined army of the Greek states, commanded by Callippus of Athens, at Thermopylae. They sacked the temple of Delphi, site of the Pythia, the Greek oracle and priestess of Apollo.

For some inexplicable reason, the Celts halted in their conquest. Their leader, Brennos, committed suicide, and the combined Celtic armies broke up. One section of them withdrew back into Celtic territory, carrying some of the treasures of Delphi, later found by the Romans near Toulouse, while another section were defeated by Antigonus Gonatas, the new Macedonian king. Some 20,000 Celtic warriors and their families were persuaded to cross into Asia Minor (modern Turkey) to serve Nicomedes of Bithynia against Antiochus of Syria.

They were eventually granted lands in central Asia Minor and established the Celtic state of Galatia, becoming the first Celtic peoples to later be converted to Christianity by Paul of Tarsus, to whom he wrote his famous Epistle. Their settlement was reinforced later by the movement of other Celtic tribes into the area.

Back in Greece, a further 4,000 warriors and their families were recruited by Ptolemy II, the Pharaoh of Egypt, and went to serve him there. Other bands of Celts decided to serve as mercenaries in armies of various kings, such as those of Carthage and Syracuse and even Syria.

The bravery of the Celts in battle was a by-word in the ancient world and Aristotle claimed that they feared nothing; 'neither earthquakes or waves'. The Classical writers have much to say on the battle tactics of the Celts, who excelled as cavalry which, with their superior iron weapons, seemed to have given them the initial edge over the Mediterranean world. The Greeks recorded several early Celtic words, like *trimarcisia* for cavalry tactics and the word *marca* for horse. The Romans began to adapt Celts weapons and even adopted the Celtic words for them into Latin. *Lanciae*, as Diodorus Siculus records, was the name of their iron-headed spears, (from which we have lance); the popular Roman short sword, the *gladius*, was named from the Celtic *clad* which we might popularly recognize in the Scottish claymore *claidheamh mór* or 'great sword', more accurately applied to the great two-edged broadsword rather than the basket-hilted sword of popular folklore.

Polybius was one of the Classical writers who mistakenly identified a Celtic tribe by the name of the Gaesatae. He recorded that they went naked into battle. In fact, they were not a tribe at all but a band of professional warriors, named from the word *gae*, meaning spear (so, 'spearmen'). As in other Indo-European or Aryan societies, the Celts produced a warrior class or caste with their own rituals; they were professionals who sold their expertise to whoever would hire their services. Their rôle might be more quickly understood by comparing them with the *samurai*, the military caste of Japan which was finally abolished in the Mejii period at the turn of this century. This Celtic warrior caste is also paralleled in Hindu society by the Kshatriya, who were the caste below the Brahmins. Like some sections of the Kshatriya, the Celtic Gaesatae fought naked because they believed this would release their *karma* to its fullest potential, enhancing their prowess and, if killed, speeding them to their incarnation in the Otherworld.

In Irish mythology, and what is referred to as 'pseudo-history', we find such a military caste with its bands of professional warriors still exists. One of the best known is the Craobh Ruadh, Red Branch warriors of Ulster. Many scholars believe the scribes confused the word *ruadh* with *rígh*, so that they were originally warriors of the 'Royal Branch'. The Fianna, warriors who guarded the High Kings and recruited from the Clan Bascna and Clan Morna, appear as another military caste and *fianna* is the modern Irish word for soldiers. Connacht had the Gamhanrhide as their military élite, while Munster had both the Degad of Cú Roi and the Naisc Niadh of the Eoghanacht kings of Cashel, the latter being warriors of the golden collar or torque, which eventually became an honour awarded by the kings of Cashel and their descendants, the MacCarthy Mór. When the MacCarthys fled into exile after the Battle of the Boyne in 1690, they continued to make the award in recognition of service during two-and-a-half centuries of exile in France, where they were recognized as Ducs de Clancarthy and the Comte MacCarthy Reagh de Toulouse. In 1926, when the MacCarthy Mór became domiciled in an independent Ireland once again, the Niadh Nask, as it had become known during the period of exile, continued to be bestowed, and it still exists today, making it one of the oldest known honours systems in Europe.

As the ancient Celts emerged into recorded history and became known to the Classical writers, it is clear that in their society four main classes had developed, as they had done initially in other Indo-

European societies: the intelligentsia, the warriors, the producers of goods and the menials or manual workers. These classes paralleled the Hindu ones of Brahmin, Kshatriya, Vaishya and Sudra. By the time the Irish law system was codified, five basic classes had emerged, which consisted of: the various forms of kings or chieftains, the intelligentsia or professionals, the officials and magistrates, the clansmen who worked the land and formed the army in time of war, and those who had forfeited their civil rights, sometimes wrongly called slaves. This last group consisted of criminals undergoing punishment, prisoners of war and hostages.

On the Italian peninsula, the Romans and Celts were still regularly clashing and Rome was threatened once again after the Celts defeated the Roman armies. As Rome began to expand in an empire which initially sought to incorporate all the peoples on the Italian peninsula, the Celts were to be found as allies of Rome's enemies, forming an alliance in 300 BC with their old adversaries, the Etruscans, then with the Samnites, achieving yet another victory over Rome in 298 BC, and again in 284 BC. When Pyrrhus of Epirius landed in southern Italy to prevent the Greek colonies falling under Roman domination, the Celts joined forces with him and were instrumental in Pyrrhus' famous victory over Rome at Asculum, in 279 BC. But Pyrrhus was eventually defeated. Rome immediately began an offensive against the Celts of northern Italy, and in 237 BC they seized the territory of the Senones Celts of Picenum, whose capital was Senigallia (Senones Gallia), and began to colonize it.

Elsewhere the Celts were being hard-pressed. Attalos I of Pegamum had thrown off Galatian Celtic overlordship and defeated them. In Iberia, Carthage was conquering Celtiberian territories to form a new empire and the Celts of northern Italy were forced to seek new allies from the Celts of Transalpine Gaul. In 225 BC, a Celtic army once again defeated the Romans but a short while later at Telamon, the Romans inflicted a major defeat on the Celts of northern Italy. Rome was now strong enough to invade and devastate Cisalpine Gaul. For three campaigning seasons the Romans, rejecting Celtic offers to negotiate, invaded and systematically destroyed Celtic settlements there.

In 221/218 BC, when Hannibal of Carthage began to make his plans to go to war with Rome, the Celts of Iberia, Transalpine Gaul and Cisalpine Gaul made alliances with him and joined his army.

Without Celtic aid, Hannibal could not have moved his predominantly Celtic army from Iberia, through southern Gaul and across the Alps into Cisalpine Celtic territory. On reaching northern Italy, 10,000 Cisalpine Celts joined his army and played a prominent rôle in his campaign against Rome from 218 to 207 BC.

Following the defeat of Hannibal, Rome renewed its systematic conquest of Cisalpine Gaul and its colonization of the conquered territory. Many writers now claimed for Latin literature were actually Romanized Celts from this territory. The campaign in Cisalpine Gaul lasted for over twenty years. When the chieftain of the Boii of Cisalpine Gaul surrendered with his family to Rome they were slaughtered by a Roman consul for personal entertainment. By 178/173 BC the Roman colonization policy had commenced but a Celtic language and Celtic customs survived in the area until well into imperial times. In 82 BC Cisalpine Gaul was declared a Roman province.

In 197 BC Rome had started a conquest of the Carthaginian empire in Iberia and its Celtic allies. The war against the Celts of Spain was to last over one hundred years, ending when the Celts finally submitted to the *Pax Romana* and were then quickly absorbed into a Latin cultural ethos. Again, many Latin writers from Iberia were, in fact, Celts.

Following their conquests over the Celts of northern Italy and of Iberia, the Romans used the pretext of protecting the Greek colony of Massilia (Marseilles) to send armies into southern Gaul and take control over an area which they named Gallia Narbonensis, or simply 'the province', which name survives as Provence.

The last record of Celts in Egypt had occurred in 186/185 BC. Galatia had become a strong power at this time but in 74 BC, Deiotaros, the ruler of Galatia, made an alliance with Rome against some of the surrounding Greek states. Deiotaros's friendship and alliance with Pompeius (Pompey) and later Mark Anthony was a political miscalculation in which he found himself on the losing side in the Roman Civil War. In 25 BC, after the death of Deiotaros, Roman armies moved into Galatia and it was declared an official province of Rome. In AD 74 it was united with Cappadocia as a single province but it was separated again in AD 106. It existed as a separate province as late as the eighth century AD. In the fourth century AD St Jerome records that Celtic was still spoken there, although many of the learned class also spoke Greek.

By the first century BC, Celtic settlements and influence had been driven back from Thrace along the Danube, out of areas such as Illyria, Pannonia, Noricum and, with Germanic tribal pressure from the north-east, the Celts were being pressed back westward over the Rhine, the great river whose Celtic name meant 'the sea'.

Only Gaul proper remained an independent Celtic territory, together with the islands of Britain and Ireland. Everywhere else the Celts had fallen either to the remorseless military machine of Rome or to the Germanic tribes.

It was inevitable that the Romans, at the zenith of their empire, would turn their attention to the last of the independent Celtic territories. Their excuse came in 58 BC. A few years earlier, Burebista of Dacia had launched a war of annexation on the Celts in the east, defeating the Boii of Bohemia, and forcing some 32,000 Boii to form an exodus to join the Celtic Helvetii in Austria and Switzerland. The Helvetii, led by Orgetorix and his son-in-law Dumnorix, brother of the chieftain and Druid Diviatiacus of the Aedui, formed a Celtic alliance and began plans for a westward migration to escape the incursions of the Germanic and now Slavic tribes.

Julius Caesar, given command of Cisalpine Gaul and Gallia Narbonesis, took the opportunity to intervene in the affairs of Gaul proper by using the movement of the Helvetii to claim it upset the peace of Gaul. Roman politicians simply used this as an excuse to conquer the entire Gaulish territory. Between 58 BC and 55 BC Caesar and the Roman armies defeated most of the Gaulish leaders. So successful were the Romans that in 55 BC Caesar was able to take an invasion force and land on the southern shores of Britain and defeat the Celtic Cantii (the tribe who gave their name to Kent). The following year, after putting down an uprising of the Treveri in Gaul and killing Dumnorix, the leader of the Gaulish resistance, Caesar took another expedition to Britain and after a fierce campaign succeeded in obtaining the formal submission of several significant southern British chieftains.

However, in Gaul, Ambiorix led a new Gaulish uprising, the leadership of which was taken over by the famous Vercingetorix. Some British Celts went to Gaul to help in this 'war of independence'. By 51 BC, after one of the bloodiest campaigns fought by the Romans, the last independent Gaulish Celtic territory, centred around the hill fort of the Aquitani of Uxellodunum, was conquered. Gaul was not entirely 'pacified' and every few years the Gauls rose in unsuccessful attempts to regain their independence. In AD 69 there was yet another major uprising in Gaul, with Tacitus recording that the Gaulish Druids were taking a leading part and prophesying the fall of Rome.

However, Rome itself was now dominant enough to attempt a more thorough invasion of Britain, one of the last two completely independent Celtic territories. A rich trading country, Britain, or its southern part, had been under the kingship of Cunobelinus who died in about AD 40–43 and was succeeded by his son Caractacus (Caradoc). The Romans used the opportunity of Cunobelinus' death to invade but it took nine years of campaigning to overcome Caractacus. Even so, Rome was never to completely conquer Britain. Eventually they gave up the idea of subduing the northern part of the island, building the famous Hadrian's Wall from coast to coast to mark their northern frontier. During the 360 years or so that southern Britain was part of the Roman empire, insurrections against Roman rule occurred, particularly among the Brigantes, occupying the territory south of the wall, who were often in rebellion.

There was now one other major Celtic territory which had not come under Roman occupation – the island of Ireland. In AD 82 Agricola, the Roman governor of Britain, welcomed some disgruntled Irish chieftains to his headquarters in Britain. They sought military aid to resolve their quarrels in Ireland and Agricola drew up plans to invade Ireland, but these were shelved due to the fact that Agricola was unable to pacify northern Britain.

By the latter days of the Roman empire, when Christianity became a state religion, Christian thought had replaced much of the pagan Celtic religion. Only Ireland and northern Britain were to remain generally pagan, until the early fifth century AD. Gaul and southern Britain had become Christian at an early stage.

By the time the Romans withdrew from Britain, and Britain re-emerged as a Celtic country once again, the Celtic world had shrunk considerably. It had nearly vanished in Cisalpine Gaul and Iberia and, certainly, along the Danube valley it existed no more. Even the Galatians, still speaking Celtic in the fourth century AD, were slowly being displaced and by the ninth century AD they would disappear entirely. Gaul itself was bilingual and we hear from Sidonius Apollinarius that it was only in the late fifth century AD that 'the leading families of Gaul' were trying to throw off 'the scurf of Celtic speech'.

New conquerors now threatened what remained of the Celtic world. Jutes, Angles and Saxons began to raid and settle in Britain, and eventually annihilated large sections of the Celtic populations in the area which was to become England, causing those that remained to migrate in large numbers, either to the western and northern areas, to Ireland, or to the European mainland. Only in Wales, Scotland and Cornwall have the Celts survived in Britain until modern times. Large numbers of Celtic refugees fled to northern Spain, others to Armorica (which became known as 'Little Britain' – Brittany – where their Celtic-speaking descendants remain to the present day). The Franks, Germanic cousins of the Angles and Saxons, were spreading through Gaul at the same time and eventually intermarried with the Gaulish Celts. A large Celtic vocabulary survives in modern French.

The Celtic peoples suffered further conquests and attempted assimilations from the English and French until today they have been pushed back into the islands and peninsulas of north-western Europe, where they constitute a population of sixteen millions of which only two-and-a-half millions still speak a Celtic language. These are the hardy survivors of the former predominant civilization of northern Europe, which once spread from one side of the continent to the other and from north to south.

We have already mentioned the Celtic caste system, no different in its early stages from other early Indo-European social systems and parallel to the Hindu system.

The ancient Celtic civilization has been represented, particularly by the Greeks and Romans, as a fierce warrior society, proud, ignorant, illiterate, taking life cheaply, given to childish amusements and often drunk. They have often been depicted as 'noble savages'. The image still remains with us today. This is far from the truth. From the initial Urnfield Culture, the Celts emerged primarily as an agricultural and pastoral people, as farmers cultivating their lands and living within a well structured tribal society. They were not nomadic, as some have argued, but once they developed ironworking among their other metalwork skills, with the start of the Hallstatt period in the eighth century BC, they were able to become mobile and surplus populations began to move with impunity in many directions. In this mobility they were again no different from the early Greek colonizers nor subsequent Romans, Germans and Slavs. Indeed, in both Greece and

Italy, when populations became too large, young people aged twenty years were often expelled to go where they pleased to form a new community. The *ver sacrum*, or 'sacred spring' of the Latins was used by Titus Livius, Livy, (59 BC – AD 17) as a means of explaining the reason for the initial Celtic migrations to northern Italy.

One of the great skills developed by the Celts was their road-building ability, once argued over by scholars but now reinforced by archaeological finds of sophisticated Celtic roadways. The myth of Roman road-building is being accorded its proper place and scholars are accepting the arguments of those who have pointed to the fact that many Latin words connected with transport were borrowed from Celtic. I have already demonstrated in *The Celtic Empire* that the evidence has always been there, especially in the writings of Caesar, for those who have wanted to find it.

Archaeology has also demonstrated the prosperity of ancient Celtic farming communities as well as their sophistication in art, in pottery making, jewellery making, enamelwork, as well as advanced metal-work, all of which found much favour in the ancient Mediterranean world. During the first century BC, before Caesar's attempted invasion of Britain, British woollen goods were eagerly sought in Rome, especially woollen cloaks (*sagi*), demonstrating just how much propaganda he worked into his description of Britain when he maintained the British Celts knew nothing of weaving.

The Celts usually used local materials with which to build. This was mostly wood but in some places they used stone, showing great architectural knowledge and skill. In Britain especially the remains of many such stone structures survive from the fourth to second centuries BC, as I have shown in *A Guide to early Celtic Remains in Britain*. One such structure survives to a height of forty feet, with lintelled entrances and inward tapering walls, sometimes fifteen feet thick, with chambers, galleries and stairs.

The basis of Celtic society was certainly tribal, and again this in no way differs from any other early Indo-European social organization. Tribes varied considerably in size. The Helvetii, whose name survives in Switzerland, numbered 390,000 when they began their migration. The Celtic law systems, handed down orally, were highly cultivated and show fascinating parallels to the Hindu law systems, demonstrating the common Indo-European origin. We have already mentioned one particular unique point of Celtic law, that of the provision of curative medical treatment, sick maintenance, and the establishment of hospitals. Under this law system, which can be described as a primitive yet sophisticated communism – or, rather, in the proper sense community-ism – there was no such concept as absolute private property nor inheritance by primogeniture. All officials in Celtic society were elected, albeit often from the same family groups. Even Caesar notes that the 'Chief Druid' of Gaul was elected by his fellow peers.

The purpose of this book is, of course, to discuss the Druids and by very definition examine the intellectual life of the ancient Celts. Therefore we will be returning to individual aspects of Celtic social organizations later. Suffice to say, at this stage, that the Celts were no simple, mindless group of savage, barbarian tribes wandering Europe willy-nilly in a ruthless and bloody orgy as many writers over the centuries would have us believe. Celtic society was highly evolved and sophisticated and the Celts formulated and developed many fascinating concepts about themselves and about the world in which they lived.

It was only at the height of the Celtic expansions that the writers of Greece and Rome began to speak of the Druids, not as priests, but as philosophers, judges, educators, historians, doctors, seers, astronomers and astrologers; in fact, as the native intellectual class of Celtic society. And we are told that the Druids were to be found throughout the Celtic world.

Nora Chadwick has argued that almost all the information from the Greek and Latin sources has survived from a period when the Druids were already in decline as an influential class. She writes:

> The decline of the Druids! This has been a battle-ground among all scholars who have seriously studied the Druids and their place in antiquity. Why did the Romans 'repress', 'persecute', 'abolish' the Druids? Pliny was the first to raise the question, and he answered it with assurance to his own satisfaction. Nevertheless, the question has been re-opened and restudied ever since. This has been, in fact, the burning question in our own day for students of the Roman Empire and the Celtic West alike . . .

Nora Chadwick's conclusion was that the 'repression' and 'persecution' of the Druids by the Romans was a creation of later scholarship, which sought a rational basis for the disappearance of the Druids, or rather, as they had not disappeared according to native Celtic literary sources but had merely undergone a change of rôle in Celtic society, the reason for this change of rôle. In Celtic sources the Druids had ceased to be philosophers, judges, educators, doctors, seers and astronomers and had become 'magicians' and 'poets'. Mrs Chadwick implies that the Druidic caste was already in the process of undergoing changes within Celtic society and that the Roman conquest simply aided that process and clouded the reasons for it. She argues:

> The evidence for suppression is not very impressive. No Roman legislation against the Druids has come down to us, and no first class contemporary evidence testifies to repressive measures. The broad answer would seem to be that the *disciplina* of the Druids perished by slow strangulation, the inevitable result of the super-imposition of a higher culture on a lower.

To accept this argument one has to accept Mrs Chadwick's almost dewy-eyed worship of all things Roman as 'civilized' and all things Celtic as 'barbaric'. But it certainly does not explain the situation in Ireland where Roman culture held no sway at this period.

However, the fact that there are no references to the Druids by those writers commenting on the Celts prior to the second century BC does raise an immediate question. Did the Druids exist in Celtic society before the second century BC? My argument will be that they did, but that no commentator used that native Celtic caste name, simply referring to them by their individual rather than their collective function.

Our next question, then, is to ask, how did the Druids emerge in Celtic society; what were their origins?

[2]

The Origins of the Druids

I T was the Greek writers who first recorded the word *Druidae*. The earliest known recorded references to Druids, as previously mentioned, survive only from the second century BC. These earliest references come down to us in third hand quotations. Diogenes Laertius, a Greek living in the third century AD, wrote *Lives and Opinions of Eminent Philosophers*. In this work he quotes earlier references, naming his sources, and is thus regarded as valuable in preserving maxims and epistles of men like Epicurus, Solon of Athens and Periander of Corinth. In his work he also quotes Aristotle (384–322 BC) and Sotion of Alexandria (fl. 200–170 BC) on the Druids. But it is now accepted that the Aristotelian work *Magicus*, to which he refers, was not, in fact, written by the famous Greek philosopher, but by an anonymous Greek writer *c.*200 BC. This still makes it one of the oldest references to the Druids.

Like *Keltoi*, the word *Druidae* is obviously a word of Celtic origin, but linguists still battle over its derivation.

Both Strabo (64 BC to after AD 24) and Gaius Plinius Secundus (Pliny the Elder, AD 23/4–79), believed that it was cognate with the Greek *drus*, 'an oak'. One should emphasize the use of *cognate* and not 'deriving from'. From a hypothesized Common Celtic word derive the modern Irish *dair* and the Welsh *dar*. Mrs Chadwick throws out an amusing idea when she says: 'It is not wholly impossible that the word *Druid* may have originated in a nickname derived from the oakwoods with which they are associated by Pliny, in which case it would have meant something like "backwoodsmen".' More seriously, some leading Celtic etymologists, such as Whitley Stokes, Rudolf Thurneysen, Henri d'Arbois de Jubainville and Holger Pedersen, among them, saw the word as deriving from the word roots *dru-wid* – 'oak knowledge' – the *wid* meaning 'to know' or 'to see' (as in the Sanskrit *vid* which occurs in the Hindu 'Vedas', the most ancient religious text in an Indo-European language). The meaning of Druid, therefore, in a non-literal sense, being 'those whose knowledge is great', or 'thorough knowledge'. The oak symbolism seems to be generally accepted although the more cautious Celtic linguists still tend to regard the origin of the name to be obscure. Dr Dáithá Ó hÓgáin, of the Department of Folklore at University College, Dublin, for example, has called the linking of the word 'Druid' with 'oak' as 'a somewhat fanciful derivation', pointing out that in an Irish context:

> The favourite tree of the Druids, however, was clearly the rowan, and it was on wattles of this tree that Irish practitioners slept in order to have prophetic visions. The hazel tree was also important, as evidenced by the Druid's name Mac Cuill ('son of hazel') and also by the lore concerning nine hazel trees at the source of the river Boyne, the nuts of which had a nucleus of wisdom.

But Dr Ó hÓgáin acknowledged that the word 'Druid' was from a Celtic word 'which would have meant "very knowledgeable".'

Oddly, however, Dr Ó hÓgáin seems to neglect the fact that the oak still played a prominent rôle in Irish mythology, as in the case of the 'Oak of Mughna' which, according to the *Leabhar Gabhála* (Book of Invasions) was the earliest sacred tree in Ireland. Indeed, oaks are frequently mentioned in an early Christian context in Ireland so that we may have reason to assume that many ancient churches were built on the site of Druidic oaks. Most famous are Brigid's monastery at Cille Daire (Kildare – church of the oak), at Daire Maugh (Durrow – plain of the oaks) and Colmcille's Daire Calgaich (Derry – the oak grove of Calgaich). However, Dr Ó hÓgáin is correct in that the yew, hazel and rowan tree are more frequently referred to in Irish mythology in connection with Irish Druids.

Sir John Rhŷs, the first professor of Celtic studies at Oxford, in his *Lectures on the origin and growth of religion as illustrated by Celtic Heathendom* (1888), comments:

> Seeing the importance of sacred trees in the ancient cult of the chief god of the Aryans of Europe, and the preference evinced for the oak as the tree fittest to be his emblem, or even the residence of divinity, I am inclined to regard the old etymology of the word Druid as being, roughly speaking, the correct one.

That is those with 'oak knowledge'.

The origin of the Druid caste had its roots in the 'food gathering age' when extensive oak forests covered Europe. We are speaking of a period prior to 4000 BC when primitive 'hunter-gatherers' saw the oak as a symbol of plenty, collecting acorns as a means of food and finding them easy to store for more difficult days. Hesiod (c.700 BC), Pausanias (fifth century BC), Galen (AD 129–199) all speak of the acorn as a food. According to Pliny, the acorn was ground and baked into bread. Publius Ovidius Naso, the poet Ovid (43 BC–AD 17), speaks of the acorn as the first food ever given to humans when they were dropped from the great tree of the sky-god Jove or Jupiter. Strabo speaks of acorn bread as a staple diet of the Celts of Iberia while the *Leabhar na Nuachonghbala*, composed about AD 1150 by Fionn Mac Gormain of Glendalough, records that in one particular bad year every ear of corn bore but one grain and every oak only one acorn, which indicates that the acorn was still regarded as an article of food classed with grain by the Irish.

Not only did the oak provide food, but these early Europeans could utilize oak wood for their fires to keep them warm and for their timber dwellings to shelter them. Examples of wooden dwellings from the period bear witness to a wise use of the resources of the vast temperate forests of Europe. These early Europeans observed that the oak was the most venerable tree of the forest, the hardiest and most useful. From this period, which probably lasted for a thousand years, there developed the veneration of the oak and the rise of 'the wise ones of the oak', which is a central belief in most ancient Indo-European religions. To have a knowledge of the trees endowed one with survival techniques and therefore wisdom. Professor Jacques Briard has pointed out in *L'Age du Bronze en Europe barbare* (1976), 'The woodman was to play an important part in Western barbarian civilizations for a long time'. Briard neglects, however, to mention that the 'woodman' not only played an important rôle in 'barbarian' European civilization but in southern European civilization – even in the societies of Greece and Rome – and that the remains of such a concept are to be found in other Indo-European societies. The Hindus considered the pipal tree (*ficus religiosa*) as sacred, a tree in which the god Brahma dwelt, with Vishnu inhabiting the twigs of the tree and each leaf assigned to one of the deities. The importance of tree worship is demonstrated by the fact that among the agricultural tribes of India every village was positioned near a sacred grove (*sarna*) reputed to be a remnant of the primeval forest, left intact for the local gods when the land was cleared to ensure better agricultural use. Even Shiva dwelt in a tree – the bel tree (*aegle marmelos*).

By the start of the first millennium BC, when the Celts began their expansions, all learned men and women in their society were designated as having 'oak knowledge'. And, in the Celtic religion itself, the oak continued to be venerated as the great symbol of vegetational increase so that, as a cult, its symbolism was retained among the Celts some time after it was lost among the Greeks and Latins.

From Irish sources we may suppose that all the Celtic tribes had their own sacred tree, the *crann bethadh* (or 'Tree of Life') standing as their totem or talisman in the centre of their territory. In ancient Ireland, a tribal raid by a rival clan would be made simply for the purpose of destroying the tree and thus demoralizing the enemy.

As John A. MacCulloch states: 'Other Aryan folk besides the Celts regarded the oak as the symbol of a high god, of the sun or the sky, but probably this was not its earliest significance.'

James G. Frazer has pointed out 'the worship of the oak tree, or the oak-god, appears to have been shared by all the branches of the Aryan stock in Europe', that is by the peoples who descended from the Indo-Europeans. In fact, the oak frequently symbolized the 'father of the gods' in various societies, perhaps because of its majestic appearance, and its size and longevity compared with other trees. In other words, the oak was an ancient phallic symbol.

The Lithuanians, or Aistians, associated the god of thunder, Perkunas, with an oak tree and came to believe that when they died their souls would take up residence in such trees. To get good crops, even in the sixteenth century, they sometimes 'sacrificed' an oak by ritual burnings. Estonians smeared the blood of animals on oaks, sacred to the god Taara, to be assured of rain and a good harvest. Throughout the Slavic nations, oak symbolism has been noticed. Among the Slavs the oak was the sacred tree of Perun, the god of thunder. His image was found on a carving at Novgorod where it is recorded that a perpetual fire had to be maintained to him. 'Holy oaks' proliferated in Lower Saxony, Westphalia and other areas of Germany, according to Jacob Grimm (1785–1863). Certainly in ancient times the Germanic peoples also worshipped the oak as representative of Thunor or Thor, the god of thunder. In England the oak was venerated by the Anglo-Saxons as part of their own religion and not, as some have thought, as an inherited part of Celtic tradition. In France, Christianity has partially claimed the oak, for we have 'Our Lady of the Oak' in Anjou and at Orthe, in Maine. And according to W.Y. Evans Wentz, quoting from Canon Mahé: 'One sees at various crossroads the most beautiful rustic oaks decorated with figures of saints'. The oak, therefore, as a symbol of veneration, is found throughout Europe and particularly as a symbol of the god of thunder. Even in England this symbolism has survived until fairly recently and there is a folk-rhyme mentioned in William Henderson's *Folklore of the Northern Counties of England* (1866):

> Beware the oak
> It draws the stroke

But, as I have already mentioned, oak veneration was not confined to the northern European peoples.

The peoples of Greece and Rome once shared that oak-cult. Remains of it are still found. Zeus was once worshipped in the oracular oak at Dodona, and at the festival at Plataea. Jupiter, the Roman equivalent of Zeus, was worshipped on the Capitol where a sacred oak tree stood. The original act of dedication to Jupiter was when Romulus won the *spolia opima* (spoils of honour) from Acron, king of Caeninenses, and hung them on the sacred oak of the Capitol in honour of Jupiter. The Temple of Vesta in the Forum had fires which had to be fuelled by oak and no other wood. But such worship developed into more complex theological ideas. So, too, did Celtic religious worship. As the Celtic social system developed, over many centuries, the learned men and women of the tribes simply retained the title of those with 'oak knowledge'.

Unlike its veneration among the Greeks and Romans, the veneration of the oak continued for a longer period among the Celts. At Séguret, in Provence, there survives the depiction of the Celtic 'father of the gods' accompanied by an oak tree. Some 150 stone monuments have been found honouring the Celtic 'father of the gods' in Gaul, such as the one at Hausen-an-der-Zaber. Each depicts a tree adorned with oak leaves and acorns. For evidence that the oak was chosen above other trees, at least by the Continental and British Celts, we observe that the majority of wooden votives from the Fontes Sequanae sanctuary were made from oak heartwood in spite of the fact that there were plenty of other suitable trees for carving on the Châtillon Plateau. Maximus Tyrius, in the second century AD, writing in his *Logoi*, claimed 'the Celtic image of Zeus is a lofty oak'.

Oak was chosen for the wooden mortuary constructions of both the Hallstatt and La Téne cultures of early Celtic society. Oak boughs were recovered from a Celtic burial in an oak coffin at Gristhorpe, Yorkshire. The symbolism of the oak is all-pervasive in ancient Celtic culture.

It will have been noted that most authorities quoted so far are resolute in their use of masculine terms for oak and those pursuing 'oak wisdom'. Of course, things were not so simple, for pre-Christian Celtic religion was not originally the masculine concept into which it later developed and which was then made into a more patriarchal system by Christianity. Like most world religions, the Celts started with a 'mother goddess' concept. In the case of the Celts, the mother goddess was Danu ('water from heaven') and it is significant that the great river Danube takes its name from her; significant, that is, because it was at the headwaters of the Danube that Celtic civiliz-ation is acknowledged to have evolved.

It can be argued that water symbolized the female element while the oak became the male symbol, and as a symbol of vegetational increase it is more reasonable to suppose water to be a fertility symbol and therefore feminine. However, the oak, in all the cultures that have used it, is definitely depicted as being a masculine symbol. That being so, we could point out that water, in the form of the mother goddess, nourished the oak and gave it birth. We shall be examining these concepts in more detail in the appropriate chapters.

From being the men and women who pursued the mysteries of their surrounding world, those with 'oak knowledge', to whom members of the 'hunter gatherer' tribes looked for their survival, how were the Druids perceived when they eventually emerged to the scrutiny of foreign observers in the second century BC?

The Druids, as we have already pointed out, appeared as the intel-lectual caste of the Celtic peoples wherever those peoples were to be found. And it is clear that they were not a male élite but consisted of both men and women. However, it does become clear that already the Celts were developing into a patriarchal society, even before

Christianity produced the final changes. The Druids were to the Celts as the Brahmins were to the Hindu people. It is obvious from their various duties in Celtic society that they encompassed many intellectual functions. I am aware that this is a contentious statement, so let us examine the arguments beginning with those who are opposed to the idea that the Druids were originally a caste developed within Celtic society.

The scholar Camille Jullian, in *Histoire de la Gaule* (1908), held that Druidism was a Celtic institution but of comparatively late appearance in the development of Celtic society which, he argues, accounts for no Greek or Latin reference to Druids before the second century BC. D'Arbois de Jubainville in *Les Druides* (1906) accepted, without question, Caesar's statement that 'the system (of Druidism) is thought to have been devised in Britain, and brought thence to Gaul'. He therefore argued that the Druids were a manifestation of the Gaelic (Goidelic) Celts which had survived when the Brythonic Celts crossed to Britain and imposed their dialect of Celtic on the original Gaelic Celtic inhabitants. The logic is that Druidism then passed back into Gaul about 200 BC where it was eventually noticed by the Greek commentators. This, according to D'Arbois de Jubainville, is why the Druids do not appear to be mentioned in a context other than Gaul or in Britain and Ireland; why no Druids are specifically mentioned among the Celts of Cisalpine Gaul (in the north of Italy) or in Galatia or Ibernia. We will be returning to this point shortly.

Sir John Rhŷs initially disagreed with D'Arbois de Jubainville's conclusion, believing the institution to be common to all Celts; and in *Celtic Britain* he concluded that Druidism was not a Brythonic Celtic invention. But by *Celtic Folk-lore* (1901) he had come to another conclusion, that the Druidic idea was formulated among a pre-Celtic population in Britain and Ireland, to which belief he finally adhered in all his later works. He argued that the Druids belonged to a civilization which was absorbed into Celtic culture.

To accept Rhŷs' contention one also has to accept Julius Caesar's comment, 'it is thought' (*existimatur*) that Druidism developed in Britain and passed to Gaul, as absolutely accurate. Sir John Rhŷs sees the Druids a 'a non Aryan priesthood'. Sir John Morris-Jones in 'Pre-Aryan Syntax in Insular Celtic' (1899) was arguing at this same time that while the insular Celtic languages were classified as belonging to the 'Aryan' languages, a term now dropped because of its imprecision in favour of Indo-European, the syntax of these languages is not so. He suggested that the syntax belonged to the Samito-Semetic group, including Arabic, Hebrew, Ethiopic, Berber and ancient Egyptian. This greatly boosted the 'British Israelite' movement which claimed the Celts as one of the lost tribes of Israel. Thus these mystical pre-Celtic peoples were said to have bequeathed the Druids to Celtic society, according to the arguments of Sir John Rhŷs, Sir George Laurence Gomme and Saloman Reinach.

But this argument has been questioned by later linguists. Myles Dillon pointed out that while Greek and Latin grammar consist of regular verbs as the norm and irregular verbs as the exception, the reverse was true of Irish. But this was also true of Sanskrit. 'It is as far as we know,' argued Dillon, 'the Indo-European system, which has therefore been best preserved in Sanskrit and in Old Irish'. Much work has now been done in demonstrating similarities of grammar construction between the language of the Vedas of Hindu culture and Old Irish. The Vedas were compiled between c.1000 BC and 500 BC. *Veda* is Sanskrit meaning knowledge and the root word *ved* or *vid* comprises the second syllable of the compound *Dru-vid*.

Having said this, Heinrich Wagner, a Professor at the Dublin Institute for Advanced Studies, and author of *Studies in the Origins of the Celts and of Early Celtic Civilisation* (1971) firmly adheres to the Rhŷs/Morris-Jones' contention. In his paper 'Near Eastern and African Connections with the Celtic World', delivered to the Toronto symposium on 'Celtic Consciousness' in February 1978, Wagner reiterated his belief in the linguistic affinities of North African languages and Insular Celtic grammar structures. According to Wagner:

> Scholars such as M. Dillon, N. Holmer, W. Meid and C. Watkins maintain that primitive Celtic was a particularly archaic Indo-European dialect. Their findings do not, however, rule out automatically, as some of these scholars seem to believe, the recognition of strong non-Indo-European elements in Insular Celtic.

The debate will doubtless continue. Many of the early arguments as to whether the Druids were non-Celtic or belonged to one particular branch of Celtic culture presupposed that the Druids were simply a priesthood. Gomme enthusiastically supported the view because he believed in a vision of the Druids practising human sacrifice which he found 'opposed to Aryan sentiment'!

Gomme seems to have entertained a belief that the Aryans were a more developed civilization, which did not indulge in human sacrifice. Of course, the Aryans, by which he meant Indo-Europeans, were as much into human sacrifice as any other ancient societies. The initial concepts of 'Aryan race purity' were being sounded out at this time. Gomme was an eager disciple of the ideas which were to give rise to Houston Stewart Chamberlain's notorious 'race history' *Die Grundlagen des Neunzehnten Jahrhundrets* (Foundations of the Nineteenth Century), 1899, which became the basis for Nazi political philosophy.

Reinach supported Rhŷs and Gomme in suggesting that the Celts accepted the 'Druidism' of the pre-Celtic 'non-Aryans' – arguing that they did so in the same way that the Romans accepted or incorporated the religions of many of the peoples whom they conquered. Further, Reinach suggested, somewhat astonishingly, that the Celts had no religion or priesthood of their own and so accepted the Druids and their ideas from conquered populations. He argued that when the Druids appeared in recorded history, the Celtic military class were in revolt against them because they were a foreign institution. There is absolutely no evidence to suggest this. The Druids of Gaul in the first century BC were certainly not in decline and Gaulish kings and military leaders, such as Divitiacus and his brother Dumnorix, were clearly Druids as well as members of the military caste. It seems that Reinach was attempting to bend things to fit his hypothesis.

Another 'non-Aryan', pre-Celtic supporter was Julius Pokorny of Vienna. Writing 'On the Origins of Druidism' in *Revue Celtique*, he argued: 'Druidism has many features quite alien to the character of an Indo-European religion.' Again, Pokorny leans towards the argument that the Celtic conquest of an aboriginal people caused an acceptance of their religion, which was 'non-Aryan' in nature. But Pokorny shows just how shaky his knowledge is when he states:

If the Celts had had Druids who were already priests of the oak before the occupation of the British Islands, they certainly would have brought that worship with them to Ireland ... *the Irish Druids are never mentioned in connection with the oak*... The Druids must have been once the priests of a people who did not know the worship of the oak. But the oak worship of the Celts is vouched for several times, therefore the Druids cannot have been originally a Celtic priesthood.

His argument is strange and confused. As we have already seen, the oak was well-known in Ireland and it is frequently used in association with places of deep religious significance. His contention must therefore fall.

John A. MacCulloch has pointed out, and rightly so I believe: 'There is no reason to believe that Druids did not exist wherever there were Celts.'

But he goes on to say that there is no trace of the institution of Druidism among the Celts of Italy, Spain or Galatia (modern Turkey) and therefore it appeared to be an institution of only late introduction in Gaul. His conclusion is that Druidism had its origin among the Belgic Celtic tribes of northern Gaul and southern Britain, and once they were conquered then Druidism disappeared as an influence in Celtic society.

However, all these arguments against the Druids being an indigenous Celtic institution, common to all Celtic peoples, rely on the argument that Caesar, and no one else, says it was thought that Druidism originated in Britain. The argument is apparently endorsed by the fact that outside of Gaul, Britain and Ireland, we have no specific references to Druids. But this is superficial for we have reference to groups who are obviously Druids by other names.

I believe that MacCulloch was right in the first instance and that Druids existed throughout the entire Celtic world.

Diogenes Laertius talks of the Gauls and the Galatians as having both *Druidae* and *Semnotheoi*. *Semnotheoi* seems to be a word preserved by Laertius from the second century BC author of *Magicus* and from Sotion, and appears to be a synonym for Druid. Clement of Alexandria clearly ascribes Druids to the Galatians as does Cyril of Alexandria and Stephen of Byzantium. Professor Stuart Piggott comments: 'If "Galatian" is accepted at face value, the place-name Drunemeton . . . might also be thought to support the existence of Druids in Asia Minor.' Drunemeton is Celtic for 'oak sanctuary'. Drunemeton was the chief city of the Galatian Celts and, although its exact location is a matter of speculation, there is reference to Pessinus, formerly a religious centre of the Phrygian kingdom, being taken over by the Tolistoboii as their main centre, which could mean that Pessinus was also Drunemeton. But Professor Piggott urges caution and points out that Strabo refers to all the Celts as Galatians. 'The whole race which is called Gaulish or Galatian . . .' [*Gallikon te kai Galatikon*]. Therefore, says Professor Piggott, one cannot talk about Druids in Galatia with the same degree of confidence as Druids in Gaul because the references might easily be applicable to anywhere in the Celtic world. Nevertheless, the naming of their centre as the 'oak sanctuary' seems fairly strong evidence. Flavius Arrianus (Arrian), a Greek of Nicomedia in Bithynia (AD 85/90, d. after 145/6), and therefore one who knew Galatia at first hand, confirms that the Galatian capital was Drunemeton, 'oak sanctuary', where twelve chieftains (*tetrarchs*) met annually with three hundred elected delegates, which formed the government of the Galatians. At Drunemeton, he says, they worshipped their equivalent of Artemis.

It has been argued that the closest parallel to Artemis, daughter of Zeus and twin sister of Apollo, was Brigit, 'the exalted one', daughter of The Dagda, 'father of the gods' and divinity of healing, crafts, poetry and divination, whose cult was widespread through the Celtic world. The Dagda was also the 'god of Druidism'. Once again we encounter the sacred oak and this time in a rather alien habitat on the central plain of what is now Turkey.

Lewis Spence posed the question: 'Were these *tetrarchs* Druids and priests as well as law-givers and administrators? I see no good reason to doubt that they were, although the evidence is much too scanty to permit of positive conclusion.'

The sad fact remains that no Greek or Latin writer composed a work solely on the Druids or was completely explicit as to their position in all Celtic societies. Or, rather, no such work has survived for us to examine. But one point cannot be impressed too many times. No Classical writer ever referred to the Druids as priests, nor is Druidism depicted as a religion.

MacCulloch comments on those writers who wish to identify Druidism as a 'non-Aryan' religious priesthood, or confine it to one branch of the Celtic peoples: 'These are the ideas of writers who see in the Druids an occult and esoteric priesthood.' On this A.H. Allcroft in *The Circle and the Cross* (1927) agrees and argues that Druidism was 'an organization (*disciplina*) which made of a religion a means to political power'.

MacCulloch also argues: 'The relation of the Celts to the Druids is quite different from that of conquerors, who occasionally resort to the medicine men of the conquered folk because they have stronger magic or greater influence with the autochthonous gods.'

Indeed, there is no historical evidence at all to show that the Druids were a non-Celtic priesthood. Even speculation should be anchored on fact. And one fact is important in our considerations: we find that the Celts had a priesthood referred to as *gutuatri*, meaning 'speakers [to the gods]', and obviously the Gaulish word is cognate with the Irish *guth*, voice. The *gutuatri* are known from some inscriptions and a reference to a *gutuatros* put to death by Caesar is mentioned by Aulus Hirtius, who added the eighth book of Caesar's *Gallic War* and who probably wrote *Bellum Alexandrinium*. Hirtius was one of Caesar's lieutenants in Gaul.

The *gutuatri*, therefore, appear as a sub-division of the Druid caste. Pokorny has attempted to argue that the Druids replaced the *gutuatri* as Celtic priests but this is demonstrably not so as Le Roux, in *Les Druides* (1961) emphasizes. The *gutuatri* were in existence well after the Roman conquest of Gaul, simultaneous with the Druids, and nearly two centuries after the Druids were first commented upon.

I make no apology for reiterating my contention by way of summary that prior to the second century BC, the Greeks and Latins had referred to the individual functions of the intellectuals they named, *sacerdotes*, *antistites*, *gutuartros* and so forth. Then came observers like Poseidonios whose work provided the source for Diodorus, Strabo and Timagenes. Poseidonios travelled among the Celts and he identified the Druids as a specific caste within Celtic society with responsibility for intellectual functions.

Joseph Vendryes demonstrated that a group of words associated with philosophy, religion and kingship had survived in Indo-Iranian on the one hand and in Italo-Celtic on the other, and he attributed their survival to the priestly caste of the Brahmins in India and the Druids in the Celtic world. Dillon and Chadwick make the comment: 'We may now go further and say that Druid and Brahmin were heirs to a common tradition of learning and culture'. They say:

The Indo-European origin of Irish metres, and the striking similarities between the Hindu and Irish systems of law, which also point to Indo-European origin, go a long way towards proving that the Irish *filid*, and therefore the Celtic Druids, were heirs to the same tradition as the Brahmins.

So before we continue to see just how the Greek and Roman commentators portrayed the Druids, let us summarize our argument. The Druids were an indigenous Celtic intelligentsia, evolving from the original wise men and women during the age of the 'hunter-gatherer' among the ancient ancestors of the Celts, losing their original functions but retaining the Celtic name of those with 'oak knowledge'. They were to be found in every part of the Celtic society but it was not until the second century BC that the Greeks realized that these individual learned functionaries had a collective name – the Druids.

[3]

Druids Through Foreign Eyes

POSEIDONIOS (*c.*135–*c.*50 BC) of Apamea, Syria, was an historian and philosopher who spent most of his life on the island of Rhodes and became head of the Stoic school there. He was a polymath who epitomized the learning of the Hellenistic age and transmitted some part of it to the Roman world. His fifty-two books of history were a continuation of Polybius (*c.*200 to after 118 BC), the Greek historian of Rome's rise to power. Poseidonios' history covered the period of Roman imperial history from 146 BC to 81 BC. Very few fragments have survived, which has been considered a particular misfortune for Classicists. He travelled widely and visited Gaul. In spite of being a Greek, Poseidonios was a fanatical admirer of the Roman empire, thinking that it embodied the Stoic view of the kinship of all humanity on the grounds that Rome sought to extend its rule over everyone in the known world. Therefore, his work represented a policy designed to uphold Roman imperial attitudes by presenting a biased and unsympathetic view of foreign society. This has to be borne in mind when he is quoted by others as the authority on the ancient Celts.

It is strongly argued that Poseidonios' work on the Celts of Gaul was used as source material by the Alexandrian, Timagenes, *c.*mid-first century BC; the Roman general and dictator, Gaius Julius Caesar (100–44 BC); Diodorus Siculus (*c.*60–*c.*21 BC), a Sicilian Greek historian; and Strabo, a Greek geographer from Amasia in Pontus (64 BC–AD 24). In fact, these four writers have been termed the 'Poseidonios School', and are among the earliest extant writers on the Druids, all, as can be seen, roughly contemporary.

Both Diodorus and Strabo divided the intellectual classes of Gaul into three categories. Strabo, in his *Geographia*, says:

> Among all the tribes, generally speaking, there are three classes of men held in special honour: the Bards, the Vates and the Druids.

The Bards are singers and poets; the Vates interpreters of sacrifice and natural philosophers; while the Druids, in addition to the science of nature, study also moral philosophy. They are believed to be the most just of men, and are therefore entrusted with the decision of cases affecting either individuals or the public; indeed in former times they arbitrated in war and brought to a standstill the opponents when about to draw up in line of battle; and murder cases have been mostly entrusted to their decision . . . These men, as well as other authorities, have pronounced that men's souls and the universe are indestructible, although at times fire or water may (temporarily) prevail.

Diodorus also makes the same categorization, pointing out that the Druids were held in great veneration and that the Ovates foretell the future by the flight or cries of birds and slaughter of sacred animals. Diodorus cites Timagenes as an authority on the Druids. In this division of the intellectual class of Gaul into three (Druids, Vates and Bards) we find a confirmation from a native Celtic source in that the same classes of intellectuals were known in Ireland (*Drui*, *Bard* and *Fili*), a fact that testifies to the common Celtic origin of the social order.

Indeed, this same division of the Gaulish intelligentsia is made by a later Greek authority from Antioch, Ammianus Marcellinus (*c.*AD 330–395) who is regarded as the last great 'Roman historian'. Ammianus also quotes the Greek, Timagenes, as his source. Timagenes was an Alexandrian, captured and taken to Rome in 55 BC where he eventually became a freeman and successful teacher of rhetoric. In disfavour with the emperor Augustus, Timagenes burnt his works and left Rome. It is thought that he died in Mesopotamia.

Ammianus Marcellinus, quoting Timagenes, mentions that the Druids had an organization, a corporate life – *sodaliciss adstricti consortiis* – and were the authorities on the history of the Gauls. 'They affirm that one portion of the Gaulish race was indigenous in Gaul, but that others had penetrated from the outlying islands and from the regions beyond the Rhine.' What a pity that Timagenes did not amplify further on the history as taught by the Druids. The one statement he makes is certainly consistent with everything we know of the history and archaeology of the Celts.

Strabo continues his observations with a chapter which is highly critical of the Celts in which he refers to the custom of bringing home the heads of their enemies from battle as trophies. Strabo has clearly not seen this custom nor does he fully understand it. He does, however, cite Poseidonios as his authority, adding that Poseidonios 'himself saw the spectacle in many places, and that although at first he loathed it, afterwards, through his familiarity with it, he could bear it calmly'. Strabo then talks about how the Gauls embalmed the heads of particularly distinguished enemies and refused to sell them. He adds, and we must remember he is writing after the Roman conquest of Gaul: 'The Romans put a stop to these customs, as well as to all those connected with the sacrifices and divinations that are opposed to our usages.'

Diodorus provides a much more comprehensive description of the Celts of Gaul than Strabo, especially in regard to their social and military customs. He also speaks of their treatment of the heads of their enemies, in a manner which is strikingly similar to Strabo, and he mentions briefly, as does Strabo, the belief in immortality of the soul, ascribing it to 'the teaching of Pythagoras'.

According to Diodorus:

They have also certain philosophers and theologians who are treated with special honour, whom they call Druids. They further make use of seers, thinking them worthy of praise. These latter by their augural observances and by the sacrifice of sacrificial animals can foretell the future and they hold all the people subject to them. In particular when inquiring into matters of great import they have a strange and incredible custom; they devote to death a human being and stab him with a dagger in the region above the diaphragm, and when he has fallen they foretell the future from his fall, and from the convulsions of his limbs and, moreover, from the spurting of the blood, placing their trust in some ancient and long continued observation of these practices. Their custom is that no one should offer sacrifice without a Druid: for they say that thanks should be offered to the gods by those skilled in the divine nature, as though they were people who can speak their language, and through them also they hold that benefits should be asked.

In fact, there can be little doubt that Strabo and Diodorus are ultimately deriving their information from a common source. They appear to be following a similar text. Strabo cites Poseidonios as his authority on the embalming of heads. But are they quoting directly from Poseidonios or from Timagenes, who could have been an intermediary reporting the works of Poseidonios to them? The Latin literary scholar Alfred Klotz believed that Timagenes was the intermediary in the conviction that Poseidonios' work had already been lost by the time Caesar, Strabo and Diodorus were writing. However, the works of Poseidonios were available to Athenaeus (fl. c.AD 200), who also names Poseidonios as his authority for quoting Celtic customs which are similar to some mentioned by Diodorus, although he uses enough original quotations to show he had the original source and was not simply repeating Diodorus. It seems likely that Strabo had access to both sources. But whether Strabo took the material directly or from the second-hand source of Timagenes, is not as important as demonstrating that both Diodorus and Strabo owe a debt to one source – the now lost writings of Poseidonios.

Moreover, it should be emphasized that Strabo's *Geographia* was a pointed attack on the Celts which was written as a justification for Julius Caesar's conquest of Gaul and the subsequent attempts to suppress the Celtic intelligentsia and their centres of learning. Poseidonios's pro-Roman, Stoic attitudes would have made his work a comfortable authority for Strabo.

So let us move on to the Roman general who actually conquered Gaul and also tried to bring the entire Celtic world under the *Pax Romana*, with the exception of Ireland. Gaius Julius Caesar (100–44 BC) certainly spent a long time among the Celts during his efforts to conquer them and he, naturally, provides us with more information than other writers.

Caesar, in *De Bello Gallico*, Book VI, says that there were three classes in Gaul – the intellectuals called Druids (*Druides*), the military caste (*Equites*) and the people (*Plebs*). Here, Caesar accords the Druids their proper caste designation but goes on, in effect, to describe a religious priesthood without naming them as such.

Of the Druids, Caesar says:

The Druids officiate at the worship of the gods, regulate public and private sacrifices, and give rulings on all religious questions. Large numbers of young men flock to them for instruction, and they are held in great honour by the people. They act as judges in practically all disputes, whether between tribes or between individuals; when any crime is committed or a murder takes place, or a dispute arises about an inheritance or a boundary, it is they who adjudicate the matter and appoint the compensation to be paid and received by the parties concerned. Any individual or tribe failing to accept their award is banned from taking part in sacrifice – the heaviest punishment that can be inflicted upon a Gaul. Those who are under such a ban are regarded as impious criminals. Everyone shuns them and avoids going near or speaking to them, for fear of taking some harm by contact with what is unclean; if they appear as plaintiffs, justice is denied them, and they are excluded from a share in any honour.

He also tells us how the Druids in Gaul were organized:

All Druids are under one head, whom they hold in the highest respect. On his death, if any one of the rest is of outstanding merit, he succeeds to the vacant place; if several have equal claims, the Druids usually decide the election by voting, though sometimes they actually fight it out. Those who are involved in disputes assemble here from all parts, and accept the Druids' judgments and awards.

We shall later discuss references in Irish sources to a similar institution in Ireland.

Caesar observes:

The Druidic doctrine is believed to have been found existing in Britain and thence imported into Gaul; even today those who want to make a profound study of it generally go to Britain for the purpose.

References to Druidic colleges or schools are also found in Irish tradition and this will be a subject for further discussion.

As to the social position of the Druids, Caesar informs us that:

The Druids are exempt from military service and do not pay taxes like other citizens. These important privileges are naturally

54

attractive; many present themselves of their own accord to become students of Druidism, and others are sent by their parents and relatives. It is said that these people have to memorise a great number of verses – so many that some spend twenty years at their studies.

One of the most important points which Caesar notes is the fact that:

The Druids believe that their religion forbids them to commit their teachings to writing, although for most other purposes, such as public and private accounts, the Gauls use the Greek alphabet. But I imagine that this rule was originally established for other reason – because they did not want their doctrine to become public property, and in order to prevent their pupils from relying on the written word and neglecting to train their memories; for it usually found that when people have the help of texts, they are less diligent in learning by heart, and let their memories rust.

A superficial interpretation and a misreading of Caesar's comments has caused many to claim that the ancient Celts were illiterate. However, examples of Gaulish, written in Greek and sometimes Latin alphabets, survive in several areas and date back to the third and second centuries BC. Inscriptions from Cisalpine Gaul, such as the Todi, Briona and Saignon stones have now been carefully studied. For a long while the intricate Calender of Coligny, dating from the first century BC, was claimed as the earliest surviving extensive text in a Celtic language until the discovery of a leaden tablet in 1983 at La Vayssière, now called the Larzac Inscription, which was written in Latin cursive and was then acknowledged as the 'longest known Gaulish text to date', ascribed to the second or first centuries BC. Then in December 1992 came yet another discovery, in northern Spain, of a Celtic text written on a bronze tablet. Modern scholars' perception of the extent to which the Celts were literate has been changing rapidly and we shall return to this theme in a discussion on 'Druidic Books'.

On the much discussed subject of the Druidic teaching of immortality of the soul, Caesar comments:

A lesson which they take particular pains to inculcate is that the soul does not perish, but after death passes from one body to another; they think that this is the best incentive to bravery, because it teaches men to disregard the terrors of death.

There speaks the cynical soldier.

Another fascinating comment, in line with other observers, is on the Druidic knowledge of astronomy.

They also hold long discussions about the heavenly bodies and their movements, the size of the universe and of the earth, the physical constitutions of the world, and the powers and properties of the gods; and they instruct the young men in all these subjects.

Caesar is clear that the prestige of the Druids in all matters public and private is paramount and their decisions are final.

In the nature and manner of their comments, although Caesar amplifies in places, it is obvious that there is a common source between Caesar, Diodorus and Strabo and that it is Poseidonios.

In spite of their bias, we can be appreciative of the comments of our pro-Roman observers. Caesar, in particular, who had personal dealings with the Celts in his war of conquest, gives important information not found in Strabo and Diodorus and not only derived from Poseidonois. The important fact to our contention is that Caesar, who is in a better position to know, names the whole intellectual class of the Gauls as 'Druids'.

We cannot leave Caesar without reference to two Druids and brothers whom Caesar knew well. Divitiacus was a chieftain (*princeps*) of the Aedui, whose capital was the hill fort of Bibracte (Mont Beuvray). It was Divitiacus who was the 'Achilles heel' causing the Roman conquest of Gaul to begin. He was looking for a powerful ally to help drive back the German incursions into Gaul. In 60 BC he went to Rome and was allowed to address the Roman Senate, pleading for military assistance. While he was in Rome he was the guest of Quintus Tullius Cicero (102–43 BC), an able soldier and administrator and younger brother of the famous orator and statesman, Marcus Tullius Cicero (106–43 BC). It is Marcus Cicero who mentions that Divitiacus was a Druid and that he was acquainted with natural philosophy and able to predict the future.

Marcus Cicero, writing to his brother, states:

The system of divination is not even neglected among barbaric peoples, since in fact there are Druids in Gaul; I myself knew one of them, Divitiacus of the Aedui, your guest and eulogist, who declared that he was acquainted with the system of nature which the Greeks call natural philosophy and he used to predict the future by both augury and inference.

When Divitiacus returned to his own land, he must have carried with him some vague promises from Rome about an alliance, for he did all he could to promote such an alliance.

But Caesar was persuading the Roman Senate to support Divitiacus' enemy, the German king Ariovistus against the Celts. It was in 58 BC that Caesar found an opportunity to intervene in Gaulish affairs and commence the conquest of what was regarded as the Celtic heartland. The Aedui had been split about Divitiacus' pro-Roman policy. The anti-Roman faction was centred in Divitiacus' younger brother Dumnorix (the name means 'king of the world') who also appears to have been a Druid as well as a chieftain. When Caesar and the Romans marched into Aeduian territory, many Aedui joined Dumnorix in a resistance movement. Caesar demanded that Divitiacus arrest his brother. Divitiacus, however, stood up for Dumnorix, pointing out that punishment of his younger brother would alienate him from the good opinion of his people. Dumnorix's 'predictive' abilities were obviously better than those of his brother, for he had foreseen that Caesar and Rome were going to seize the whole of Gaul. In the wake of the defeat of the Belgae confederation, Divitiacus, king and Druid, vanished from the historical scene. Until this point he had been the constant companion of Caesar in Gaul, urging his fellow Celts to submit peacefully to Rome. Caesar, in his work, includes what he claims to be a verbatim report of speeches made by Divitiacus, although these appear to be Caesar's own impression of what Divitiacus should say about Rome's interest in Gaul. Indeed, if we accept that Divitiacus was a Druid, there seems little of the qualities associated with a Druid in his speeches. In fairness, Caesar never refers to him as a Druid, but Cicero is a good authority. Nora Chadwick argues:

In all probability, however, in view of Cicero's statement, he may well be typical of the Druids at their best and in their best period, and his influence with Caesar, and the important political help which he rendered him, almost entitles him to the description of the political power ascribed to the Druids by Dio Chrysostom.

It is hard to accept that the moral code of Divitiacus, who seems to have had no compunction about selling out his fellow countrymen – indeed, the whole of Gaul to Rome – represented what was best in the Druids, unless one is a doctrinaire pro-Roman. And, indeed, we may ask the question whether Divitiacus, when he vanished from the historical scene in 54 BC, simply died or was assassinated by Gaulish patriots?

In 54 BC it was Dumnorix who emerged as chief of the Aedui and a hostage of Rome. Caesar intended to take Dumnorix on his attempt to invade Britain because he realized that if there was an uprising in Gaul while he was away then it would be Dumnorix who would lead it. Waiting on the Channel shore for favourable weather to sail, Caesar found that Dumnorix and his retinue had eluded their captors. Caesar dispatched some cavalry to chase after him and the Gaulish leader was overtaken. He refused to surrender, was overpowered and slain crying out that he was a free man of a free nation. His death became a rallying point for the Gauls to rise up in a war of liberation, which the Romans were unable to quell for four years.

That Dumnorix was an Aeduian chieftain and military leader of exceptional ability, we have ample proof. Yet what proof do we have for asserting that he, like his brother, was a Druid? Firstly, we have argued that the Druids were an intellectual caste like the Brahmins, which later degenerated into a mere priestly rôle. Dumnorix was clearly of this caste as well as the Celtic military caste. Importantly, Dumnorix, in seeking excuses not to accompany Caesar to Britain, put forward several pretexts. One was that he had religious functions to perform in Gaul during this period. The use of the plural *quo religionibus impeditri sese diceret* is important because it implies that these religious commitments were priestly functions which only he was able to carry out.

Nora Chadwick has little doubt that Dumnorix was a Druid:

That Divitiacus was a Druid we are not left in doubt and we may accept his word that he was versed in [philosophy] and augury, which are associated in our earliest authorities with the Gaulish Druids. Whether he remained a Druid after coming under Roman influence we do not know. Probably he did not. This would account for Caesar's silence on the subject, though other explanations are possible. A more difficult question arises in regard to Dumnorix. He is never stated to be a Druid; but one wonders. His background is in all probability the same as his brother's. He evidently enjoyed the confidence of those Gaulish chiefs who were opposed to Caesar, and enjoyed unbounded popularity among the common people. What are the *religiones*, the 'religious responsibilities' which – so he alleged to Caesar – precluded his crossing over to Britain? His extreme conservatism and dedication to the Gaulish cause in implacable opposition to Roman influence was completely consistent with the political attitude of the Druids as we gather this from later writers. In fact, apart from what we learn of Divitiacus from Cicero, and surveying the evidence for Druids as a whole, Dumnorix, as he comes before us in the pages of Caesar, answers more closely to our latest reports of the Druids inciting the Gauls against the Roman conquerors than his elder brother.

It has been argued that rather than Caesar being one of the Poseidonios school of writers on the Druids, he, in fact, gave birth to his own traditional school in which many writers followed him. Certainly Pomponious Mela of Tingentera (c.AD 43), and Marcus Annaeus Lucanus (AD 39–65), a grandson of Seneca the Elder, seem so close to Caesar as to indicate free borrowing from his text.

It can be also argued that Pliny the Elder, who came from a family of Roman colonists in Cisalpine Gaul, who also held the office of procurator in Gaul, owed much to Caesar's work. Pliny was suffocated by fumes during the famous eruption of Vesuvius in August AD 79, which buried Pompeii and Herculaneum. In his *Naturalis Historia*, his chief and only surviving work, Pliny gives one of the fullest accounts of the Druids ever to survive, presenting them as natural scientists, doctors of medicine, and magicians. Pliny was fascinated by magic himself and it is, perhaps, understandable that he should dwell on this aspect of his perception of the Druids.

It was, perhaps, this fascination with magic which caused Pliny to talk about *anguinam*, the 'Druid's eggs' or 'serpent's eggs'. He says that in the reign of Claudius, a chief of the Gaulish Vocontii was put to death when attending a lawsuit in Rome because it was found that he carried a 'serpent's egg' on his person. Pliny claims that the Druids saw it as a talisman which brought victory in law courts. It has been pointed out that, whether true or not, it does indicate that anyone connected with Druidism, however remote, was liable to punishment by Roman law. Pliny says he has seen one of these 'Druid's eggs', which was like crystal and about as large as a moderate-sized apple. Pliny also says the egg was produced by the foam of hissing snakes meeting together. The foam from their mouths formed a viscous slime which became a ball tossed in the air and which, if caught by a Druid, could be used to counteract incantations. Celtic deities carry eggs, such as Sirona, the goddess of fertility, healing and rebirth, whose image at Horchscheid in Germany carries a bowl with three eggs. Sirona, interestingly enough from the viewpoint of 'serpent's eggs', is seen with a serpent coiled around her arm, reaching out to take the eggs. Clearly eggs are seen as a powerful fertility symbol. In one grave of a Gaulish warrior chieftain, eggs were actually buried as grave goods. Eggs also appear in Celtic mythology. The Irish goddess Cliodna possessed two Otherworld birds, red in colour with green heads who laid blue and crimson coloured eggs. If mortals ate of them, then they turned into birds, growing feathers.

Indeed, the idea of Druid's eggs appears in most Celtic folklore. In Scotland the *glain-nan-Druidhe* or Druid's crystal was spoken of. William Camden in his *Britannia* (1586) mentions *gemmae anguine* as 'small glass amulets, commonly about as wide as our finger rings, but much thicker, of a green colour, usually though some of them are blue, and others curiously waved with blue, red and white'. Thomas Kendrick says they 'were called "snake-stones" in Cornwall, Wales and Scotland, and it is reported that in Wales and in Ireland they were also sometimes called Druid's Glass'. The crystal Kendrick believes Pliny saw was a conglomeration of tiny ammonites.

Pliny goes on to tell of numerous eminent physicians in the early part of the first century BC who were either natives of or who had received their training in Gaul before the Druidic colleges were proscribed. Crinias of Marseilles, who combined astrology and medicine, Charmis of Marseilles, and Alcon, all trained in Gaul, are cited with the implication that Gaulish physicians were pre-eminent until the Roman conquest and prohibition of the Druids. We shall be returning to the Celtic medical traditions, as well as astrology, later in this work.

It is from Pliny that we first hear about the oak groves and mistletoe.

> The Druids – for so they call their *magi* – hold nothing more sacred than the mistletoe and the tree on which it grows provided that it is an oak. They choose the oak to form groves, and they do not perform any religious rites without its foliage, so that it can be seen that the *Druides* are so called from the Greek word.

Pliny now follows with a passage that has become one of the most widely known and accepted descriptions of the Druids. Speaking of the Druids in their oak-groves, Pliny relates:

> Anything growing on those trees they regard as sent from heaven and a sign that this tree has been chosen by the gods themselves. Mistletoe is, however, very rarely found, and when found, it is gathered with great ceremony and especially on the sixth day of the moon . . . They prepare a ritual sacrifice and feast under the tree, and lead up two white bulls whose horns are bound for the first time on this occasion. A priest attired in a white vestment ascends the tree and with a golden pruning hook cuts the mistletoe which is caught in a white cloth. Then next they sacrifice the victims praying that the gods will make their gifts propitious to those to whom they have given it. They believe that if given in drink the mistletoe will give fecundity to any barren animal, and that it is predominant against all poisons.

Nora Chadwick has pointed out that this passage is a 'picturesque fantasia'.

> It ranks with the stories of King Alfred and the cakes, of Cnut and the waves, and of Bruce and the spider, among the classics of universal popular knowledge . . . taken with the uncritical nature of Pliny's writings generally, should make us hesitate to attach too grave a credence to the passage of the mistletoe in association with the Druids.

Indeed, so far as the Irish Druids are concerned, the mistletoe was not a native Irish plant and was only introduced into Ireland towards the end of the eighteenth or early nineteenth century. However, if the Gaulish Druids revered mistletoe, and this ceremony was as important as Pliny indicates, then it is interesting that no other source corroborates this. Pliny himself cites Polyhistor (Alexander Cornelius, b.*c.*105 BC) as an authority on oaks and mistletoe but Polyhistor does not corroborate, nor is he the source, for Pliny' oak-grove Druid fantasia.

Pliny becomes the first writer to introduce the oak-grove into the picture of the Druids. Apart from the derivation of the name, when the Druids emerge in the writings of Poseidonios and his followers, forests do not feature as part of their world until Pliny nor are they significantly present in native Celtic tradition. But following Pliny, the floodgates are opened.

Lucan echoes Pliny when he refers to the Druids dwelling in deep groves and uninhabited woods, practising barbarous rites and a sinister mode of worship. Lucan, in his epic poem, *Pharsalia*, describes a wood near Marseilles as an eerie, enchanted wood: 'The people never frequented the place to worship very near it, but left it to the gods . . . The priest himself dreads the approach and fears to come upon the lord of the grove.' However, Lucan does not go so far in this to describe it as a *Druidic* grove, although the implication is obvious. While, of course, the *Pharsalia* is not history, we cannot leave it without mentioning the fact that Lucan says that the wood of the trees of this oak grove was crudely sculptured to represent gods (*simulacra maesta deorum*). In 1963 some 140 pieces of wood carving, dating from the second century AD, were discovered in the vicinity of a Gaulish sanctuary in the marshland sources of the Seine, devoted to Sequana, thought to be goddess of the source. They are now in the Musée Archéologique, Dijon. The significance, linking them to what Lucan says, is that they are carved from pieces of oak wood. The items, some whole statues of gods and goddesses, are claimed to be votive offerings.

Lactantius Placidus in his commentary on the *Thebais* of Caecilius Statius (*c.*AD 45–*c.*96), notes: 'The Druids are those who delight in oaks'. Statius mentions a grove 'dense and ancient, untouched by human hand and impervious to the beams of the sun. Here the pale and uncertain light serves only to increase the awe and the ominous silence. The divine presence of Latona (the Latin name for the Greek goddess Leto, one of the Titans who was mother of Apollo and Artemis) 'haunted the grove, and the wood in its sacred shadows hides her effigies in the cedar and oak'.

Now it would be very easy to accept the Roman writers and assign the Druids to dark oak groves, especially since, as we know, forest groves were considered sacred places among most Indo-European cultures, even surviving in Hindu culture. But some questions do arise.

Publicius Cornelius Tacitus (b. AD 56/57 – d. after 117) seems to support Pliny by referring to the dark groves on the island of Anglesey devoted to barbaric superstitions which were then destroyed by Suetonius Paulinus around AD 61. However, Tacitus was not a witness to this so was he working from the new Pliny tradition? Of course, one has to remember that Tacitus' father-in-law was Gnaeus Julius Agricola (AD 40–93), who did his early military service in Britain with Suetonius before he himself became governor of the province. But there is still one worrying aspect of Tacitus' work, especially in *Germania*. Attributes he claims to be German seem, on the contrary, to be Celtic. Or were he and other Roman writers so totally confused about the Gaulish Celts that they mixed many customs of the Celts with those of their German neighbours and vice versa? Tacitus says it was the Germans who prefer to dwell in deep forest groves and held them sacred.

> Woods and groves are the sacred depositories; and the spot being consecrated to those pious uses, they give to that sacred recess the name of the divinity that fills the place, which is never profaned by the steps of man. The gloom fills every mind with awe; revered at a distance and never seen but with the eye of contemplation.

Pliny the Younger (Gaius Plinius Caecilius Secundus – AD 61–113) echoes this but attributes to the Germans: 'We adore the gloom of the woods, and the silence that reigns around us.' So, in fact, have the Romans, starting with Pliny, mistakenly put the Celts into the German sacred groves? A mistake that has reverberated throughout centuries of scholarship?

Of one group of Germans, Tacitus makes an obvious mistake when he declares 'their language has more affinity to the dialect of Britain'.

Those he spoke of were clearly Celts and not Germans. He also says: 'The Germans abound with rude strains of verse, the reciters of which, in the language of the country, are called *bards*.' He is again clearly confused between Celts and Germans. He also designates Veleda as a German prophetess. But the name is clearly Celtic and we will discuss her further under the section, 'Female Druids'. The cutting of auguries from trees in sacred groves by German priests seems to be an echo of the Elder Pliny's Druids and their sacred mistletoe.

Nora Chadwick has, however, put forward another plausible theory to explain the sudden appearance of oak groves in reference to the Druids in the works of Latin writers in the first century AD. Gaul, we must remember, had fallen to Rome in the first century BC and, for reasons which can be debated, the emperors Augustus, Tiberius and Claudius are said to have attempted to suppress the Druids. If so, driven from their open position in Gaulish society, from their colleges, and from the retinue of the chiefs and kings, were the Druids forced to hide out in the more inaccessible reaches of the forests of Gaul, there to teach and practise their beliefs? Indeed, the idea is given some credence by Pomponius Mela, writing some fifty years after this suppression of the Druids, who states: 'They teach many things to the noblest of the race in sequestered and remote places during twenty years, *whether in a cave or in secluded groves.*'

The passage actually reminds us of the 'hedge schoolmasters' of Ireland who, when an attempted suppression of native education was engineered under the Penal Laws in the late seventeenth century, would gather their pupils in secluded spots and teach while a pupil took a vantage point to warn of the approach of English soldiers. We shall be discussing this subject more fully when we discuss the Druidic colleges.

It is, however, Cornelius Tacitus who gives us invaluable information on the Druids as historians when, in his *Histories*, he cites a prophecy of the Gaulish Druids made at the time of Vespasian, which also shows that they had not been entirely suppressed at that time. In December, AD 69, the emperor Aulus Vitellius was defeated and killed by Vespasian who then claimed the throne. According to Tacitus:

The Gauls began to breathe new life and vigour, persuaded that the Roman armies, wherever stationed, were broken and dispirited. A rumour was current among them, and universally believed, that the Racians and Sarmatians had laid siege to the encampments in Maesia and Pannonia. Affairs in Britain were supposed to be in no better situation. Above all, the destruction of the Capitol announced the approaching fate of the Roman empire. The Druids, in their wild enthusiasm, sung their oracular songs, in which they taught that, when Rome was formerly sacked by the Gauls, the mansion of Jupiter being left entire, the commonwealth survived that dreadful shock; but the calamity of fire, which had lately happened, was a denunciation from heaven, in consequence of which, power and dominion were to circulate round the world, and the nations on their side of the Alps were in their turn to become masters of the world.

Tacitus cynically observes: 'Thus the Druids declaimed in their chantings of vain superstitions'. The prophecy may have been three hundred years too early but, one can't help pointing out, certainly the Germanic peoples north of the Alps did become masters of the known world when Rome fell.

One particularly interesting point is that the Druids of AD 69 still remembered, whether by oral tradition or written record is unclear, the Celtic defeat of the Roman army at Allia on 18 July c.390/387 BC. This was the event in which Brennos and his Celts sacked Rome but failed to capture the Capitoline. Negotiations led to Rome paying a ransom for Celtic withdrawal from Rome. This history, Tacitus demonstrates, was remembered by the Druids, and thus he confirms Ammianus Marcellinus, quoting Timagenes on the rôle of the Druids as historians.

We have, so far, dealt with the Classical sources which were supportive of the Roman empire, whether from Latin writers or Greek apologists. Apart from those Greeks who devoted their services to the Roman empire, there emerged another school of Greek observers. These were scholars who had been educated in the School of Alexandria, writing from the first century AD but also using older source materials. This group were concerned with gathering sources and traditions, meticulously citing their authorities, compiling encyclopaedias rather than producing first-hand accounts. Professor Stuart

Piggott, one of the most recent Druidic scholars, is inclined to dismiss these works as: 'all second-hand library work, with no new empirical observations from first-hand informants or from field work among the Celtic peoples'. Professor Piggott believes the texts of the Alexandrian School fall to an idealizing of the Druids as the 'Noble Savage' and created the romantic image of the Druids which enraptured seventeenth and eighteenth century French and English scholars.

Certainly these writers were not overly concerned in writing justification and propaganda and their tone is more respectful towards the Celts and the Druids, who are, indeed, openly compared, for the first time, to the Brahmins of India. Mrs Chadwick has remarked that the Alexandrian tradition is therefore an important one, even though she tends towards an idealization of Rome.

Dio Chrysostom (c.AD 40 – d. after AD 111), properly Dion Cocceianus, known as Chrysostomos – 'golden mouthed' – who came from Bithynia, is the first figure of importance in this new school. He travelled to Rome, came in conflict with the emperor Domitian, and then set out to travel widely through Greece and Asia Minor, encountering the Celts in Galatia.

Dio Chrysostom in his *Oratio* is highly respectful of the Druids. It is he who first compares them, accurately in my estimation, to the Brahmins of India and mentions both their political influence in Celtic society and their intellectual attainments, crediting them with advances in mantic art and other branches of ancient wisdom.

> The Celts appointed Druids, who likewise were versed in the art of seers and other forms of wisdom without whom the kings were not permitted to adopt or plan any course, so that in fact it was these who ruled and the kings became their subordinates and instruments of their judgment, while themselves seated on golden thrones, and dwelling in great houses and being sumptuously feasted.

It is from the Alexandrian school that we hear of the comparisons of the Druids to Pythagoreans, especially in their teachings on the immortality of the soul, which we will discuss later. It was Hippolytus (c.AD 170–c.236) who claims that the Druids adopted this teaching through the agency of Pythagoras' slave Zalmoxis. Hippolytus was then contradicted by Clement of Alexandria (c.AD 150–

211/216) who argued that Pythagoras developed his ideas from the
Celts. Diogenes Laertius (fl. AD 225/250) took Polyhistor as his main
authority for the doctrines of Pythagoras. Polyhistor wrote a special
work on Pythagoras which is now lost but which Diogenes obviously
had access to. Diogenes was aware of the arguments of Clement but
takes the side of Hippolytus. Clement's argument revolved on the
curious concept: 'It was from the Greeks that philosophy took its
rise: its very name refuses to be translated into foreign speech.'

Apart from Dio Chrysostom, Hippolytus and Diogenes Laertius,
Origen (c.AD 185–255) and Cyril of Alexandria (archbishop of the
city in AD 412–444) have also added to the discourse on Druids as
philosophers. Origen, who was Clement's successor as head of the
Christian school at Alexandria, claimed that the Druids taught
monotheism. All these themes will be studied in our discussion on
the Druids as philosophers.

It is from the Alexandrian writings that we have references to
earlier writers who had studied the Celts and the Druids but whose
works no longer survive in their entirety. Timaeus (c.356–260 BC)
was used extensively as an authority by Diogenes Laertius and
Clement of Alexandria. Sotion of Alexandria (fl. 200–170 BC), a
philosopher, was a major source for Diogenes Laertius on the
Druids. Greek writers from Herodotus (c.490–425 BC) of Halicarnassus to Alexander Cornelius Polyhistor (b.c.105 BC) are quoted
but not as mentioning the Druids by that name.

Also among the authorities cited was Aristotle (384–322 BC), the
famous pupil of Plato. But the work, as I have mentioned before,
quoted by Diogenes, called *Magicus* was identified by V. Rose (in
Aristotles Pseudepigraphus, Leipzig, 1863) as being falsely ascribed.
However, the work was certainly written in the second century BC,
making it one of the earliest works to mention Druidic philosophy,
and therefore, whether attributable to Aristotle or not, worthy of
consideration. The wrong identification of Aristotle as the author
came through a misreading of Diogenes' quotation of Polyhistor and
this was corrected by R.D. Hicks in his work on *Diogenes Laertius*
(1958). It was Diogenes Laertius who claimed that the Druids taught
in triads and the basis of their tradition was 'to honour the gods, to
do no evil, and to practise bravery'.

While Professor Piggott acknowledges that the Alexandrian writers
were engaged in works of synthesis and collation, preserving many

important earlier texts which are otherwise lost, he does tend to be more appreciative of the Poseidonios tradition 'mainly derived from first hand information on Celtic manners and customs'. He is inclined to dismiss the Alexandrian tradition as portraying 'a romantic image of barbarian philosophers, and we move from Druids-as-known to Druids-as-wished-for'. Yet it is clear that most of the information given in the writers of the Poseidonian tradition is merely repetitive of information from Poseidonios himself. Even Caesar, who was in a position to have tremendous first-hand knowledge, tends to use Poseidonios as his base, though it is true he adds to our knowledge with some original observations. But, as already made clear, Caesar is not entirely to be trusted. His comments on Britain, for example, are ridiculously wrong.

> But many of the inland Britons do not grow corn. They live on milk and flesh and are clothed in skins. All the Britons stain their persons with a dye that produces a blue colour. This gives them a more terrible aspect in battle. They wear their hair long, shaving all the body except the head and upper lip.

The Celts were fastidious in personal appearance. Diodorus Siculus points out that soap (*sopa*) was a Celtic innovation and word. During Caesar's time, Britain was renowned in the Roman world for its woollen trade and for a Roman to own a British woollen cloak was regarded with the same prestige as many would have regarded the ownership of a Harris Tweed suit a few decades ago. This is not the place to go into a detailed rebuttal of Caesar's jaundiced views. Even Caesar's contemporary Strabo pointed out that because Britain was a leading commercial centre outside the Roman empire, trade on an equal footing with Britain would produce more revenue for Rome than would accrue if the island were to become a Roman province and the Roman treasury had to pay for a standing army and civil service to run the country. This is hardly a view compatible with the savage country Caesar tried to portray as justification for invasion and conquest.

There is another point about the Poseidonian writers. They do not tend to acknowledge their sources, whereas the Alexandrian writers do so meticulously. So both groups are citing other writers with very few actually observing Celtic society at first hand and with the Poseidonians clearly writing to support the ethics of the Roman empire.

These schools, the Poseidonians and Alexandrians, therefore constitute our Classical sources on the Druids. In dealing with these sources we have to keep uppermost in our minds that, whether they are clearly anti-Celtic or sympathetic, they still consist of observations made by people whose cultural and social concepts were foreign to the Celts. Therefore, even the most sympathetic observer could totally misinterpret the subject on which he was writing. How a fact can be drastically changed by mistaken interpretation was brought home to me when researching my book *MacBeth: High King of Scotland* AD 1040–57 (1980). In pre-eleventh century AD Scotland, Celtic law prevailed in that there was no such concept as primogeniture, that is, the succession of the first-born son. When it came to kingship, High Kings were elected, not by the people at large, but under a limited hereditary system first by the *derbhfine* of the clan and then by sub-kings and chieftains. How would this system seem from an observer imbued in the system of primogeniture? We have the example of a comment from the distinguished nineteenth century English historian, Professor A.J. Church. Church ingenuously observed that the struggle for kingship in Scotland must have been a remarkably *bloodthirsty* affair *for hardly ever did a son succeed his father to the throne!* As Celtic law provided that the best candidate from the family could succeed rather than simply the son of the former king, we can see how easy it is to totally misinterpret social and cultural concepts and imagine mayhem and bloodshed where there was none. The Greek and Latin commentaries are certainly valuable but they must not be treated without question.

[4]

Druids Through Celtic Eyes

B Y the time the Celts started to commit their fabulous wealth
of learning, their mythology, history and philosophies to writing, not only had their world become very much reduced in
size but they had become Christian. In fact, the very act of becoming Christian was the means whereby the Druidic proscription
against committing their knowledge to writing was overcome.
Yet in this process, the general Christian attitude to the Druids
was inimical. They were obviously portrayed as opponents of
Christianity, upholders of the ancient religion, and thereby were
relegated to the rôle of shamans, magicians and 'witch doctors',
although this prejudice varied from writer to writer. Dr Douglas
Hyde, in his seminal *Literary History of Ireland* (1899), has
pointed out: 'There existed a sufficient number of persons in
early Christian Ireland who did not consider the Druids wholly
bad, but believed they could prophecy, at least in the interests of
the saints.'

With the Continental Celtic world overcome by the Roman Empire
and its heirs, it is the Insular Celts who have preserved, to varying
degrees, the native traditions of the Druids, albeit through Christianized eyes. Our two basic sources in this respect are the Irish
sources and, to a far lesser extent, the Welsh sources.

In medieval Ireland, the classes recognized by the Romans in Gaul
continued to have their equivalents. Druid (*druî*), vates (*fáith/fáidh*
or *filî*) and bard (*bard*). In Irish terms of this period, these equated
to 'magician', 'prophet' and 'poet'.

The *Leabhar Gabhála* (Book of Invasions) hails Amairgen, a son
of Milesius, as the first Druid of the Gaels in Ireland. His wife Scena
died on the voyage to Ireland and was buried at Inverkscena (Ken-
mare River, Co. Kerry). It is Amairgen who pronounces the first
judgement delivered in Ireland by deciding that Eremon should
become the first Milesian king of the country. Three poems are

accredited to Amairgen and perhaps the most famous is the extraordinary incantation of self used as the opening quotation to this work. In this 'song' Amairgen subsumes everything into his own being with a philosophical outlook that parallels the declaration of Krishna in the Hindu *Bhagavad-Gita*. The incantation is echoed by a poem attributed to Taliesin in the sixth century AD, of which the following is a comparative section:

> I have been a blue salmon
> I have been a wild dog,
> I have been a cautious stag,
> I have been a deer on the mountain
> and a stump of a tree on a shovel
> I have been an axe in the hand
> A pin in a pair of tongs
> A stallion in stud
> A bull in anger
> A grain in the growing
> I have been dead, I have been alive
> I am a composer of songs
> for I am Taliesin.

Of course, the tradition of Amairgen is far older than Taliesin and it could well be that the composer of the Taliesin poem was influenced by the Irish source. It should also be borne in mind that many traditions and poems have been attributed to Taliesin which are demonstrably spurious.

For those who turn to the opening Amairgen incantation at the start of this work, it should be explained that Tethra was a mysterious Fomorii sea-god who owned the sword Orna which could speak and recount its deeds. Ogma claimed it, having killed Tethra at the second Battle of Magh Tuireadh (Moytura). The 'cattle' which Amairgen sings of were, in fact, fish as befitted an ocean god. As the Rees brothers point out, like Krishna, 'Amairgen on the ocean of non-existence embodies the primeval unity of all things. As such he has the power to bring a new world into being, and his poems are in the nature of creation incantations.'

Another of Amairgen's poetical incantations is directed to Ireland herself:

I invoke the land of Éire:
much coursed by the fertile sea.
Fertile is the fruit strewn mountain,
fruit strewn by the showery wood,
showery is the river of waterfalls,
of waterfalls by the lake of deep pools,
deep is the hill-top well,
a well of tribes is the assembly.
an assembly of the kings is Tara
Tara of the hill of the tribes,
the tribes of the sons of Míl
of Míl of the ships –
Like a lofty ship is the land of Éire
lofty land of Éire darkly sung
and incantation of great cunning
the great cunning of the wives of Bres
the wives of Bres of Buaigne
but the great goddess Éire –
Eremon has conquered her.
I, Amairgen, have invoked for her.
I invoke the land of Éire.

Again, here is a creation incantation for the new Ireland.

If Amairgen was regarded as the first Druid of the Gaels, it does not mean that he was the first Druid known in Ireland. Partholón, who, according to the *Leabhar Gabhála* (Book of Invasions), was leader of the third mythical invasion of Ireland, had three Druids. Once again we encounter the mystical number three, so predominant in Celtic tradition. These Druids were named Fios, Eolas and Fochmarc. All three names mean 'knowledge'.

According to the same source it was a Druid of the Nemedians, named Mide, who lit the first Druidical fire at Uisneach (Ráthconrath, Co. Westmeath), which spot was claimed to be 'the navel of Ireland', the exact centre of the country. The first fire burnt for seven years and it was from this sacred fire that every fire in Ireland was supposed to have been lit. Thereafter, the Druids gathered every year to light the famous Fires of Bel (Beltaine, on May 1) at Uisnech where stood the Stone of Divisions (*Aill na Mirenn*). Veneration of Bel was widespread in the Celtic world, cognate with Belenus, Beli and Bilé, a solar deity found on many Gaulish coins whose duties included gathering the souls of the people and accompanying them to the Otherworld.

In Ireland, Uisneach was also where the High King, Tuathal Techtmhair, built a great palace and created a fifth province, Midhe (Meath) or the Middle Province, as the territory of the High King at Tara, a neutral territory, where he might dwell in order that the concerns of his own province would not outweigh the concerns of the other provinces of Ireland. High Kings were chosen from one or other of the four provincial kings of Ireland. Significantly, it is Uisneach which is claimed as 'Mount Killaraus' from which Geoffrey of Monmouth states that Merlin, the archetypal Druid of the Arthurian saga, took the stones with which he is credited as building Stonehenge.

It is interesting that the custom of the annual gathering of the Druids at Uisneach, as the centre or 'navel' of Ireland, coincides exactly with what Julius Caesar reports about the Druids of Gaul: 'On a fixed date in each year they hold a session in a consecrated spot in the country of the Carnutes, which is supposed to be the centre of Gaul.'

The Tuatha Dé Danaan, the Irish gods and goddesses themselves, also had their Druids. In the earliest reference we hear that the Children of Danu come to Ireland from four fabulous cities; Falias, Gorias, Finias and Murias. In each city they have been taught by Druids or 'wise men' – Morias, Urias, Arias and Senias. So the gods, too, had to learn their wisdom at the hands of mystical Druids. Ogma, son of The Dagda, the Father of the Gods, becomes the god of eloquence and poetry as well as being regarded as god of the Druids themselves. The Druids of the Dé Danaan conjured storms in an attempt to drive away the invading Milesians.

It was a Milesian Druid, Caicher, who prophesied the victory of his people over the Dé Danaan.

The most interesting Druid in Irish saga is Mug Ruith (sometimes given as Magh Ruith) who is variously described as Chief Druid of Ireland and even Chief Druid of the World. According to Thomas O'Rahilly: 'Originally the Sun-god, he has been euphemized in our texts into a wonder-working "Druid" or magician (drui).' Mug Ruith is a euphemistic form of Roth, meaning wheel which is a representation of the sun. He is said to have lost an eye. He is also able to dry up waters, which is a significant attribute of sun gods. He lives through nineteen reigns and is known as *mac Seinghesa* 'son of ancient wisdom'. He drives a chariot of white metal with lustrous gems, the light of which makes night into day, and in this he can travel through the air like a bird. The chariot is, of course, the sun itself. Mug Ruith carries a solar wheel, the *Roth Fáil* or 'wheel of destiny', which can blind those who see it. Mug Ruith fights Cormac Mac Art and drives the High King out of Munster after doing battle with the Druid Ciothruadh in a fabulous aerial combat. His traditions lie in Munster. Anroth, 'the glowing wheel', is found as the name of a mythical ancestor of the Eoghanacht kings of Cashel. He is also identified by the name of Rothechtaid Rotha 'great traveller of the wheel'. Mug Ruith is also claimed as the ancestor of the Fir Maige Féine, who gave their name to the barony of Fermoy in Co. Cork.

Many fascinating Druids appear in the Irish myths and annals. There is Findgoll Mac Findemas, Druid to Bres, who briefly ruled the gods. And Trosdan, who devised an antidote against the poisoned arrows used by some invaders of Ireland. There is Cabadios, grandfather to Cúchulainn. Morann, chief judge and Druid of Ulster, who was born with a caul on his head. His father ordered him to be drowned but he was rescued and raised by a smith. His most famous judgement was on who should foster Cúchulainn. Tages, father of Murna, mother of the famous warrior Fionn Mac Cumhail, was also a Druid. Lamhderg, a hermit Druid, lived on an isolated Donegal mountain. Dadera was slain by the Munster king Eoghan. Eoghan himself married Monchae, the daughter of the Druid Treth moccu Creccai. Monchae gave birth to his son Fiachu Muillethan, from whom all the kings of Munster claimed descent. Olc Aiche, another Druid, prophesied the death of Cormac Mac Art. Cormac choked to death on salmon bones because of the Druid's curse when he announced his conversion, so we are told, to Christianity. Fiachu Sraibtine (Fécho), a king of Tara and ancestor of Niall of the Nine Hostages, voluntarily chose defeat and dishonour when his Druid foretold that this was the only way he could ensure the succession of his descendants. Crond ba Druí, another Druid, is considered the ancestor of the Cruthin (or Picts) of Ulster. Cáthair Már, a King of Leinster, is able to declaim to his people:

> I am Cáthar the triumphant
> I am your Druid and your father

In the Irish cycle concerning Fionn Mac Cumhail, as another example, there appears Fir Droirich, 'the Black Druid' who turns Fionn's future wife Sibh, the mother of Oisín, into a fawn. Hence when Oisín was born he was so named the 'little deer'.

The Druid Sitchenn figures importantly in the story of Niall of the Nine Hostages. Niall and his four brothers are sent to him to see what their future holds. Sitchenn entices them into his forge and sets fire to it to see what items they would rescue from the flames. While the others come out with sledge hammers, a pail of beer, bellows, spearheads and dry sticks, Niall emerges with the anvil and from this Sitchenn prophesies that he will be the greatest High King of Ireland.

Perhaps the most sympathetic Druid to appear in Irish mythology is the figure of Cathbad, Druid and counsellor of Conchobhar Mac Nessa, king of Ulster, in the Red Branch Cycle. Dr Dáithí Ó hÓgáin has stated that some of the original status of the Druids permeates this early text. We learn that no one is allowed to speak in the assembly of the Ulster kingdom, not even the king himself, until Cathbad has spoken. In one passage in the '*Mesca Ulad*', or 'the intoxication of Ulster', in the version given in the *Leabhar na hUidri* (Book of the Dun Cow, compiled in AD 1100 at Clonmacnoise), Conchobhar stood up in the assembly to speak. No man could speak before him but he could not speak before his Druid. There was a silence. We are told that a needle falling from roof to floor would be heard. But Conchobhar, under the powerful *geasa* (prohibition) was unable to say anything. Finally, Cathbad asks: 'What is the matter, o king?' After which Conchobhar could speak for his Druid had uttered the first words. So, in many ways, Cathbad the Druid has actual status above that of the king. The passage reminds us of the comment by Dio Chrysostom that the Druids were so highly placed socially that 'the kings were not permitted to adopt or plan any course' without consulting them 'so in fact it was they who ruled and the kings became the subordinates . . .'

Incidentally, we learn in one version of the story that Conchobhar is actually the son of Cathbad by a liaison with Ness, daughter of

Eochaidh Sálbuidge. Cathbad has earlier prophesied the greatness of his son.

Druids make appearances in the making of the Irish kings such as those associated with the semi-legendary Cormac Mac Art, Eoghan Mór and Conall Gulban. Conall, for example, receives his name from the Druid of Muireadhach Meann, king of Calraighe (Co. Sligo) and, when wounded, is healed by Dúnadheach, the Druid of the princess Doireann who has fallen in love with him. The High King, Laoghaire, sends his two daughters to be educated by two Druids at Cruachan in Connacht.

In the seventh century AD, Muirchú Moccu Machteni of Armagh wrote a *Life of St Patrick*, which survives in a corrupted form in the *Book of Armagh*. In this he tells of Patrick's confrontation with the Druids at Tara:

> It came to pass in that year, that on the same night as the holy Patrick was celebrating Easter, there was an idolatrous ceremony which the gentiles [pagan Irish] were accustomed to celebrate with manifold incantations and magical contrivances and with other idolatrous superstitions when the kings, satraps, chieftains, princes and great ones of the people had assembled, and when the Druids, singers, prophets and the inventors and practitioners of every art of every gift, had been summoned to Laoghaire, as once to king Nebuchadnezzar, at Tara, their Babylon.

The Tripartite Life of Patrick says that Tara, the seat of the Irish High Kings, was 'the chief [seat] of the idolatry and Druidism of Ireland'.

In fact, the story of Patrick's conflict with the Druids at Tara is clearly modelled on the confrontation between Daniel and the prophets of Baal. For better effect, Muirchú has changed the date of the Beltaine fire ritual from 1 May to coincide with the Paschal celebration and also changed the location from Uisneach to Tara, so that Patrick can light his rival fires on the Hill of Slane. Lucet Mael (the first name means a follower of Lugh, god of arts and crafts, and the second 'bald', or more likely, 'tonsured') prophesies, with another Druid, Lochru, the end of their power and the coming of new ways in the form of Patrick's Christianity. These are the Druids who contend with Patrick and are patterned on the Biblical wizards of

Nebuchadnezzar. In Muirchú's version Laoghaire is converted but in the version given by Tirechán, also written in the same century, Laoghaire refuses baptism and when he dies he is buried in the traditional pagan warrior manner, upright and fully armed in the ramparts of Tara, his face towards his hereditary enemies – the kingdom of Laighin (Leinster).

Lucet Mael is typical of the new Christian image of the Druid, seen as a wizard for his ability to cause snow to fall at will, create illusions, interpret dreams, cure illness, curse people and give shrewd military advice. We also find, in the ninth century AD *Tripartite Life of Patrick*, a reference to an assassination attempt on Patrick by nine Druids, instigated by Amalgaid, son of Fiachra-Ealgach, whose land was Hy-Amhalgaidh near Killala. In Tirechán's *Life of Patrick* we are told that Amalgaid's Druid, one Rechrad, and eight companions (all Druids?) wore white tunics (Druidic vestments?) when they attempted to kill Patrick.

Two more Druids appear more benignly in the St Patrick story; Ida and Ono, Druids of Corchachlann, near Roscommon, who gave Patrick their house, Imleach Ono, which he then converted into the religious foundation of Elphin (*Ailfinn*, white stone).

Colmcille (St Columba, *c*.AD 521–597) was said to have been a descendent of Niall of the Nine Hostages. Some manuscript references have him as receiving his initial education from a Druid. The accounts vary. In one version it was his mother who took him to the Druid, in another, the cleric is charged with his upbringing. In the fifteenth century compilation, the *Book of Lismore*, the Druid is simply called a prophet (*flaidh*). He is initially asked when would be an auspicious time for Colmcille to start his education. When the Druid 'had scanned the sky' (astrology?) he answered that Colmcille should start at that moment and asked that the alphabet be inscribed on the top of a cake, which the boy was told to eat. From the way Colmcille ate his cake, the Druid then foretold he would be famous both in Ireland and in Scotland.

The High King at this time was Diarmuid Mac Cearbaill, reigning between AD 545–568. He is said to have had both Druids and Christian advisers at his court in Tara. His chief Druid was Beag Mac Dé (sometimes given as Bec Mac Dé), whom later writers converted into a Celtic 'saint'. Diarmuid is an interesting combination of Christian and Pagan according to the texts.

It was he who forced Colmcille into exile in Scotland, about which we will hear more later.

When one of Diarmuid's men was killed by a chieftain named Aodh Guaire, related in fosterage to St Ronán, Diarmuid sent his men to arrest Aodh. St Ronán hid him and so Diarmuid had Ronán arrested in his stead. The High King was then condemned by the Christian ecclesiastics for this act and Ronán is said to have uttered his famous curse: 'Desolate be Tara for ever!' The story goes that Tara was abandoned never to achieve its former splendour. Although a nice dramatic story, archaeological evidence shows that Tara flourished for many centuries after this period.

When Diarmuid's wife, Mughain, had an affair with Flann Mac Dima, Diarmuid had Flann's fortress burnt over his head. Sorely wounded, Flann sought to avoid the flames by climbing into a vat of water, where he drowned. St Ronán prophesied that a roof beam would fall on Diarmuid's head in retribution and kill him. In another version St Ciarán foretells that Diarmuid would suffer the same death as Flann.

However, it is Beag Mac Dé, the Druid, who pronounced the most interesting prophecy of all, which is an example of the mysticism of the Threefold Death which emerges in Celtic mythology. His prophecy was that Diarmuid would be killed by Flann's kinsman, Aedh Dubh mac Suibni, in the house of Banbán of Ráith Bec, a small ring fort east of Antrim. His death would only be encompassed on the night when he wore a shirt grown from a single flax seed, when he drank ale brewed from one grain of corn, and when he ate pork from a sow which was never farrowed. The manner of his death would be by burning, by drowning and by the ridge-pole of a roof falling on his head. The prophecy seemed so unlikely that Diarmuid scorned it, although he did have Aedh Dubh banished from Ireland and sought other ways to protect himself from any event by which the prophecy could come true.

However, a day arrived when Banbán invited the High King to a feast. Diarmuid ignored the prophecy and went to his fortress.

At Banbán's house, his host suggested that since the king's wife, Muighain, had not accompanied him, his own daughter would 'this night be your wife'. The girl brought Diarmuid a nightshirt, food and ale. The prophecy began to be fulfilled. Realizing his impending doom, Diarmuid sprang to the door. Aedh Dubh was there and stabbed him. Wounded, Diarmuid fled into the house. Aedh Dubh's men set fire to it. Seeking to escape the flames, Diarmuid scrambled into a vat of ale. A burning ridge-pole fell on his head. The prophecy was fulfilled in all its aspects.

Druids as symbols of knowledgeable or wise people continued for a long time in Irish literature. The poet Blathmac, son of Cú Brettan (fl. AD 750–770), who was a monk, was able to write of Jesus Christ:

ferr fáith, fisidiu cech druí
rí ba hepscop, ba lánsuí

Better He than prophet, more knowledgeable than any Druid, a king who was bishop and full sage.

Also of interest among the Irish references to Druids is the fact that there is mention of a tribe called the Corco Mo-druad ('seed of my druid') in north Clare and on Beare Island in Cork. And, of course, we have already mentioned the Fir Maíge Féne at Fermoy who were said to have been descendants of the Druid/solar deity Mug Ruith.

'It is pretty certain, indeed, that the Druidic systems of Gaul, Britain and Ireland were originally one and the same,' comments Dr P.W. Joyce. However, instead of calling into question the accuracy of Caesar's accounts, Joyce accepts them as infallible and then explains the differing picture shown by native Celtic records in Ireland and Britain by arguing that they 'were separated and isolated for many centuries from the Celtic races of Gaul; and thus, their religious system, like their language, naturally diverged, so that the Druidism of Ireland, as pictured forth in the native records, differed in many respects from that of Gaul.'

Joyce agrees that the Druids were the intellectual class in Ireland as well as Gaul and that 'they combined in themselves all the learned professions'. It is also interesting that Joyce actually agrees on eight points of similarity between the Irish and Gaulish druids – the latter as depicted by the Classical sources. 1) That both classes were known by the same name – Druid. 2) Both Gaulish and Irish Druids were regarded as seers, prophets, judges, poets etc. 3) That they were the only learned class of the Celts. 4) That they were teachers, especially of the children of kings and chiefs. 5) That their disciples underwent a long course of training during which they learnt a great number of verses by heart. 6) That they were advisers to the kings, influenced and often took precedence even over the kings, being held in great respect. 7) That both the Irish and Gauls had Druidesses. 8) That they worshipped a great number of gods.

We will be coming to the subject of female Druids, or Druidesses, shortly.

The male Druids in Irish sources had a tonsure. It seems obvious that the Druids of Britain also had a similar form of haircut although it is not specifically stated. The concept of a tonsure appears in many cultures and religions. Buddhist and Jaina monks, also Hindus, cut their hair as a form of religious initiation. In early times, a Hindu boy at the age of two years would undergo the *cudakarana* ceremony, having a tonsure cut to show his transition from infant to child. Today the *cudakarana* is more symbolic than actual. Therefore, it is not surprising to find a Druidic tonsure in ancient Celtic society.

The scholar Maud Joynt discusses the Druidic tonsure in her article '*Airbacc giunnae*' (*Eriu*, X, 1928, pp. 130–34). Tirechán is one of our first authorities to mention such a tonsure. Lucat Mael and Caplait, two Druids who were the tutors of the High King Laoghaire's daughters, Ethne and Fidelma, are said to have cut their hair in the fashion known as *airbacc giunnae*, which P.W. Joyce believes meant 'fence cut of the hair', implying the cut left a sort of eave or fence along the head, cut from ear to ear, leaving the front part of the head shaved. Joynt, however, believes this to mean 'frontal curve of the tonsure'. The name Mael, 'bald', as we have mentioned before, could equally imply 'tonsured'. The Latin writers refer to Lucat Mael as Lucat Calvuc, obviously from the Latin *calvus*, bald.

When Christianity took hold among the Celts, this Druidic tonsure was preserved and became the tonsure of the Celtic Christian religieux, although in Ferfesa O'Mulchonry's glossary (*Annales Ríoghachta Éireann*), the name of the tonsure became *berrad mog* or the *tonsura civilis*. The most explicit description of the tonsure is given in Ceolfrid's letter to Naiton, king of the Picts, who describes it as shaven at the front of the head, on a line from ear to ear, with the hair growing long at the back. Of course, later Celtic Christian writers did not claim a Druidic origin for this tonsure, arguing it was the tonsure of St John.

The Roman opponents of the Celtic Church, particularly Aldhelm of Malmesbury, argued it was the tonsure of Simon Magus. Both the *Tripartite Life of Patrick* and Tirechán's *Life of Patrick* claim that when Cass Macc Glais, the swineherd of the High King Laoghaire, was baptized by Patrick, his hair was cut in this fashion. But according to Dom Gougard, Patrick opposed the Celtic tonsure and ordered excommunication of those Irish clerics who refused to shave themselves *more Romano*. Dom Gougard's excellent study is firmly entrenched in his Roman doctrine and we must allow for this attitude in his work. If Dom Gougard is correct, we have to conclude that Patrick was unsuccessful in his attempt and that he, himself, finally accepted the Celtic tonsure.

The Celtic tonsure was one of the causes of argument during the conflict between the Celtic and Roman advocates at Whitby in AD 664. The Council of Toledo in AD 633 had already condemned the tonsure of the British Celts, who had settled in Galicia and Asturias. However, it was still worn in Brittany as late as the year AD 818 at Landévennec, when Abbot Marmonoc was ordered to institute the rule of Benedict to supersede that of Guénolé, also known in Cornwall as Winwaloe. Landévennec was the intellectual centre of the Celtic Church in Brittany.

According to the *Annals of Tigernach*, the Roman tonsure was not accepted at Iona until about AD 714. And beyond this time the British Celts were still wearing the Celtic tonsure. How long the fashion lasted among them it is difficult to say. There are even some references to Culdees, *Cele Dé*, Servant of God, an order formed by Mael Ruain, founder of the monastery of Tallaght (d. AD 792), who are said to have worn the Celtic tonsure, wandering Scotland as late as the fourteenth century AD.

In accepting the conception of the Druids purely as 'priests', commentators have found it difficult to work out why other people, not simply religious functionaries, also wore a tonsure. 'Doubtless,' says Dom Gougard, 'the tonsure was not the exclusive privilege of the Druids. It was very likely affected by certain other classes of ancient Celtic society'. But I would argue that this merely confirms the contention that the Druids were not simply a priesthood. However, there is another argument. In many parts of the world, a tonsure was made as a distinctive mark of the warrior caste as well as intellectual or priestly caste. In Celtic society we also find that certain champions of the Breton king, Waroc'h II (*c*.AD 577–594), shaved their head with the same Druidic tonsure. Waroc'h successfully united Brittany against the attacks of the Franks.

The popular romantic image of Druids today is of venerable men clad in white robes. The Druids of history, as we will examine in more detail, were both men and women and they married and had children. Indeed, references to the children of Druids in the ancient Irish sagas are numerous and ancient texts would confirm that the Druids were a hereditary caste. Pliny gives the first reference that the Druids wore white robes. We read in Tirechán that Rechrad and his eight companions, the nine Druids of Amalgaid, who Patrick destroyed by bringing down a magical fire on them, were also clothed in white robes. Yet Strabo says that Druids were attired in variegated garments embroidered in gold. Some writers have argued that these 'variegated garments' might be an early form of tartan. Druids were also entitled, from descriptions in the Irish texts, to wear golden torcs, usually associated with heroes. Tulchinne, another Druid of Tara, wore a speckled cloak and gold earrings and he was able to juggle with the nine swords which he carried. When the celebrated Mug Ruith went to do magical battle he wore a 'dark grey, hornless bull hide and a speckled bird headpiece'. Whereas Strabo portrayed the Druids with bare feet, in the *Táin Bó Cuailnge* the Druids wore sandals, and the ArchDruid usually wore an oak garland on his head surmounted by a golden tiara inset with 'snake stones' (the Druids' eggs of Pliny). When he went to perform a rite, he donned a white cloak fastened by a golden brooch.

While the references in Irish literature are the main source for the native Celtic traditions of the Druids, there do occur references to Druids in the other literary traditions of the Celtic world.

It is easy, for example, to presume the presence of Druids on the Isle of Man (Ellan Vannin), which was settled extensively by the Irish in about the third and fourth centuries AD, imposing their language on a Brythonic Celtic-speaking population. But Manx records, as distinct from Old and Middle Irish manuscripts, did not start until the sixteenth and seventeenth centuries. However, Manx folklore and place-names are full of references to the pre-Christian gods of the Celts. The island is said to have been named after the sea god Mannánan Mac Lir. In one folkloric tale, recorded by A.W. Moore in *Folklore of the Isle of Man* (1891), Mannánan Mac Lir is seen as 'a famous Druid who kept, by necromancy, the Land of Mann, under mists, and, if he dreaded any enemies, he would make of one man to seem an hundred by his art magic.'

It is from the *Tripartite Life of Patrick* that we hear of Mac Cuill (Latinized as Maccaldus) who was a thief in Ulster. Coincidentally, or perhaps not, the name Mac Cuill (son of the hazel) is also given as a Druid's name in Irish mythology. He was converted by Patrick but had to submit to the Brehon law for judgement for his previous life of crime. His crimes must have been serious for he was cast adrift on the sea in a curragh without food or sail or oars. The *Senchas Mór* states that being cast adrift on the open sea in a boat, without sail, oar or rudder, was the punishment for a homicide if the perpetrator could not pay the victim's family the necessary compensation. Hugh de Lacey, the Anglo-Norman earl of Ulster (d. AD 1243) is recorded as using this Brehon law by casting those who had betrayed John de Courcy adrift in a ship.

Mac Cuill, after drifting for some time, was washed ashore on the Isle of Man. The law said that he had to serve the ruler of the territory on which the shoreline was situated unless he paid a fee for his release. But the *Tripartite Life* says that two men, Conindri and Romuil, who were Christian missionaries on the island, 'when they saw Mac Cuill in his curragh, they took him from the sea and received him with a welcome and he learnt the divine rule with them until he took the bishopric after them.'

Mac Cuill certainly began to preach Christianity on the island and became St Maughold (from the distortion of the Latin version of his name, Maccaldus). Many topographical features on the island still bear his name. He is acclaimed as a founder of a Celtic monastic community which for centuries was the premier monastery on the island until replaced when Rushen was founded in AD 1134. Importantly, to our later discussion on Druidic ritual, Dudley Wright, in *Druidism* (1924), records a tradition from early Christian writers that when Mac Cuill, or Maughold, came to the island, the Druids were making a human sacrifice in the Lonan stone circle, near Baldrine. A stone was being heated with fires on which the sacrifice was being compelled. Mac Cuill threw holy water on the stone and it split asunder. This was a scientifically possible act. The Druids fled and the sacrifice was released.

The conversion of Mac Cuill by Patrick is also given in the *Liber*

Ardmachanus (Book of Armagh), compiled by Feardomhnach about AD 807. More interesting, in support of a Druidic identity for Mac Cuill, we find him appearing in the Latin *Incipiunt cronica regum Mannie & Insularum & episcoporum & quorundam regum Anglie, Scotie, Norwegie* (popularly known as the Chronicles of the Kings of Man and the Isles) compiled in the thirteenth century. St Maughold or Mac Cuill appears in a more popular Druidic rôle striking an enemy dead with the use of his staff. A further story of Maughold is contained in *Trias Thaumaturgae* (1647), a work on the lives of early Irish saints written by Seán Colgan of Donegal, professor of theology at Louvain (1590–1658) in which he is given a more miraculous gloss.

A stone found near Port St Mary on the island, carved in Ogham, has *droata*, the genitive of *druadh*, carved on it. William Sacheverell, in his *An account of the Isle of Man* (1703), believed that the island, which shared the Latin name Mona with Anglesey, was, in fact, the principal seat of the Druids, pointing out that it was also anciently known as *Sedes Druidarum* and *Insula Druidarum*. But the evidence for this assertion is tenuous to say the least, being based on legends such as the tradition that Dothan, a king of Alba, sent his three sons to be educated by Druids in the island, and that Corbed, another mythical king of Alba, was educated by the Druids there. In his *History of the Church of Scotland* (1655), John Spottiswood, Archbishop of St Andrews, surmises from church traditions that the island was a centre of Druidism which was governed by an elected ArchDruid. This appears to be the source of the story repeated by Sacheverell.

When Colmcille was banished from Ireland, he founded a monastic centre on Iona (I-Shona, the Isle of Saints). This was part of the Dàl Riada settlement which had been made in Caledonia during the fourth century AD by Irish settlers. Irish sources claim that after a famine in Munster, a chieftain named Conaire, son of Riada, was driven north and founded a kingdom in Co. Antrim. The name Dàl Riada meant 'followers of Riada'. After a quarrel among the Dàl Riadans, some of them crossed to Caledonia and formed a second kingdom along the coast which was to become known as Airer Ghàidheal (Argyll), the seaboard of the Gael. Colmcille eventually left the Dàl Riada settlement and pressed into the hinterland of the native Caledonians, who have become more popularly known to us by their Latin nickname, the Picts (*Picti* – painted people). He found that the Cruthin, the name by which the Picts called themselves, had Druids. John Hill Burton, in his *History of Scotland* (1853) averred that there is no tradition or reference to Druidism in Scotland. But the body of evidence is unquestionable. D'Arbois de Jubainville in *Les Druides* points out that the existence of Druids in Scotland is an undeniable fact of history. Druids are also referred to long before the arrival of Colmcille when Cormac Mac Art sends to the Druids of Alba to ask their assistance against the troublesome king of Munster.

The ruler of the Picts at the time of the arrival of Colmcille in Scotland was one Bruide Mac Maelchon (c.AD 556–584), regarded as the first historical king of the Picts. Adomnán mentions Bruide several times in his work and points out that he was never converted to Christianity in spite of Colmcille's best efforts. His death is recorded in the *Annals of Ulster*. It is clear from Adomnán that Bruide's capital was near where the river Ness flows into the Moray Firth, possibly the hill fort of Craig Phádraig (Patrick's Rock). Colmcille journeyed to Bruide's capital via the Firth of Lorn, the Great Glen and Loch Ness itself. Colmcille came away from his first meeting with the king of the Tuatha Cruthin with a negotiated treaty providing a safe conduct for Christian monks and missionaries travelling through Pictish territory.

In the *Lives* of Colmcille we find a powerful figure: the Druid Broichán, tutor of King Bruide, and Colmcille's main antagonist. We find Colmcille engaging in magical contests with him and other Druids. Colmcille is even able to raise a young man from the dead to astound the local Picts. He had converted a Pictish family and a few days later one of its members, a youth, fell ill and died. When the Druids proclaimed it a punishment for their act of infidelity to the old gods, Colmcille raised him to demonstrate his magic as more powerful than the Druids. Even Broichán is said to have been taken with an illness which Colmcille cures on condition that the Druid would free an Irish female prisoner.

One of the poems attributed to Colmcille demonstrates his anti-Druidism:

> It is not with the sneeze our destiny is,
> Nor with the bird on the top of the twig,

Nor with the trunk of a knotty tree.
Nor with an act of humming.

I adore not the voice of birds,
Nor the sneeze, nor a destiny on the earthly world,
Nor a son, nor chance, nor woman;
My Druid is Christ, the son of God.

The references are interesting in this poem, for we have a tradition Druids could divine by a sneeze (*sreod*) and also by an act of humming (*sordán*). According to the traditions related in Willliam F. Skene's *Chronicles of the Picts and Scots* (1867), the Druids were driven into Alba (Scotland) from Ireland by Patrick. He says 'from them are every spell and every charm and every *sreod* (sneeze) and voices of birds and every omen'. But there is nothing to support the contention that Druids were not a native institution among the Celtic tribes of Caledonia before the arrival of the *Scotti*, as the Irish Dàl Riadan settlers were called.

From the accounts of the magical contests between Broichán and Colmcille we find that the people of Bruide worshipped at a certain fountain and drank and bathed of its waters which helped with leprosy or partial loss of sight. Colmcille immediately blessed the fountain so that it was harnessed for Christianity.

Within the next century the Cruthin, or Picts, had become Christian. They were one of the last Celtic peoples to adopt the new faith. By AD 625 we find that Nechtán, king of the Picts, had become the patron of a group of nuns from St Brigit's house of Kildare who went to Scotland to establish a 'daughter house' at Abernethy.

Lewis Spence believed several Druidic rituals survived as folkloric traditions in Scotland. In 1656 the Presbytery of Applecross, Ross-shire, took action against certain persons for sacrificing bulls on 25 August, 'which day is dedicated, as they conceive, to St Mourie, as they call him'. In 1678 the Presbytery of Dingwall took action against four Mackenzies for sacrificing a bull on an island in Loch Maree. Thomas Pennant in his *Tour in Scotland and a Voyage to the Hebrides in 1769* (1771) noticed an oak tree on this island of Inis Maree into whose trunk nails and coins were driven as 'offerings'. Further, local people took oaths in St Maree's name. Spence believes that Mourie or Maree was 'an earlier divinity'. He overlooks the name of the celebrated Druid of Dairbre (Valentia in Kerry), whose name was Mug Ruith (Mow-rih). As we have seen, Mug Ruith, sometimes given as Magh Ruith, was originally a solar deity who was euphemized into a Druid.

Another ritual Spence points out is that rite of *taighairm*, which survived in many parts of the Highlands, in which a seer, wrapping himself in the hide of a newly slain bull, waits for a vision to come. We will discuss such survivals further when we consider Druidic rites and rituals.

When the Druids of Wales make their appearance in native Welsh literary tradition, they have become transformed into a bardic, poetic class.

Sir John Rhŷs pointed out in his *Celtic Britain* (1904) that 'Druidism is far harder to discover in the oldest literature of the Welsh' than it is in Irish records. The word *derwyddon* (Druids) appears in a poem in the *Book of Taliesin* applied to the Three Wise Men who visit the infant Jesus. In fact, most references to Druids in Welsh literature are to them as poets and wise prophets. The literary sources are mainly from twelfth to fourteenth century AD texts. There is one interesting historic reference by the early ninth century AD Welsh historian Nennius who wrote *Historia Britonnum* (History of the Britons), about AD 829. Nennius devotes eighteen chapters to the career of Vortigern (*Vawr tigern*, overlord), the king of southern Britain in the wake of the Roman departure in the mid-fifth century AD. He says that when St Germanus of Auxerre excommunicated Vortigern for adhering to Pelagian heresy, Vortigern engaged twelve Druids to advise him. We will return to the significance of Pelagianism when we consider the Druids as philosophers.

In an elegy on Madog of Powys, Gwalchmai ap Meilyr (AD 1130–1180) writes: 'Would to God the day of doom were arrived, since Druids are come bringing the news of woe'. And in a panegyric on Owain Gwynedd, king of Gwynedd (AD 1137–70), Cynndelw Brydydd Mawr (fl. AD 1155–1200), writes 'Bards are constituted judges of excellence, even Druids of the circle, of four dialects, coming from the four kingdoms (of Wales)'. He goes on to speak of 'Druids of the splendid race, wearers of the golden chains' as though they still existed in the twelfth century. Cynndelw addresses a poem to Owain Cyfeilcawg, Prince of Powys (c.AD 1149–1195), and repeats the concept of the Druids as a group still in existence.

Llywarch ab Llewelyn (AD 1160–1220) speaks of the prophecies of the Druids in a manner that also indicates that they were still part of the everyday cultural life of Wales. And Filip Brydydd (1200–1250) speaks of the Druids in a similar fashion.

In the *Red Book of Hergest* (compiled c.AD 1375–1425) there is a poem known as 'The Wand of Moses' which has the lines, 'Each exalted woman's praise hath been sung by some of the Druids'.

There does not seem to be any mention of the Druids in the Welsh law system, the laws of Hywel Dda, codified in the tenth century AD, in the same manner as the Druids of Ireland were accorded a specific social place in the Brehon law system. If, as the poems of Wales seem to indicate, the Druids were still a recognizable group in medieval Wales, then they were a group not recognized by law.

It appears from the evidence then, that by the twelfth century, the Druids in Wales had survived merely as a poetic fraternity. Sir Thomas D. Kendrick, in his pioneering study, *The Druids: A Study in Keltic Prehistory* (1927) observes: 'The basic assumption that the medieval Welsh bards were a continuation of the Druidic hierarchy ... is not by any means an extravagant or ridiculous belief.' Certainly, there emerges in Wales a continuation of the 'bardic class' from early Celtic Britain. According to Lewis Spence: 'we have good reason to believe that it must have retained and preserved much of the lore of the Druidic *cultus* with which it had once been contemporary and closely allied.'

Before William Borlase wrote his *Antiquities of Cornwall* (1754), in which he quite rightly rejected William Stukeley's theory that the Cornish quoits were Druidic altars, there appeared to be no traditions of Druids surviving in Cornish literary sources. In spite of the countless *Lives* of Cornish saints there seem to be no accounts of conflicts between Christian missionaries and Cornish Druids. But there is one reference to Christian martyrs in Cornwall in the sixth century AD. A fourteenth century *Life of St Gwinear* records that he was an Irish missionary who led a group to Cornwall, landing at the mouth of the Hayle. His sister Piala was one of his party. The local ruler was named Teudor (Tewdrig), and also appears in the Cornish *Bewnans Meriasek* (Life of St Meryadoc) as a Muslim! *Bewnans Meriasek*, the only full-length medieval saints' play surviving in a Celtic language, was written in AD 1504. But in the *Life of Gwinear*, we are told that Teudor 'fearing lest they might convert his people to the faith of Christ' puts Gwinear,

Piala, and some of their companions to death. Others, such as Ia (St Ives) manage to escape. It has been argued, by Henry Jenner among others, that Teudor was probably just 'a slack Christian'; he was certainly not a Muslim. However, there is an obvious alternative, that Teudor was not only a king but a Druid and defender of the old faith. The fact that the same source says that Teudor beheaded Gwinear, picked up the head and took it with him as a trophy, conjures up the images supplied not only by Classical writers, but native Celtic traditions, in which the head is a symbol. The pagan Celts venerated the heads of their enemies, the place where they believed the soul reposed. Teudor obviously believed in the old ways.

According to F.E. Halliday, in his *A History of Cornwall* (1959):

... although the Druids have left no certain, visible monuments of their religion, they appear to have left enduring memorials in the minds of men. The belief that passing children through the hole of Men-an-Tol will cure them of rickets could be a superstition of the Druids, derived perhaps from an even earlier age, and their art of divination may be preserved in the old custom of placing two crossed pins on top of the stone and foretelling fortunes by their movements. And again, the fire festivals so dear to the Cornish are probably the sacrificial fires of the Druids in modified form. It used to be the custom to draw the figure of a man on Christmas 'stocks' or Yule logs, before setting them alight, and at the great Celtic festival of Midsummer, when fires were lighted on the hilltops, as they still are, children were swung through the flames, sometimes so perilously close as to singe their clothes.

Among the Druidic traditions of Brittany there occurs a story in the ninth century *Life of St Guénolé* written by Wrdistan, a monk of Landévennec. Guénolé was a sixth century AD saint also known in Cornwall as both Gunwalloe and Winwaloe. He founded the great Breton monastery at Landévennec. The tradition recorded by Wrdistan shows the Druids in sixth century Brittany as having almost disappeared, as elderly adherents to a dead religion. But, significantly, they are depicted with great sympathy.

The story concerns the semi-legendary king of Kernev (Cornouaille) in south west Brittany, which stretches south from the Monts d'Arrée and east to the River Ellé. The king, Gradlon, is dying and sends for Guénolé. As the monk approaches the king he finds a Druid there. Gradlon tells the monk not to be harsh with him for the Druid knows the depth of suffering: 'The ills I have endured are as nothing to the agonies through which he has passed . . . he has lost his gods! What sorrow can compare with this sorrow? Once he was a Druid; now he mourns a dead religion.'

Gradlon dies and both the Christian monk and 'the last worshipper of the Teutatès' intone their various psalms and dirges. In the morning, the body of Gradlon is washed in a nearby spring and wrapped in linen perfumed with vervain in readiness to be taken to Landévennec. The Druid then addresses Guénolé as 'brother, for are we not sprung from common ancestors?' The Druid asks Guénolé to raise a church 'to the Sorrowful Mother of your God' on the spot, so that sick persons might find health and 'the heavy laden, peace':

> There was once a time, I was young then, when a block of red granite stood here. Its touch gave sight to the blind, hearing to the deaf, hope to hearts in distress. May the sanctuary that you raise inherit the same virtues; it is my wish, the wish of one conquered but resigned to the changing order of the times, one who feels neither bitterness nor hatred. I have spoken.

We are told that Guénolé felt great sympathy for the Druid in spite of a brief theological argument when the Christian saint offered to teach him 'the Word of Life' and was rejected by the Druid who, pointing to the blue sky, observed that when the time came for one or the other of them to pass into the Otherworld either one might find 'perchance there is nothing but a great mistake'. Guénolé was scandalised. 'To believe is to know,' he argued in Christian fashion. His compassion for the Druid leads him to offer him refuge in the abbey at Landévennec. The Druid declines saying he prefers his woodland paths. 'Do not all tracks lead to the same great centre?' is his parting shot. It is a philosophy that our modern intolerant world finds difficult to accept.

The encounter with, symbolically, the last Druid of Brittany, written by a Christian monk in the ninth century, is fascinating in that the Druids are still held as worthy of respect by Christians, who display an understanding and forbearance lacking in subsequent times.

[5]

Female Druids

S EVERAL Greek and Latin writers speak of *Dryades* or
Druidesses, and the existence of such female Druids is certainly
confirmed by Celtic sources. One has to bear in mind the fascinating rôle of women in Celtic society as opposed to their position in
other European cultures. The rights and position of Celtic women
far exceeded those of Greece or Rome.

In Greece women had no political rights at all. They could take
no part in the running of society. And their social rights were severely
limited. They could not inherit nor hold property or enter into any
transaction which involved more than the value of a bushel of grain.
The woman's husband, father or male guardian took complete charge
of her affairs. If her father died without male issue, the daughter
'went with the property' to the next of male kin who would accept
her as a wife. In other words, she was regarded as an 'inheritable'
chattel. Women were kept in seclusion at home. Indeed, they had
their own separate quarters in the house. This was the reality of their
life, in spite of a Greek woman's life sometimes being more vigor-
ously depicted in the Greek epics, where the heroines' behaviour was
governed by literary convention. Aristotle seems more progressive
than his fellow Greeks when he argues that men and women should
have the same education and training. But life for Greek women was
extremely restricted.

In Rome women were generally allowed more rights than in
Greece, but the *paterfamilias* still had complete control over his wife
and it was necessary for women to have a male guardian to conduct
affairs of business. Property was a male-dominated concept. Married
women in Rome did not, as in Greece, live in seclusion but took
their meals with their husbands, were free to leave the house, provided they wore the *stola matronalis* to indicate their status, and
could visit shops, law courts and theatres and other public places.

In Celtic society, however, the position of women was vastly different. From history we find numerous female figures of supreme authority, for example Boudicca (Boadicea), the ruler of the Iceni, who was accepted as war leader by the southern British tribes in AD 61. She is, perhaps, the most famous of the female Celtic rulers. According to Dio Cassius, Boudicca appears as a priestess of the goddess 'Andrasta', described as a goddess of victory. This seems to be the same goddess as Andarte, worshipped by the Vocontii of Gaul. An argument could, therefore, be made that Boudicca was a Druidess as well as a queen. But Boudicca was no isolated case of a female ruler. Indeed, Tacitus says in his *Annals*: 'it is not the first time that Britons have been led to battle by a woman'.

The sagas support the idea of women as warriors. Female warrior-queens appear in many stories, notably Medb of Connacht who commanded her army and personally slew the hero-warrior Cethren in combat. Scáthach, a female champion, was the principal instructor of the martial arts to Cúchulainn. Her sister, Aoife, was another famous female warrior and, as great as the hero Cúchulainn was, he had to resort to trickery to overcome her prowess. Among Fionn Mac Cumhail's Fianna, that élite band of warriors, we find the female champion Credne. Art finds himself hard-pressed to overcome the female warrior Coinchend. A female champion named Estiu plays a prominent part in the story of Suibhne Geilt during his time at Snámh Dá Én (Swim Two Birds), which was the inspiration for the title of Flann O'Brien's classic comic novel *At Swim Two Birds* (1939).

Returning to history, we find that contemporary with Boudicca was Cartimandua ('the sleek pony'), ruler of the British Brigantes c.AD 43–69. She emerges as a strong and determined personality. She was married to Venutios. Venutios attempted to take over her kingdom. Cartimandua divorced him and married his charioteer, Vellocatos. Venutios, leading bands of dissidents, seems to have been finally defeated by the Roman governor, Petillius Cerialis, about AD 72.

We hear of the earlier Gaulish chieftainess, Onomaris, who commanded the Celtic tribes in their wanderings into Iberia. Other powerful Celtic women emerge into history. From both Tacitus and Plutarch (the Greek historian Ploutorches – c.AD 46–c.120) we learn the story of a Gaulish woman of distinction, Eponina. The name relates to the Celtic horse goddess Epona and perhaps she was a priestess of her cult. Eponina's husband, Julius Sabinus of the

Lingones, took part in the Gaulish uprising of AD 69. When it failed, in order to elude his Roman pursuers, Sabinus arranged matters to appear as if he had committed suicide. Eponina hid him, smuggling food and clothing to him for nine years. At the same time she sought to obtain a Roman pardon for him, even going to Rome to plead his cause. When Sabinus was finally caught, the emperor, Vespasian, had both Sabinus and Eponina executed.

Plutarch also relates that the historian Polybius met and talked with Chiomara, wife of Ortagion, chieftain of the Tolistoboii, who united the Galatian Celts into a powerful state against Rome at the time of the invasion led by Gnaeus Manlius Volso in 189 BC. Chiomara was captured by the Romans and a centurion raped her. He then discovered that she was of high rank and demanded a ransom which Ortagion duly sent. The exchange was to take place on the banks of a river, always a significant site in Celtic tradition. While the centurion was collecting his gold, Chiomara had him decapitated and took his head, in Celtic fashion, to her husband. The Greek report of their conversation, according to Doctor Rankin, 'preserved genuine, gnomic, Celtic idiom':

'Woman, a fine thing (is) good faith.'
'A better thing only one man be alive who had intercourse with me.'

Plutarch tells us another story of a Celtic heroine of Galatia who was clearly a Druidess, Camma, priestess of the goddess Brigit (if we accept that Brigit, Brigantu in Gaulish, was the Celtic equivalent of Artemis). Camma, an hereditary priestess, according to Plutarch, of the Celtic equivalent of Artemis, was married to a chieftain named Sinatos who was murdered by a man called Sinorix who then forced Camma to marry him. But, as the ceremony involved drinking from a common cup, Camma contrived to put poison into it. She allayed Sinorix's suspicion by drinking first and so accepted death herself, as well as her would-be husband, Sinorix.

It is also from Plutarch's essay, 'On the Virtues of Women', that we learn that Celtic women were often appointed ambassadors. They were involved in a treaty between the Carthaginian general Hannibal and the Celtic Volcae. Rome had already sent to the Volcae to demand their neutrality if Hannibal marched through their country.

The Celts were obviously not enamoured of Rome's demands. Hannibal was being supported by other Celtic tribes. Plutarch also says that women took part in the Celtic assemblies, frequently smoothing quarrels with their careful diplomacy.

According to Irish sources, Macha Mong Ruadh (Macha of the Red Hair), daughter of Aed Ruadh, became ruler of all Ireland from 377–331 BC. Female rulers appear in the Irish and Welsh texts as well as the ideal queens of the Otherworld which, as Professor Markle, in *Le Femme Celte*, has pointed out were 'symbols of an attitude of mind that patriarchy could not uproot from the ancient Celtic spirit'. Goddesses occur with great frequency in Irish mythology and are associated with the Irish south-western province of Munster more than anywhere else. Perhaps this is because Mumham (the *ster* is a Norse addition) is depicted as a primeval world, a place of origin, the place where several of the mythical invaders land and which becomes the gathering place for the dead. Mug Ruith, the solar deity turned into a Druid, comes from Munster, while his daughter Tlachtga is depicted as a goddess in some stories before she, like her father, is turned into a mere Druidess. The Christian writers have her raped by three sons of Simon Magus and she produces three sons at one birth, in the process of which she dies. She was buried at the Hill of Tlachtga, now the Hill of Ward (*Cnoc an Bháird* – the Hill of the Bard) near Athboy, Co. Meath, which became associated with the Samhain Festival and sacred Druidic fires.

Tacitus comments in his *Annals*, in some apparent bemusement, that the Celts had no objection to being led by women and he repeats this point in his *Agricola*. 'In Britain,' he says, 'there is no rule of distinction to exclude the female line from the throne, or the command of armies.' As Dr Rankin points out: 'The city states of Greece and Rome had highly organised political structures which allowed no place for women in power. Greeks and Romans were all the more astonished at the relative freedom and individuality of Celtic women.' Certainly Pausanias makes a special mention of the notable courage of Celtic women.

The position of women, as it emerges in the Brehon Law system of Ireland, at a time when women were treated as mere chattels in most European societies, was amazingly advanced. Women could be found in many professions, even as lawyers and judges, such as Brigh, a celebrated woman-Brehon. Women had the right to succession and, as we have seen, could emerge as a supreme authority, though kingship, in the historic period, was mainly confined to males. A woman could inherit property and remained the owner of any property she brought into a marriage. If the marriage broke up, then she not only took out of it her own property but any property that her husband had given her during the marriage. Divorce, of course, was permitted and a woman could divorce her husband just as a husband could divorce his wife. If a man had 'fallen from his dignity', that is, committed a crime and lost his civil rights or been outcast from society, it did not affect the position of his wife. A woman was responsible for her own debts and not those of her husband.

As Professor Markle has pointed out: 'The Romans looked upon women as bearers of children and objects of pleasure, while the Druids included women in their political and religious life'. Greeks and Romans could not understand the freedom of Celtic women and their more open attitudes to sexual relationships. 'The Greek and Roman writers express little more than a prejudiced and impressionistic notion of the rôles of women in the Celtic societies that they discuss,' says Dr Rankin. For example, Strabo makes the wild claim that the British Celts not only cohabit with the wives of others but with their own mothers and sisters and then, half-heartedly, admits that he has absolutely no evidence for such a statement. The phrase 'it is said . . .' could excuse many wild speculations. Caesar and Dio Cassius mention the practice of polyandry and communal marriage. What we are actually looking at is a more permissive and open society, not fully understood by the foreign observers.

This is not to say that the Celts had an ideal society at the beginning of the Christian era. Their society had already started to disintegrate into patriarchy. As we shall later discuss, changes from the initial 'mother goddess' concept had altered into a 'father of the gods' idea and slowly the male warrior society was replacing earlier perceptions. The introduction of Christianity, particularly the displacement of Celtic Christianity by Rome, gave the last kick to what had once been the equality of male and female in Celtic society. The uniqueness of ancient Celtic society lay in the fact that such concepts had lasted so long.

Bearing in mind this unique position of women in Celtic society, Dr Rankin observed: 'The range of rôles possible for women in ancient Celtic societies was wider than that permitted in Greece or

Rome. The Irish tradition, which presents us with a picture of an archaic Iron Age tradition, speaks not only of women warriors, but women prophets, Druids, bards, doctors, and even satirists.'

Just what do we know of these female Druids?

We have already mentioned that the fourth century AD Gaulish writer, Ausonius Decimus Magnus, who wrote his works in Latin, and some epigrams in Greek, had an aunt called Dryadia, whom he mentions in his *Parentalia* (no. XXV). Why would his aunt be called 'Druidess' so many centuries after it was claimed that the Romans had stamped out the caste? The answer – that she was of that caste.

Tacitus mentions women on the island of Mona (Anglesey) running among the Celtic warriors, dressed in funeral garments, hair streaming, carrying torches, while nearby (*circum*) the Druids poured forth maledictions with raised hands. Tacitus does not say that these women were female Druids. However, he later mentions a 'prophetess' of the Bructeri, which he says was a 'Teutonic' tribe, called Veleda, in the time of Vespasian AD 69–79. Veleda certainly has a Celtic name which seems to derive from the root *gwel*, 'to see' (cognate with the Irish *filí*), and Veleda seems to be a common Continental Celtic noun for 'seeress'. She is described as a virgin ruling over a wide territory. 'Her name was held in veneration ... Veleda, at the time, was the oracle of Germany.' Now the Romans sometimes had difficulties identifying Celtic and Germanic tribes as we have already discussed. Oddly enough, the very word Teutonic is derived from the Celtic word for tribe, *tuath* in Irish. The god recorded as Teutates is, as we shall see in the next chapter, the title of Celtic tribal gods. There can be little doubt that Veleda was a Celt and a Druidess and this is confirmed by Dio Cassius.

Veleda was a force in politics and was chosen to arbitrate between the Tencterians and the Agrippinians on opposite banks of the Rhine, together with Claudius Civilis. Tacitus says that no ambassadors were allowed to see Veleda in person. 'The deputies, however, were not admitted to the presence of Veleda. To increase the veneration paid to her character, all access to her person was denied. She resided in the summit of a lofty tower. A near relation, chosen for the purpose, conveyed to her several questions, and from that sanctuary brought back oracular responses, like a messenger who held commerce with the gods.'

Veleda reminds one of the female prophet in the story of Fíngin

Mac Luchta of Munster in Ireland who, on every feast of Samhain, would visit a similar Druidess who was able to relate all the occurrences in the kingdom on that night and the results which would issue from them during the next twelve months.

Tacitus, in his *Germania*, in which he is clearly muddling Celts and Germans, identifying, for example, Ambiorix of the Eburones as a German, and speaking of their 'sacred groves', mentions other female prophets:

> There is, in their opinion, something sacred in the female sex, and even the power of foreseeing future events. Their advice is, therefore, always heard; they are deemed oracular. We have seen, in the resign of Vespasian, the famous Veleda revered as a divinity by her countrymen. Before her time, Aurinia and others were held in equal veneration; but a veneration founded on sentiment and superstition, free from that servile adulation which pretends to people heaven with human deities.

It is my belief that Tacitus is continuing to muddle Celts and Germans in this passage.

Dio Cassius does not muddle Celts and Germans when he refers to Ganna, 'a virgin among the Celts', who succeeded Veleda as the oracle and who is said to have accompanied Masyos, king of the Semnones, on a embassy to the Emperor Domitian, the younger son of Vespasian who became emperor in AD 81–96. Ganna, whose name seems to derive from a Celtic word meaning 'intermediary' (the word appears to survive in modern Welsh as *canol*), was received by the emperor, honoured by him and returned home. This is confirmed by Flavius Vopiscus who identifies Ganna as being of the Gaulish tribe of the Tungri (modern Tongres, near Liège, Belgium).

Pomponius Mela in *De Chorographia* mentions nine virgin priestesses on the island of Sena off Pointe du Raz, on the western coast of Armorica (Brittany) who knew the future and gave oracles to sailors. But again he does not specifically call them Druidesses but *Gallicenae*. In Breton tradition these women were called the *Groac'h* or *Grac'h*, the Breton words implying they were 'fiery headed'. J.F. Campbell, however, sought to make the word cognate with the Scottish Gaelic *gruagach* which was the word for a female brownie; used adjectivally, this meant having a beautiful head of hair. He believes that the brownies were originally the Druidesses and representatives of the Celtic solar deities relegated to a new fairy rôle in Christian times. The *Gallicenae* certainly have the attributes of Druidesses as depicted in insular Celtic literature where they had become 'sorceresses' and 'wizards'.

Most fascinating is the fact that the Larzac inscription contains the names of nine 'witches' (druidesses). The lead tablet was found in tomb no. 71 among the 115 tombs found in a necropolis near Millau. It is dated to AD 90–110. According to Lejeune's translation (*Études Celtiques*, No. XXII, 1985) the text is a 'magic formula' to preserve the dead from the curse of 'witches'. Seven names are mentioned in one place while a further two are mentioned elsewhere. Lejeune toys with the idea of an association of seven 'witches' but becomes confused by the mention of the other two names, forgetting that the number 'nine' is equally as significant as 'seven' and forgetting the nine *Gallicenae*.

The nine *Gallicenae* also have a parallel in the legend of nine female magicians who guard the thermal waters of Gloucester, who appear in the Welsh tale of Peredur.

Strabo mentions an island similar to that of Sena, which he places near the mouth of the Loire where women called Namnites served a deity resembling Bacchus, the Roman name for Dionysus, god of wine and ecstasy. Interestingly, traditions have been retained in Norse sagas of women prophets and priestesses inhabiting the Channel Islands. Strabo, probably repeating Poseidonios, emphasises that Gaulish priestesses were very independent of their husbands, thus also confirming marriage among the priesthood.

Aelius Lampridius, one of the authors of the *Historia Augusta*, written *c.* fourth century AD, has a *Dryades* foretelling the defeat of Alexander Severus before he set out on his expedition in AD 235. Lampridius puts these words into the mouth of the Druidess: 'Go forth but hope not for victory nor put your trust in your warriors.' The Druidess makes her prophecy in Gaulish Celtic. According to Flavius Vopiscus, another of the *Historia Augusta* authors, Gaius Aurelius Diocletian (AD 284–305) was residing in an inn in the land of the Tungri of Gaul. He was then a simple soldier of humble birth. When he came to settle with his hostess she upbraided him on his apparent meanness in haggling with his account. He retorted that he would be more liberal with his money if he was emperor. To this

jocundity the hostess, who was a Druidess, replied: 'Laugh not, Diocletian, for when you have slain the Boar, you will indeed be
emperor.' Diocletian rose in rank and slew the prefect Arrius, nick-
named 'the Boar', and became emperor of Rome. He carried out a
notorious persecution of the Christians. Vopiscus gives another
example of a Druidess when he says the Emperor Aurelian (Lucius
Domitius Aurelianus – c.AD 215–275) consulted 'Gaulish Druidesses' (*Gallicanas Dryadas*) as to whether his children would retain
the imperial crown. The Druidesses gave an negative answer.

We have discussed Plutarch's story of the Galatian priestess serving
the equivalent Celtic goddess to Artemis. In Gaul, several inscriptions
speak of priestesses at Arles and at Le Prugnon where the goddess
Thucoliss was venerated. An inscription near Metz speaks of '*Arete
Druis Antistita, somno monita*', Druidic priestess.

In Celtic tradition the existence of female Druids is quite explicit.
References to the *bandruaid*, Druid women, occur, and more frequently to *banfhlaith* or *banfhilíd*. According to Seathrún Céitinn,
the virgin guardians of the sacred fires held office in Ireland and their
functions were taken over by Christian religieuses. The rôle of
women Druids is mentioned in the Rennes *Dinnsenchus* and many
individual Druidesses feature in Irish epics. E. Gwynn, in his study
of the *Metrical Dindshenchas* (1913), identifies a woman named
Gáine as Chief Druidess in one story. Before the second battle of
Magh Tuireadh two Druidesses promise to enchant 'the trees and
stones and sods of the earth, so that they shall become a host and
rout their enemies'. Aoife, the wicked step-mother of the children of
Lir, not to be confused with the warrior sister of Scáthach, turns
them into swans by means of a Druidic wand. Aoife is clearly a
Druidess. Bíróg was a Druidess who helped Cian gain access to the
crystal tower of the evil Fomorii ruler, Balor. He had imprisoned his
daughter Ethlinn in it for it had been prophesied that his own grandson would kill him and he sought to prevent the birth of such
a grandson. Bíróg was also instrumental in saving the life of the
child, the issue of Cian and Ethlinn, when Balor had it cast into
the sea. The child grew up as Lugh Lámhfada, god of arts and
crafts.

T.D. Kendrick refers to a tradition that at Cluain Feart (Clonfert)
there existed a community of Druid women who could raise storms,
cause diseases and kill their enemies by supernatural curses. Many

names of Druidesses, real or mythical, are preserved in early Irish literature. Bodmall was the Druidess who raised Fionn Mac Cumhail when in hiding from his father's killers. Smirgat prophesied that if Fionn drank from a horn he would die so he was always careful to drink from a goblet or bowl. Milucrah transformed Fionn into an aged man at Loch Slieve Gallion. In Donegal there lived the Druidess Geal Chossach (white legs).

In the most famous epic in Irish mythology, the *Táin Bó Cuailnge*, The Cattle Raid of Cuailnge, Medb, the queen of Connacht, consults a Druidess named Fidelma from the *sidh* of Cruachan. An interesting reflection of Caesar's statement that the Gauls went to study the Druidic lore in Britain is the fact that Fidelma says she has just returned 'from learning verse and vision in Albion'. Asked if she possesses the *imbas forasnai*, the Light of Foresight, Fidelma says she does, and is then asked to prophesy how Medb's army will fare against the armies of Conchobhar Mac Nessa of Ulster. Fidelma prophesies its defeat at the hands of Cúchulainn.

Fidelma is a young girl. In Thomas Kinsella's translation of the *Táin* she is described thus:

> She had yellow hair. She wore a speckled cloak fastened around her with a gold pin, a red embroidered hooded tunic and sandals with gold clasps. Her brow was broad, her jaw narrow, her two eyebrows pitch black, with delicate dark lashes casting shadows halfway down her cheeks. You would think her lips were inset with Parthian scarlet. Her teeth were like an array of jewels between the lips. She had hair in three tresses; two wound upward on her head and the third hanging down her back, brushing her calves. She held a light gold weaving rod in her hand, with gold inlay. Her eyes had triple irises. Two black horses drew her chariot, and she was armed.

The epic is of uncertain date although the first reference to it being written down is in the seventh century AD. Surviving texts are from much later, and are contained in the eleventh century *Leabhar na hUidhre* (Book of the Dun Cow), the twelfth century *Leabhar Laighnech* (Book of Leinster), and additionally in the *Leabhar Buidhe Lecain* (Yellow Book of Lecan).

Fidelma is not the only interesting woman in this saga. We have

the 'sovranty goddess' figure of Medb and mention of the Macha
Mong Ruadh, who pronounced a curse on the warriors of Ulster,
whose symbolism we shall return to shortly.

We come across another fascinating female figure who is also a
Druidess in the story of the death of the High King Muirchertach
mac Erca (*c.*AD 512–533), recounted in the *Leabhar Buidhe Lecain*.
The king is out hunting when he meets a beautiful girl and is
enamoured with her. Although married already with children, he
asks her to come as his mistress to his royal palace of Cletach, Cletty
on the Boyne near Rosnaree. She agrees on condition that no Christian cleric should ever set foot in the palace while she resides there
and that the king must submit to her will in all things. On asking
her name, she gives the name Sín. She also gives a series of words
which are used as synonyms for her name: sigh, rustling, storm,
rough wind, winter night, cry, tear, groan. Indeed, in Old Irish, the
word *sín* does signify 'bad weather' or a 'storm'. Is the girl warning
the king of 'the storm' to come? The king asks whether she believes
in the Christian god, for he now realizes that she possesses great
powers. She answers:

> Never believe the clerics
> For they chant nothing save unreason
> Follow not their unmelodious stave
> Cleave not to the clerics of churches
> If you desire life without treachery
> Better am I as a friend here
> Let not repentance come to you.

Installed in Cletach, Sín ousts Muirchertach's wife, Duailtech, and
his children, who go to the Christian bishop, Cairnech, to demand
that he intervene. Cairnech orders Muirchertach to send the girl
away. The king refuses and Cairnech curses him in a ritual that
appears more Druidic than Christian. However, Muirchertach's followers side with him against the bishop. After a while, Muirchertach
begins to be awed by the feats of magic which the girl performs and,
afraid, he goes to Bishop Cairnech and confesses his sins and
promises to leave Sín. He returns to eject her from Cletach but falls
under her power, for she evokes a vision which mesmerizes him. We
find, however, that Sín is torn between wanting vengeance

for Muirchertach's betrayal of her to the Christian bishop, and her genuine love for the king. Vengeance wins, as it must in all great epics, and Muirchertach awakes to find his fortress ablaze. Seeking to escape, Muirchertach climbs into a vat of wine but drowns, which it rather like the motif found in the story of King Diarmuid. Now we discover another theme. Sín's entire family, her mother, father, sister and cousins, had been slaughtered by Muirchertach during the battle of Atha Síghe (Assey) on the Boyne. She had planned her vengeance on the king using her Druidical powers to ensnare and destroy him. But she had genuinely come to love Muirchertach and after his death she is overcome with grief and dies. Once more we come away with a feeling of sympathy for the Druidess in spite of the Christian presentation.

We find in the *Tripartite Life of Patrick* that, in his canons, Patrick warns kings not to accept the advice of Druids or Druidesses and in his *Hymn* asks God especially to protect him from Druidesses.

According to the *Rennes Dinnsenchus*, Brigit was a *ban-druí* before she converted to Christianity. Brigit is said to have been born *c.*AD 455 at Faughart, near Newry, Co. Down. Her father is named as a Druid called Dubhtach. Her birth and upbringing, according to legendary tradition, were steeped in Druidical symbolism and she was supposed to have been nourished on the magical milk of Otherworld cows. She became a Christian and was ordained by Mael ('bald' or 'tonsured'), the bishop of Ardagh. She is recorded as founding her first religious settlement at Drumcree under the shadow of a high oak. Her foundation at Kildare was also based on oak symbolism, being *cill-dara*, the church of the oak. She died there in AD 525. As early as *c.*AD 650 Cogitosus wrote a biography of the saint *Vitae Brigitae*. Symbolically, Cogitosus mixed her cult together with the ancient Irish goddess of fertility, Brigit, after whom she had obviously been named. Druidic symbolism permeates the traditions of her life. St Brigit's feastday was grafted onto the festival of Imbolc (sometimes given as Oímelg – literally, parturition), sacred to the goddess Brigit. This was on the eve of 31 January and on 1 February, remembering Celts counted their time periods by night followed by day. The feast was connected with the coming into milk of the ewes and therefore a pastoral or fertility festival. The goddess Brigit ('the exalted or high one') was also known as Brigantia in northern Britain and Brigantu in Gaul. She was a daughter of The Dagda and was a divinity of healing, poetry and arts and crafts. The goddess was renowned for her powers of divination.

The saint took over many of the powers of the goddess, particularly her fertility symbolism.

St Brigit's mother, Broiseach, is given in ninth century AD hagiographies as the slave of Dubhtach and is sold by him to a Druid. Brigit is therefore brought up by the Druid who later sends her back to Dubhtach. An eighth century account actually gives the name of this Druid as Maithghean and says that he knew from the sound of the chariot in which Broiseach was being conveyed that she had a marvellous child in her womb. This account says that Brigit was born as her mother brought milk into the Druid's house at sunrise, but Broiseach had one foot on the threshold and one outside so that the child was born 'neither within nor without the house'. This 'neither nor' motif is a favourite recurring theme in Celtic mythology.

According to Dr Ó hÓgain:

It is therefore probable that a pagan sanctuary at Kildare was Christianized by a holy woman of the Fotharta (Faughart). This would have meant that the cult of that sanctuary became attached to her, including the goddess name Brighid which probably was a title borne by the chief Druidess there.

In many stories potent 'fairy women' or 'witches' are mentioned and these were undoubtedly relegated to this rôle from that of the Druidess by the Christian writers. The concept of the Druidesses relegated to sorceresses perhaps gave birth to the world's three most famous 'witches'.

'Thunder and lightning. Enter three witches.' This is the opening simple stage direction of William Shakespeare's famous play *Macbeth* (1606). MacBeth, High King of Scotland from AD 1040–57, was one of the most interesting Scottish monarchs. He had come to power legitimately under the Celtic law system, ruled over a Scotland which was prosperous and peaceful and could even afford to leave his kingdom and go on a pilgrimage to Rome. Envious English rulers used the ambitions of the son of a former king, there being no such concept as primogeniture in Celtic law, to send armies into Scotland but it took several years to overthrow him. Conquerors always write the history and so we arrive at Shakespeare's distorted version of MacBeth's life. It was Andrew of Wyntoun, the Prior of St Serf's in Loch Leven in Fife, who wrote about MacBeth (c.AD 1395–1424) and introduced into the stories of the monarch the very typical Celtic motif of three sorceresses who prophesy MacBeth's rise to greatness and the circumstances of his fall from power. This motif was followed by Shakespeare.

The motif occurs many times in Celtic sagas. Conaran had three sorceress daughters who ensnared people by spinning a magic web. The warrior Goll Mac Morna killed two of them but the third, Irnan, begged for mercy and promised to release the warriors. Irnan changed into a monster and placed a *geis* on Goll and his companions that they had to accept single combat with her. Goll eventually slew her after Oisín, Oscar and Celta all refused to do battle.

In a Breton tale we have another example of a woman, undoubtedly a Druidess adhering to the old religion, who is then transformed into a sorceress by Christian scribes. In this tale we find Dahud-Ahes, the daughter of the semi-legendary sixth century king of Kernev (Cornouaille), Gradlon, in the rôle of a Druidess, 'the shameful daughter of a worthy king'. She is consistently opposed to Christianity, possesses magical powers, and is opposed by St Guénolé. Her opposition causes her city of Ker-Ys to be destroyed by a flood but Guénolé turns her into a mermaid as she sinks beneath the waves, proving his magic is just as good as that of any Druid! It is interesting that the traditions of Dahud-Ahes in the Pointe du Raz area, off which point Ker-Ys is said to have been situated, are those which portray Dahud-Ahes as a 'good witch'. In addition the site of Ker-Ys, in the Baie des Trépassés (Bay of the Dead) off the Pointe du Raz is where Sena, the island of the nine Gallicenae, the prophetesses of Pomponius Mela's reference, was situated.

According to Professor Markle:

Apart from representing paganism in opposition to Christianity, however, she [Dahud-Ahes] also symbolises the rebellion against masculine authority ... The full significance of this act becomes clear when one considers her dissolute life as contrary to the teachings of the Christian Church, here represented by St Gwénnolé, himself the very symbol of masculine authority.

In Welsh saga we have the fascinating tale of Ceridwen, the wife of Tegid Foel of Penllyn. She is clearly depicted as the Christian concept of a Druidess; a sorceress, who has given birth to two extremely ugly sons. One of them, Morfan, who is said to have fought with Arthur at the battle of Camluan, is so ugly no one would challenge him to combat because they thought he was the devil. Ceridwen's other son, Afagddu, which name means 'utter darkness', was known as the ugliest man in the world. To compensate for this, Ceridwen decides to boil a cauldron of inspiration and science in order that Afagddu should drink of it and know the mysteries of the world so that everyone would respect his knowledge.

The cauldron, the prototype 'Holy Grail' which Christian monks developed from the Celtic myths, was to be boiled for a year and a day. After which only three drops (again, the mystical number 'three') would be ready. Morda, a blind man, is ordered to keep the fire stoked while Ceridwen employs the son of Gwreang of Llanfair, a lad named Gwion Bach, to stir the cauldron. As he does, the three drops of the magic distillation fall onto his finger and he sucks it. One is immediately reminded of the tale of Fionn Mac Cumhail and the Salmon of Knowledge. Gwion Bach obtains wisdom, the secrets of the past, present and future. Enraged, Ceridwen chases him. During the chase Gwion Bach transforms himself into a hare, fish, bird, and a grain of wheat. Ceridwen turns into a greyhound, otter-bitch, hawk and finally a hen, swallowing Gwion Bach as a grain of corn. The result of all these transmutations is that Ceridwen, transformed back into her human shape, finds herself pregnant. When she has the child, the reincarnated Gwion Bach, she puts him into a sack and throws him in the sea. But he is rescued and becomes the poet/mystic Taliesin. As Professor Markle observes: 'That child was to be the bard Taliesin, the true incarnation of Druidism, and famous for his knowledge of the world.'

MacCulloch says:

The existence of such priestesses and divineresses over the Celtic area is to be explained by our hypothesis that many Celtic divinities were at first female and served by women, who were possessed of the tribal lore. Later, men assumed their functions, and hence arose the great priesthoods, but conservatism sporadically retained such female cults and priestesses, some goddesses being still served by women – the Galatian Artemis, or the goddesses of Gaul, with their female servants.

If women had no part in the priestly functions of the religion of the early Celts, then the Celtic religions would indeed be unique in the world's history. But, as we have seen, women not only played a co-equal rôle in the activities of the Druids but their very position in Celtic society was highly advanced compared to their position in other European societies. Changes in patriarchal society were taking place, however, and the prominent rôle of Celtic women was given a *coup de grâce* by the coming of Roman Christianity. Even so, in the early years of what we define as the Celtic Church, their rôle was still a prominent one, as the evidence of the vast numbers of female Celtic saints compared with the number of such women in other societies demonstrates. But as Rome began to exert more and more influence in church matters, the rôle of women began to diminish. According to Mary Condren, in *The Serpent and the Goddess: Women, Religion and Power in Celtic Ireland* (1990): 'We can trace a gradual change of emphasis whereby what formerly was held sacred became profane and the new expression of sacredness took on an increasingly male character.'

Female church leaders were initially seen as equal with their male counterparts as they had been under the pre-Christian Celtic religion. This is apparent from the authority that the female Celtic saints had. Brigit, according to Cogitosus in the seventh century, presided over members of both sexes in her community as did the Irish trained Northumbrian St Hilda. In the early Celtic Christian church the communities were often double-houses or *conhospitae* in which men and women, and their children, lived as an extended family working in the name of the new god, perhaps carrying on traditions of the Druid communities. Women were able, initially, in accordance with Celtic philosophy, to celebrate the 'divine sacrifice of Mass', as well as the male priests. This incensed the sensibilities of the Roman Church, whose long struggle for domination over the Celtic Church is well documented. Rome first seemed to notice the practice in Brittany and in about AD 515–520 three Roman bishops wrote a letter to two members of the Breton clergy named Lovocat and Catihern: 'you celebrate the divine sacrifice of the Mass with the assistance of women to whom you give the name of *conhospitae*. . . We are deeply

grieved to see an abominable heresy . . . Renounce these abuses . . .'
Mary Condren observes:

> One of the main problems that the Christian Church had with
> these religious women was that the god of the Christians was very
> different from their god. Just as the Israelites overthrew the gods
> of the Canaanites when they developed their patriarchal forms of
> social organisation, so too the Christian priests would formulate
> a concept of god that would reinforce and encourage their new
> patriarchal consciousness. In its initial stages, the church may well
> have counteracted the power of the warriors, but in many respects
> its priestly practitioners were blessed with an equally virulent form
> of male reproductive consciousness. Although the Christian god
> would have control over nature, this was not his primary concern.
> He was much more concerned with abstract rules and concepts
> like justice, law and righteousness.

The lives of several early Irish saints begin to depict the rising conflict
in the social position between men and women. The *Life of Maedoc*,
or Aidan of Ferns (d. AD 626), whose reliquary was preserved in
Dublin to the eleventh century, details several interesting misogyn-
istic conflicts with women. Other examples are found in the *Lives* of
Kevin (Coemgen), the 'Glendalough saint', Declan, Molasius, Moling
and even Colmcille. We find stories of the early Irish saints accepting
Roman misogynism. Enda of Aran (c.AD 530), for example, would
only speak to his sister, St Faenche, through a veil when she came
to visit him. Maighenn, abbot of Kilmainham, would never look on
a woman lest he see the devil. Ciarán (future abbot of Clonmacnoise)
studied at the school of Finian of Clonard. Among his fellow pupils
was the beautiful daughter of a chieftain but he would never allow
himself to gaze on her nor, indeed, any other maiden, according to
the *Vita Ciarani*.

According to one's interpretation, the 'law of the innocents', proposed by Adomnán, and accepted by the Synod of Birr in AD 697,
emancipated Celtic women from the savage hardship of serving in
battle. It is true that Adomnán's *lex innocentium* was designed to
protect non-combatants in war, such as the elderly, women and children as well as clergy and, again, was highly advanced compared with
customs in other European societies. The law also forbade women to

be warriors, or military commanders. According to a life of Adomnán, he was moved to propose the new law, known as the *Cáin
Adomnáin* after an appeal by his mother, Ronnat, when they were
crossing a battlefield together and saw the terrible sight of a beheaded
woman with her child still suckling at her breasts; 'a stream of milk
on one of its cheeks and a stream of blood on the other'. Ammianus
Marcellinus records a fight in which an enraged Celtic woman fought
alongside her husband. Another interpretation of the *lex innocentium*
would be that it took away some rights of women to authority and
command.

The rôle of women in Celtic society had been drastically altered
by the tenth century AD when the Welsh law system was codified in
the reign of Hywel Dda.

According to *The Welsh Law of Women*, edited by Dafydd Jenkins
and Morfydd E. Owen (1980), 'Welsh law is considerably less gener-
ous to women (than Irish law), only allowing them such an equality
of status while they remain indistinguishable from men.' This meant
until the girl reached the age of puberty at twelve years. Under the
new patriarchal development, encouraged by Roman Christianity,
the Welsh law did not recognize the female in the same way as Irish
law. This is not to say that, under Welsh law, the position of women
in Celtic society had degenerated to the same level as it had in other
European cultures. They had not reached the position of mere chattels. Welsh women could still be *gwraig briod* (women of property);
and if a woman divorced she became entitled to half the marriage
wealth, a concept introduced into English law only in the closing
decades of the twentieth century! As in Irish law a woman widowed
or divorced was entitled to the status of the man with whom she last
cohabited. But a position of female inferiority was beginning to
emerge in the new Christian patriarchal society. The rôle of Celtic
women was changing.

Perhaps an echo of the vanishing independence of Celtic woman
can be seen in a story concerning Macha, a triune goddess. She
appears in several different forms in Irish myth. She is also identified
as Macha Mong Ruadh, the seventy-sixth monarch of Ireland, reigning in 377 BC, but this might simply be a confusion of name or
tradition. The annals accord Macha Mong Ruadh with having established the first Irish hospital, Bron-Bherg (House of Sorrow), and
with building Ard Macha (Macha's Height), which is the city of

Armagh, which Patrick made into the seat of the primacy of the Christian church in Ireland. This is hardly the tradition of a 'war goddess'. I am therefore inclined to believe that the traditions of the goddess Macha and that of Macha Mong Ruadh are two separate ones. A careful examination of the deity Macha shows her initially to be a 'mother goddess' figure who became subverted to a 'goddess of war'.

In the saga of 'The Debility of the Ulstermen', Macha appears as the mysterious wife of Crunnchua mac Agnoman. She is pregnant by him. He goes to a horse race at the feast of Samhain in which the two horses of the king of Ulster defeat all challenges. Crunnchua boasts that even his wife can outrun the king's horses and he is overheard by the infuriated king. The king orders Macha to be brought to the assembly and orders her to race against his horses, saying that otherwise he will kill Crunnchua. Macha is in the last stages of pregnancy and pleads with the king to delay his demands until she has given birth and recovered. He refuses and she cries to the assembled people: 'Help me, for a mother bore each one of you!' They heed her not.

The race is started and Macha wins but, as she reaches the winning post, her babies, twins – a boy and girl, are born. Then she pronounces a curse on all the men of Ulster, specifically excluding children as well as women.

> From this hour the ignominy that you have inflicted upon me will redound to the shame of each one of you. When a time of oppression falls upon you, each one of you who dwells in this kingdom will be overcome with weakness, as the weakness of a woman in childbirth, and this will remain upon you for five days and four nights, to the ninth generation it shall be so.

Like all myths, the story is open to several interpretations. Mary Condren sees the story as symbolizing the last pagan appeal to true motherhood as the basis for public social ethics, and a curse on the patriarchal age that had dawned.

> The Goddess was effectively saying; Although you may develop sophisticated doctrines of rebirth; although you have taken to yourselves the right of life and death; although your efforts might

seem logical and plausible in the light of patriarchal culture, your efforts cannot but be doomed to failure so long as they are based on the subordination of women. Speaking the language of peace and common good with the one hand, with the other, you are calling the troops to war against women and the earth.

This certainly is as valid an interpretation as any offered for this intriguing story, and one feels distinctly sympathetic to it.

MacCulloch has observed:

Irish mythology points to the early preeminence of goddesses. As agriculture and many of the arts were first in the hands of women, goddesses of fertility and culture preceded gods, and still held their place when gods were evolved. Even war goddesses are prominent in Ireland. Celtic gods and heroes are often called after their mothers, not their fathers, and women loom largely in the tales of Irish colonisation, while in many legends they play a most important part. Goddesses give their name to divine groups, and even where gods are prominent, their actions are free, their personalities still clearly defined. The supremacy of the divine women of Irish tradition is once more seen in the fact that they themselves woo and win heroes; while their capacity for love, their passion, their eternal youthfulness and beauty are suggestive of their early character as goddesses of ever-springing fertility.

In order to explain the change from feminine deities to masculine ones, Sir John Rhŷs claimed that the supremacy of goddesses was a pre-Celtic conception, a notion which 'the masculine orientated' Celts incorporated. MacCulloch has already dismissed this as nonsense. 'It is too deeply impressed on the fabric of Celtic tradition to be other than native, and we have no reason to suppose that the Celts had not passed through a stage in which such a state of things was normal. Their innate conservatism caused them to preserve it more than other races who had long outgrown such a state of things.' MacCulloch speaks unfortunately with the complacency of masculine arrogance, implying that a female orientated society was primitive and a masculine one a more mature state of affairs.

In any study of the Druids, inasmuch as they represent pre-Christian Celtic religious concepts and philosophy, one has to acknowledge not only the importance of the rôle of women but, indeed, the very centrality of their position enshrined as the supreme 'mother goddess', the symbol of knowledge and freedom, and as the moral pivot of Celtic society. It is not by chance that in the Irish sagas sovranty is consistently portrayed in the person of a woman. The woman usually appears in the form of a hag until the hero embraces her and is then hailed as the rightful ruler, with the woman turning into a beautiful woman. The union between the king and the goddess of the land was essential and, in this act, ancient Ireland is no different from other civilizations such as that of Mesopotamia where the Sumerian kings married symbolically with the goddess Innana. Medb of Connacht comes out of the myths as the wife of nine kings of Ireland in succession.

Here turning to Hindu myth again, we find that the Indian goddess Laksmi, Indra's consort, appears as 'sovranty', and in the wedding process she prepares Soma, 'the drink of which none tastes who dwells on earth', by chewing some leaves. Indra drinks this Soma from the goddesses' own mouth. When we turn back to Medb we find that her very name means 'an intoxicating liquor', and is the origin of the English mead. Medb is the daughter of Conan of Cuala and an ancient poem says that no one can be king in Ireland unless they drink of the mead of Cuala. When the goddess of sovranty gives Niall of the Nine Hostages a drink she says: 'smooth shall be the drink from your royal horn, it will be mead, it will be honey, it will be strong ale'.

The northern British Celtic tribes, the Cruthin of Caledonia, popularly known by their nickname as the Picts, are said to have had a matrilineal succession of kingship. There are two sources for this argument. The most quoted source is the Northumbrian historian Bede (d. AD 735), in his *Historia Ecclesiastica gentis Anglorum*, where he says that the Pictish kings and chieftains took Irish wives on the condition that the kingship passed through the female line. The second earlier source being an Irish one which affirms this. This is obviously Bede's source. Lloyd and Jenny Laing in *The Picts and the Scots* (1993) believe this was probably a piece of Irish propaganda that really related to Irish claims over the Pictish kingship. 'As things stand, the case for Pictish matriliny is not proven, and would not appear to be supported in any way by the evidence that survives, except in the very curious succession pattern.' This 'very curious succession pattern' is nothing more than the usual electoral method of Celtic kingship, ignoring the primogeniture system.

The Scottish, and, to some extent, Irish king lists purport to claim a succession back to a female named Scota whose traditions separate her into two different identities. In one tradition Scota is the daughter of an Egyptian Pharaoh named Cingris who became the wife of Niul, a wise teacher and obviously a Druid, who was invited to settle in Egypt where he befriended Aaron. Niul and Scota's son was named Goidel and was healed from the bite of a serpent by Moses himself. Goidel was the progenitor of the Gaels and thus it was foretold that no serpent could live in the lands in which the children of Goidel lived. This is clearly a story conjured by Christian scribes to explain the absence of venomous snakes in Ireland. The other Scota tradition was that she was the daughter of the Egyptian Pharaoh Nectanebus, who became wife of Míl and was killed fighting the Dé Danaan and was buried in Scotia's Glen, three miles from Tralee in Co. Kerry. From a combination of the two Scota figures descended Eber Scot who was the 'father of the Scots' as applied to modern Scotland. The name *scotti*, as recorded by the Romans, was thought to mean a 'raider'. Scota, however, at one time stood for the symbolism of sovranty of Scotland.

The name of Ireland itself, Éire, is the name of one of the triune goddesses; her sisters being Banba and Fotla. Each goddess asked the Milesians to remember her by naming Ireland after her. Banba and Fotla were often used as synonyms, particularly in poetry, for Ireland. But the Druid, Amairgen, promised the goddess Éire that the children of the Gael would use her name as the principal name of the country.

[6]

Religion of the Druids

'To summon a dead religion from its forgotten grave and to make it tell its story, would require an enchanter's wand,' comments J.A. MacCulloch in his seminal *The Religion of the Ancient Celts* (1911). He explains:

> No Celt has left us a record of his faith and practice, and the unwritten poems of the Druids died with them. Yet from these fragments we see the Celt as the seeker after God, linking himself by strong ties to the unseen, and eager to conquer the unknown by religious rite or magic art. For the things of the spirit have never appealed in vain to the Celtic soul, and long ago Classical observers were struck with the religiosity of the Celts. They neither forgot nor transgressed the law of the gods, and they thought that no good befell men apart from their will. The submission of the Celts to the Druids shows how they welcomed authority in matters of religion, and all Celtic regions have been characterised by religious devotion, easily passing over to superstition, and by loyalty to ideals and lost causes. The Celts were born dreamers, as their exquisite Elysium belief will show, and much that is spiritual and romantic in more than one European literature is due to them.

There are several things which one can take issue with MacCulloch about, especially his assertion of the submission of the Celts to religious authority and the abrogation of their will to that of the deities. One has to remember that MacCulloch was a religious minister and speaking more of religious attitudes of his time than of those in pre-Christian or early Christian times. The very fact of the conflict between Free Will and Predestination, encapsulated in the Pelagian/Augustine conflict, which we will come to later, shows that the Celts were not inclined to abrogate their will to anyone but themselves.

The Celts, in spite of the Romantic writers, particularly the French, of the eighteenth and early nineteenth centuries, were polytheists and not monotheists. The idea that the Celts were monotheists comes from a quotation by Origen (AD 185–254), who succeeded Clement as head of the Christian school of Alexandria. In his textual criticism of the book of *Ezekiel*, he claimed that the Druids of Britain had 'worshipped the one god . . . previous to the coming of Christ'. The Celts, he goes on, 'had long been predisposed to Christianity through the doctrines of the Druids . . . who had already inculcated the doctrine of the unity of the godhead.'

But the idea that they were monotheists is not substantiated. The reader should be warned immediately that no clear knowledge of the Druidic system of worship or ritual has come down to us in spite of romantics such as Edward Davies, in *Mythology of the British Druids* (1809) or Herbert in *The Neo-Druidic Heresy* (1838). Davies claimed to have resurrected the Druidic esoteric system from the bardic poetry of Wales. We must take his claims with a Druidical pinch of salt.

But, having said this, fragmentary as the evidence is, we can glimpse some of the religious ideas and rituals connected with the pantheon of the Celtic deities and their rôles by studying the insular Celtic literatures and comparing them with the archaeological evidence and place-name references.

It is a fact that there are extant some 374 names of Celtic gods and goddesses throughout the vast area once inhabited by the Celts in Europe. Of these names, some 305 occur only once and have been thought to be names of local deities (*teutates*), particular to each tribe. However, twenty names occur with great frequency in those areas where the Celts were domiciled. Although more work needs to be done in making a demographic study of such names, I would go so far as to argue that the main Celtic pantheon of gods numbered thirty-three. The Hindu gods and those of Persia were also thirty-three in number. The Vedas speak of thirty-three gods as 'all the gods' (*visve-devab*). Thirty-three seems to be a number of significance shared with other Indo-European cultures, even Rome.

Does this number thirty-three have any significance in Celtic culture? Indeed, we find that the Irish gods and goddesses, the Children of Danu, have thirty-three leaders at the battles of Magh Tuireadh, although only five of them, another significant figure, confer before the battle. But the Fomorii also have thirty-three leaders. Nemed lost thirty-three ships on his voyage to Ireland. Cúchulainn slays thirty-three opponents in the Otherworld. In the *Táin Bó Cuailnge* the men of Ireland are mustered in companies of thirty-three. In the story of 'Bricriu's Feast' thirty-two heroes accompany Conchobhar Mac Nessa to Bricriu's Hall (making thirty-three) and in 'The Dream of Maxen Wledig' thirty-two kings accompany Maxen in a hunt which leads to his vision. The Dési have to wander thirty-three years after their expulsion from Meath. The Druid/solar deity, Mug Ruith, was said to have studied with Simon Magus for thirty-three years. The Cruithin (or Picts) had thirty-three pagan kings and thirty-three Christian Kings. The children of Calatín, of Fergus, of Morna and of Cathair Mór numbered thirty-three each. In some versions of the Welsh historian Nennius, the great cities of Celtic Britain are listed as thirty-three, not twenty-eight accounted in other versions. It is obvious that the numeral is, therefore, of significance.

Pomponius Mela states that the Druids 'profess to know the will of the gods' which, if we accept the statement, clearly means that the Druids were the 'middle-men' and 'middle-women' between the mortal and immortal world. But, as already argued, this was only one of their functions.

One thing is evident, confirmed by Caesar and the insular Celtic literatures, that the Celts did not look upon their gods as their creators but as their ancestors – more as supernatural heroes and heroines, in which form they also appear in Hindu myth and saga. We must therefore ask whether the Celts had a concept of 'creation'. Certainly in Old Irish there occurs the concept *isin chétne tuiste* (in the primal creation). According to O'Curry there is a passage in the ancient texts in which Conlaí of Connacht convened an assembly of Druids at which a claim was made that they were creators of the world. Conlaí mocked this claim and challenged them to alter the course of the sun and of the moon so that they would appear in the opposite areas of the sky. The Druids are said to have retired in complete confusion. Probably this is but a bellicose Christian hand recording the story.

The story of Conlaí is reiterated in a gloss to the *Senchus Mór* which records that the Druids, like the Hindu Brahmins, once boasted that they had made the sun, moon, earth and sea. In Vedic mythology, creation began with space (*aditi*) in which sky and earth were formed, and were regarded as the original male and female elements. The sky was personified as Varuna. The first man appeared as Manu and his daughter Ida was born of the food which Manu offered as a sacrifice to Vishnu in gratitude for being protected from the great flood. But we have some trace of an earlier Hindu 'mother goddess' figure in Aditya to whom we shall return shortly.

The earliest recorded creation myth is that of the Sumerians of Mesopotamia in which Nammu, the primeval sea, gave birth to the sky god, An, and the earth god, Ki. Their offspring was Enlil, the air. He begat Nanna, the moon, who in turned fathered Utu, the sun. Enlil impregnated Ki, who gave birth to Enki, god of water and of wisdom. Enki ordered the universe. His sister Nintu then created man by moulding him out of clay.

The creation myth of the Babylonians is contained in *Enuma el'ish* (War of the Gods), in which Marduk forms man out of the blood and bones of the slain god Kingu. In Egypt the solar deity Ra created himself out of Chaos by calling his own name, an example of the power of the Word, which we will discuss later. Naming as a process of creation does occur in Irish mythology for the *Leabhar Gabhála* is careful to provide the name of the first to accomplish things, ranging from landing in the country to churning butter, making mead, building a house, cultivating the land and so on. There is another Egyptian creation myth that the god Atun stood on a mound in the primeval waters and gave birth parthenogenetically to the other gods and allotted them parts of the world to embody. The Hebrew/Christian myth is familiar from *Genesis*, in which Yahweh created the universe and man in seven days. The earliest Greek creation myth appears in the *Theogony* of Hesiod in which, after the creation of the elements from the original Chaos, Prometheus moulded the first men and women from clay.

The problem with the Celtic myths is that when they came to be written down the writers were Christian monks who were endeavouring to reconcile them with the new Christian beliefs based on the Hebrew creation myths. Therefore, we have the Hebrew God creating the earth with a liberal borrowing from Biblical sources. Alas, we have no record of the original Celtic creation myths. The earliest native 'origin' book is of course the *Leabhar Gabhála* in which the five invasions of Ireland are recounted and these invasions provide the genesis of all crafts and knowledge, commemorating each occasion.

The first invader was Cesair, daughter of Bith who was son of Noah of the Hebrew myth. Bith was denied a place in the Ark and so Cesair advized him to build an idol with his companions Fintan and Ladra. The idol then told them to build a ship as Noah had done and take refuge in it. The idol could not advize them as to the specific time that the Deluge would occur. But they built the ship and sailed off. After seven years they came to the shores of Ireland. Cesair became the wife of Fintan but he eventually abandoned her. The Deluge came and Bith and Cesair were drowned with their followers. Fintan, however, survived the Deluge by turning himself into a salmon. There is some similarity in this story to that of the Hindu survival of Manu, saved from the flood by a large fish. This, of course, is not exactly a creation myth, but one of rebirth.

According to MacCulloch:

Certain folk-beliefs, regarding the origin of different parts of nature, bear a close resemblance to primitive cosmogonic myths, and they may be taken as disjointed memory of similar myths held by the Celts and perhaps taught by the Druids. Thus sea, river, or springs arose from the micturition of a giant, fairy, or saint, or from their sweat or blood. Islands are rocks cast by giants, and mountains are the material thrown up by them as they were working on the earth. Wells sprang up from the blood of a martyr or from the touch of a saint's or a fairy's staff. The sea originated from a magic cask given by God to a woman. The spigot, when opened, could not be closed again, and the cask never ceased running until the waters covered the earth . . .

The stories are numerous as to how plains, mountains and other natural features assumed their identity, particularly in the period of the second invasion led by Partholón and the third invasion led by Nemed. Both Partholón and Nemed are descendants of Magog, son of Japhet. The reason that the Christian scribes chose Japhet as an ancestor figure is because he was one of the three sons of Noah. Japhet had seven sons whose descendants were said to occupy the 'isles of the Gentiles' (*Genesis 10:5*). Both Partholón and Nemed are said to have invaded Ireland separately and found the Fomorii there, the evil gods of the Irish myths, whose name means the 'under-sea dwellers'. Interestingly, we are not given any account of their origin. Partholón and his followers perished from plague while Nemed was also killed and his followers dispersed. Only when the children of Danu, the mother goddess, invaded Ireland was the power of the Fomorii broken at the second Battle of Magh Tuireadh and the good gods prevailed.

It is here that we might glimpse, albeit briefly, a Celtic origin myth in the story of Danu, the mother goddess, and her children, the Tuatha Dé Danaan. Most religions of the world have their 'mother goddess' figure. As Professor Markle has pointed out: 'The Druidic religion was no exception to this rule. Its mythology, like all other mythologies, contains traces of a mother goddess.' Danu's name is also that of the great River Danube at whose headwaters, significantly, the Celtic peoples are said to have evolved before commencing their expansion throughout Europe at the start of the first millennium BC. The name seems cognate with the Sanskrit, the nearest we can come to our hypothesized Indo-European language, *Dana* meaning 'waters of heaven'. The Irish form now indicates 'swift flowing'. Moreover, the name is to be found in several river names, such as the River Don in Durham and Yorkshire, the Don in Scotland and in France. We have another comparison to Hindu culture in that, according to the *Rigveda*, Aditya is not only an early mother goddess but the name of a mythical river which is the source of all the waters of the world. Could it be that the Danube, the river of the mother goddess Danu, providing the 'waters of heaven', occupied that same rôle in the early Celtic world? A place which the Ganga, or Ganges, still occupies in the Hindu world today? Ganga was a mother goddess who in later Hindu tradition becomes one of the wives of Shiva. As Joseph Campbell remarked: 'The idea of the sacred river, the Jordan, the waters that pour from heaven, becomes translated into the idea of the grace of the divine, flowing inexhaustibly out of some source. In India the very source of the Ganges, up in the Himalayan area, is a very sacred place.' We find that the ancient Irish bards deemed that the river's edge, the brink of the water, was always that place where *éicse*, wisdom, knowledge and poetry was revealed. It was also a word that meant divination.

We find that Danu, or rather her children, on arriving in Ireland, have to struggle against their enemies, the evil Fomorii, whose own 'mother goddess' is Domnu. Significantly, Domnu not only means 'the world' but the 'deeps' of the sea. Irish epic contains many episodes of the struggle between the Children of Domnu, representing darkness and evil, and the Children of Danu, representing light and good. Moreover, the Children of Domnu are never completely overcome or eradicated from the world. Symbolically, they are the world. The conflict is between the 'waters of heaven' and the 'world'.

It is a significant point to note that the Celtic chieftain, Viridomar (Virdomarus) who led thirty thousand Gaesatae against Rome in 222 BC, called himself a 'son of the Rhine', meaning, in my opinion, that the goddess of the Rhine had been his ancestor. Conchobhar Mac Nessa is varyingly said to be the son of the Druid Cathbad or Nessa's lover Fachtna. But in the *Stowe MS 992*, there is a third more interesting version. Nessa brings Cathbad a drink from a river. He sees that there are two worms in the water and forces her to drink it in punishment. She becomes pregnant and gives birth to Conchobhar who is then named after the river. Has the goddess of the river taken the form of worms to be reborn as Conchobhar?

As the Celts spread through Europe, did they, at that time, consider themselves all children of the great mother goddess/divine river, Danu? Certainly, there is a Welsh equivalent of Danu in the person of Don, whose name, as Donwy, also occurs in Welsh river names as Dyfrdonwy and Trydonwy. Other river names with the same derivation are found in England, Scotland and France.

But Welsh sources do not have the creation myth traditions as in the Irish tales. We can only speculate on how much the Christian/ Hebrew tradition of the writers of the Celtic sagas intruded on, and distorted, the original traditions.

Only when the Tuatha Dé Danaan invaded Ireland do we clearly recognize a pantheon of gods and goddesses and these are certainly paralleled by the Children of Don in Welsh saga.

Both Irish and Welsh mythology and saga are 'heroic', for, by the late first millennium, the Celts had made their gods and goddesses into heroes and heroines and their heroes and heroines into gods and goddesses. In the lives of these gods and heroes, goddesses and heroines, the lives of the people, in their emerging patriarchal society, and the essence of their religious traditions were mirrored. The gods and heroes, goddesses and heroines, were no mere physical beauties with empty heads. They had to have intellectual powers equal to their physical abilities. They were totally human and were subject to all the natural virtues and vices. They practised all seven of the deadly sins. Yet their world was one of rural happiness, a world in which they indulged in all the pleasures of mortal life in an idealized form; love of nature, art, games, feasting, hunting and heroic single-handed combat.

Caesar, unfortunately as it turns out, sums up the gods of Gaul with a Roman identity in a short passage:

> They worship chiefly the god Mercury; of him there are many symbols, and they regard him as the inventor of all the arts, as the guide of travellers, and as possessing great influence over bargains and commerce. After him they worship Apollo and Mars, Jupiter and Minerva. About these they hold much the same beliefs as other nations. Apollo heals diseases, Minerva teaches the elements of industry and the arts, Jupiter rules over the heavens, Mars directs war . . . All the Gauls assert that they are descended from Dispater their progenitor.

By trying to equate the Celtic gods with Roman equivalents, Caesar's evidence is almost worse than useless. No less than sixty-nine different Celtic gods have been coupled in Latin inscriptions to that of the Roman Mars. The reference to the Gaulish Celts asserting they were descended from Dispater is, however, interesting and is a confirmation that the Celts saw their gods as ancestors. Dis, in the Roman religion, was the equivalent of the Greek god Pluto, and the ruler of the Underworld which, in classical Roman literature, becomes a symbol of death. We can only interpret Caesar's assertion that Dispater (Father Dis) was seen as the ancestor of the Gauls, as meaning that the Celts held a 'father of the gods' as their progenitor. It therefore follows that by this stage in their development, the Celts had inserted their perception of a 'mother goddess' as the source of their existence into a patriarchal mode of expression.

There is indeed a 'father of the gods' in insular Celtic literature which equates with a native god in Gaul. But this is not a god of death or the underworld. The analogous god of the dead in Irish myth is Donn, the eldest son of Midir the Proud and his abode was at Tech Duinn (House of Donn) on a island off the southwest coast of Ireland where he assembles the dead before they set off on their journey westward to the Otherworld. He is not to be confused with Don of Welsh myth, who is the Welsh equivalent of Danu, the 'mother goddess'. Significantly, in Welsh myth, the equivalent of Tech Duinn is also envisaged as an island to the southwest coast of Wales (Lundy). In fact, both the Irish kingdom of Munster and Dyfed in Wales, both in the southwest of their respective countries, are associated with the Otherworld and appear as places of origin, as primeval worlds. More importantly, these areas are associated with more female deities than any other area.

Henri D'Arbois de Jubainville, however, identifies another Celtic god, Bilé, cognate with Bel and Belenus, as the Dispater. His feastday was on 1 May (Beltaine), which month in modern Irish still bears his name. It may also be significant that Uisneach was the place where one of the four major festivals of Ireland was celebrated in his name. It is true that he also appears as a 'god of the dead' and has sometimes been referred to as 'Father of Gods and Men'. He is portrayed as Danu's consort. The cult of Bilé was widespread under the equivalents Bel or Belenus. Belenus was venerated in Gaul for many centuries after the Roman conquest.

There are many places named after Bilé throughout Europe. In London, Belenus' Gate has come down to us as Billingsgate (Bilé's gate). Presumably the heads of the dead of the original Celtic settlement, and later the Roman occupied city, were taken through this gate to the river Thames — *tamesis*, the dark or sluggish river — where they were used as votive offerings or simply placed for Bilé to transport to the Otherworld. Hundreds of skulls from the Celtic period have been discovered in the Thames, around London, with other votive offerings.

One has to remember that the ancient Celts believed that the soul reposed in the head, not in the region of the heart as Western Christians now have it. This is why the head was so venerated and prized in ancient Celtic society. When Bran the Blessed was mortally wounded he urged his companions to remove his head and take it back to the Island of the Mighty (Britain) for burial. It takes many years and Bran's head eats, drinks and instructs them on the journey back. The head is buried (legend has it that the site was Tower Hill in London) looking towards his enemies so that, in accordance with Celtic custom, he could protect the land against invasion. Many other examples of talking heads of slain heroes are found in Celtic myth.

Connecting the many human skulls found in the Thames, together with exquisite swords, shields, helmets and other votive offerings, Professor Richard Bradley, of Reading University, in a 1990 BBC television documentary, put forward the argument that the Thames could have been a sacred river for the British Celts, occupying the same role as the Ganges. I have already mentioned this in *A Guide to early Celtic remains in Britain* (1991). It is certainly an acceptable theory although the emphasis must be that it was *a* sacred river not *the* sacred river.

Once again, we find this worship of rivers, springs or wells as part of an ancient Indo-European custom. In central India the tribes of Chota Nagpur, in what is now the Maharashtra state, offer sacrifices to the deities of wells and rivers in much the same way that their Christian Indo-European counterparts in Ireland, Wales and Brittany still do today.

D'Arbois de Jubainville's candidate for the Dispater, Bilé or Belenus, had his name incorporated in many personal Celtic names. Perhaps the most famous of these was the king of Britain who ruled just before the Roman invasion of AD 43 – Cunobelinus. The name means 'hound of Belinus' whom Shakespeare later made famous in the form of Cymbeline.

I would argue that The Dagda is portrayed more often than Donn or Bilé as the 'father of the gods'. And I would argue that this is also significant because The Dagda is Danu's son by Bilé. Therefore Danu still takes precedence as the primary source of life. As the sacred 'waters from heaven', Danu watered the oak, which was Bilé the male fertility symbol, and gave birth to The Dagda, 'the good god' who fathered the rest of the gods. What makes me link Bilé with the oak? Because Bilé is the Old Irish word for a sacred tree which was also used to denote a 'noble warrior'. We find Biliomagus in Gaul as a place meaning 'the clearing of the sacred tree'. The name survives in place names such as Billé and Billom in France and Billum in Denmark. When the sacred tree of Medb of Connacht is mentioned in the *Táin* it is as Bilé Meidbe.

Bilé's rôle in transporting the souls of the dead Celts to the Otherworld takes on another significance. Transportation is usually via water, rivers like the Thames, or out to the sea. He is, in fact, transporting them to the 'divine waters' – his consort Danu 'the mother goddess'. It is no accident, therefore, that his main centre of veneration in early times was the Hill of Uisneach whose very name, as we will discuss further when studying Druids as astrologers, is composed of the root word for water, *uisce*.

The Dagda is father of nearly all the Irish gods and is also known by the names of Eochaidh Ollathair (Father of All), as Aedh (Fire) and as Ruadh Rofessa (Lord of Great Knowledge), making him a triune divinity. Professor Myles Dillon points out that the name Eochaid has an equivalent in Sanskrit of Pasupati, which is one of the names of the Hindu god Shiva, the supreme spirit who is also known as Mahadeva (the great god).

The Dagda appears as the patron of Irish Druidism. He is visualized as a man carrying a gigantic club which he drags on wheels. One end of his club can slay while the other can heal. He has a black horse named Acéin, or Ocean, and his cauldron, called Undri, is one of the major treasures of the Dé Danaan, brought from the fabulous city of Murias. It provides food so that no man went away from it hungry. It is the 'cauldron of plenty' which later generations of Christianized Celts developed into the Holy Grail of Arthurian myth. The Dagda also possesses a magic harp.

The Dagda has also been equated with Cernunnos, whose cult is found in both Britain and Gaul. Representations of Cernunnos show his club, like The Dagda, and he sometimes sits in a characteristic Buddha posture. The hill figure at Cerne Abbas, south west England, which is also a near replica of a Celtic carving found at Corbridge, Northumberland, is thought to represent Cernunnos. But usually Cernunnos is represented as having a stag's antlers and is accompanied by a serpent with the head of a ram. In this form he appears on a panel of the Gundestrup Cauldron (National Museum, Copenhagen). This figure also occurs on a silver coin of the Belgic Remi, now in the British Museum. As well as clasping the serpent in his left hand, he is surrounded by numerous and diverse animals. This has led some scholars to claim him as 'Lord of the Animals'. As previously mentioned Dillon has shown that Shiva was also known as Pasupati, meaning 'Lord of Animals' and when the archaeologist, Sir John Marshall, was excavating at Mohenjodaro, in north-west India, he found a seal on which Pasupati was represented. 'The general resemblance between the Cernunnos panel and the Mohenjodaro seal (now in the New Delhi Museum)·is such that one can hardly doubt their common origin,' says Dillon.

When the Children of Danu arrive in Ireland, Danu is no longer with them. Did they leave her behind in the form of the Danube when they began their expansion across Europe? We learn that the Children of Danu have come from four fabulous cities, Falias, Gorias, Finias and Murias, and brought with them special treasures from each of these cities. The Lia Fáil (Stone of Destiny) from Falias; a sword from Gorias (the forerunner of the famous Excalibur), the spear of victory from Finias and The Dagda's 'cauldron of plenty' from Murias. Moreover, we learn that in these four cities were 'four Druids who taught the Children of Danu skill and knowledge and perfect wisdom'. Morias dwelt in Falias; Urias 'of the noble nature' lived in Gorias; Arias the poet resided in Finias and Senias had his abode in Murias. Were these 'cities' real places along the banks of the Danube from which the Celts began their first migration at the start of the first millennium BC? And were Morias, Urias, Arias and Senias a folk memory of real people who had instructed the Children of Danu before they departed on their first great migration from the headwaters of the Danube?

There is confusion in that The Dagda is not their leader at the time the Children of Danu arrive in Ireland. The leader is Nuada, who also appears in Welsh myth as Nudd, which is also cognate with Lludd Llaw Ereint and is obviously also Nodens, whose name survives in a temple from the Roman occupation of Britain at Lydney by the Severn. Nuada, in the battles with the Fomorii, first has his hand severed, which is replaced by a silver one by the god of medicine, Dian Cécht, and then by a real one by Dian Cécht's son, Miach, and is finally slain, in another battle. Nuada is not to be confused with the Nuada who is the chief Druid of Cahir Mór, the ancestor of Fionn Mac Cumhail. When Nuada can no longer lead the Children of Danu, because of his injury, he is replaced by Bres, who is the son of Elatha, a Fomorii king, and a woman of the Dé Danaan who became consort to the goddess Brigit, a daughter of The Dagda. Bres is a tyrant and soon deposed, fleeing to the Fomorii. After these events The Dagda becomes the leader of the gods and goddesses and remains so until they are driven underground.

Among the names of the Celtic gods which appear most frequently is that of Lugh in Irish, Llew in Welsh and Lugus in Gaulish. The inscriptions and monuments to him are more numerous than to any other Celtic god, and it is generally accepted that when Caesar spoke of the Gaulish 'Mercury' it was to Lugus that he referred. The name appears in place names in many of the former Celtic territories: Lyons, Léon, Loudan and Laon in France; Leiden in Holland; Liegnitz in Silesia; and Carlisle (Luguvalum in Roman times) in England. It has been argued that the name of London, now the capital of England, also derived from Lugdunum, as did Lyons, in France. Hence the Latin form Londinium. Some scholars have argued, however, that the name could equally derive from the Celtic root *londo* signifying 'the wild place'. Other dedications to Lugh occur at Arranches in Switzerland and at Asma (Tarragona) in Spain, as Lugoues and Lugoubus. At Lyons (Lugdunum) the Gaulish Celts celebrated an ancient feast of Lugus. Following the Roman conquest, during the reign of Caesar Augustus, the feast was dedicated to the emperor. This same feast occurs in insular Celtic tradition. In Ireland it was known as Lughnasadh, held on 1 August. It was one of the four major pre-Christian festivals and basically an agrarian feast in honour of the harvesting of crops. The name still survives as Lúnasa (August) in Irish, in Luanistyn (August) in Manx, and in Lúnasad for the Lammas Festival in Scottish Gaelic. Lugh in Irish myth, the son of Cian and Ethlinn, was the god of all arts and crafts and, from the splendour of his countenance, he was also known as Find (Fair One). In this form he also survives on the Continent as Vindonnus and in some place-names such as Uindobona (Vienna).

Lugh was, says Professor Dillon, the greatest of all the gods. The Dagda actually yields command to him at the second battle of Magh Tuireadh. He is commonly known as Lugh Lámhfhadha or Lugh of the Long Arm or Hand, whose counterpart in Welsh myth is Lleu Llaw Gyffes. Now the fascinating thing is that in the *Rigveda* the Hindu god Savitar is called *prthupani*, 'of the large hand'. The Hindu perception of the sun rising, with its beams of light, and its setting, was likened to a great hand. 'The god with the great hand stretches up his arms so that all obey'. Not only was Lugh claimed as a solar deity but so was Savitar, who was able to stretch out his hands to command day and night. Do we have a common Indo-European link again?

Professor Dillon was a student of Paul Jules Antoine Meillet, author of such pioneering works as *Les dialects indo-européens*

(Paris, 1908). Meillet was particularly interested in the subject of taboo words in languages, a subject we will return to when discussing the Druids as astronomers and astrologers. Meillet pointed to the fact that there seemed to be no identifiable common Indo-European root for the hand or arm and concluded that the word was a subject of taboo. The word for hand/arm varies so much in each Indo-European language (the English *hand*, representing the Germanic group, *cheir(o)* in Greek, *manus* in Latin and *lamh* in Irish indicate the widely differing words) suggesting, says Meillet that a euphemism was used in each language. He pointed to this being due to an ancient Indo-European cult of a god with a large hand or long arm. This cult was discussed by Hermann Güntert in *Von der Sprache de Götter und Geiser* (1921). The 'god with the large hand' is known from rock carvings and paintings dating back to the Bronze Age and geographically from Sweden to the Punjab.

Lugh was called *samildánach* in Ireland, possessing many crafts. One craft was that of shoemaking and one dedication to Lugh at Asma, Tarragona, Spain, is by an ancient guild of cobblers while, as Professor Dillon points out, equally fascinating is the fact that at Backa, near Brastad in Sweden, the 'god with the large hand' is known as 'the shoemaker'. Paul-Yves Sebbilot, in *Le Folklore de France* (1904–07) says that the Bretons of Morbihan still called the sun *sabotier* ('shoemaker') as a euphemism. Is it coincidence that Lleu Llaw Gyffes, in the *Mabinogion*, comes to visit his mother in the disguise of a cobbler? And, finally, in Ireland, as the old gods were driven underground by Christianity Lugh diminished in people's minds, becoming simply a fairy craftsman – *Lugh chromain*, 'little stooping Lugh'. Now all that is left of this potent patron of Celtic arts and crafts is the Anglicized version of *Lugh-chromain* – the leprechaun, a fairy cobbler!

Another god with a widespread following was the Gaulish Ogmios, identified by the Greek poet Loukianos – Lucian (*c.*AD 115 – after 180) – as 'Heracles'. Ogmios had his equivalents in Ireland (Ogma) and Britain (Ogmia). In Britain, for example, a piece of pottery from Richborough depicts a figure with long curly hair and sun rays emanating from his head with the name Ogmia inscribed. In Ireland, Ogma was the god of eloquence and literature, and a son of The Dagda. He is credited with the invention of Ogham script, named after him, the earliest form of Irish writing. His daughter married the god of medicine, Dian Cécht. His parentage and adventures in many ways make him a comparative figure to Heracles, who was the son of Zeus, father of the Greek gods.

We find Irish gods and goddesses, such as Badb, Brigit, Bron, Buanann, Cumal, Goibniu, Manánnan, Mider, Nemon, Nét and Nuada, all have recognizable equivalents in Britain and Gaul.

Lucan adds to our knowledge of Celtic gods by stating that Esus, Taranis and Teutates were also worshipped. He refers to 'uncouth Esus of the barbarous altars' who has to be propitiated by human sacrifice. Esus appears in the guise of a muscular woodcutter on a relief dedicated to Jupiter c.AD 14–37, rediscovered in 1711 under the choir of Notre Dame cathedral in Paris. A similar depiction was found from the same century at Trier. The other gods Taranis and Teutates are more easily identified for Taran means 'thunderer' (*taran* in Welsh and *torann* in Irish) and he is obviously a god of thunder, like Thunor or Thor. On dedications Taranis is often equated with Jupiter. Monuments to him survive in Chester (England), Böckingen and Godramstein (Germany), Orgon, Thauron and Tours (France) and Scardona (in the former Yugoslavia.) Taran occurs in Welsh mythology as the father of Gluneu, one of the seven survivors of the ill-fated battle between Bran and Matholwch. As for Teutates, mentioned by Lucan, the name signifies a people or tribe (echoed by *tuath* in Irish and *tud* in Welsh). Toutatis is a variant spelling. From the dedications, it is clearly a title rather than a name. Teutates was used with another name such as 'Mars Toutates Cocidius' in Carlisle. Therefore a Teutates was a tribal god. From its meaning, it has been argued that when the Germanic peoples began to encroach on the eastern borders of the Celts, the Celts referred to them as 'the people' (Teutons), in much the same way that in the nineteenth century southern Africans became known as the Bantu from the native word which simply meant 'men'.

Many Celtic gods were worshipped in triune or triple form. The concept of a three personality god seems to have its roots in Indo-European expression. In Hindu belief the Trimurti consisted of Brahma, the Creator, Vishnu, the Preserver, and Shiva the Destroyer. Pythagoras saw three as the perfect number of the philosophers – the beginning, middle and end – and used it as a symbol of deity. Indeed, the ancient Greeks saw the world ruled by three gods – Zeus (heaven), Poseidon (sea) and Pluto/Hades (underworld). Three permeates Greek myth: the Fates are three, the Furies three, the Graces three, the Harpies three, the Pythia or Sibyl (the Delphic oracle) sits on a three-legged stool, the Sibylline books are three times three, the Muses are three times three and so on.

As in the Greek world, so among the Celts, who saw *homo sapiens* as body, soul and spirit; the world they inhabited as earth, sea and air; the divisions of nature as animal, vegetable and mineral; the cardinal colours as red, yellow and blue and so forth. Three was the number of all things. Most of their gods were three personalities in one. Combinations of the figure three occur often in Celtic tales such as nine (three times three) and thirty-three.

Ireland itself is represented in the female triune goddess – Éire, Banba and Fótla. There were three Celtic craft gods – Goibhniu, Luchta and Creidhne. The goddess of fertility, of smiths and of healing and poetry, even The Dagda himself were worshipped in triune form. The most famous war goddess was the Mórrígán, sometimes Mórrígú, 'great queen', and she also appears interchangeable as Macha, Badb and Nemain. She embodies all that is perverse and horrible among the supernatural powers.

Mother symbols were also worshipped in triple form; in Gaul the title *matres* or *matronae* was used, because the dedications on the monuments survive only in Latin. Mother Earth was the symbol of fertility and figures with children, baskets of fruit and horns of plenty are found all over the Celtic world. From Vertault in Burgundy comes a triple mother goddess sculpture with a baby held by one while the other holds a towel.

Christianity later adopted this triune godship (Father, Son and Holy Ghost) – not from Judaic culture, to which it is alien, but from the Greek interpretation aided by the concepts of early Christian Fathers. The Gaulish Celt, Hilary, bishop of Poitiers, (c.AD 315–c.367) is regarded as one of the first native Celts to become an outstanding philosophical force in the Christian movement. And his great work was *De Trinitate*, defining the concept of the Holy Trinity, which is now so integral to Christian belief.

Diogenes Laertius observed that the Druids taught in the form of Triads. This is confirmed by the literary traditions of both Ireland and Wales.

The great rivers of northern Europe tend to still bear Celtic names, many associated with goddess figures. We have already dealt with

The Gundestrup Cauldron, a silver-plated bowl dated to the first century AD. Cauldrons had a special place in pre-Christian Celtic religious ideas and practices. Modern observers associate the cauldron with the Druids.

This bronze from Haute-Marne represents Taranis, the Celtic god of thunder, carrying his solar wheel.

Part of the Celtic Calendar of Coligny, on bronze plates and dated to the first century BC. It demonstrates the sophisticated Druidic calendrical observations.

It has been suggested that the base plate from the Gundestrup Cauldron shows the divination concept of the 'bull feast' (tarbhfheis) used by Druids.

An early Celtic chariot burial in which the dead were buried with all the accoutrements needed for life in the Otherworld.

Dead warriors lining up to be plunged into the cauldron of rebirth, a typical Celtic motif.

On 1 August 1984, at Lindow Moss on the southern outskirts of Manchester, a human torso was found preserved in peat. It was 2000 years old. Drs Ross and Robins claimed it was the body of a Druid Prince who had been ritually slaughtered.

William Stukeley's fanciful drawing of a Druid's
appearance, 1740.

Roman propaganda portrayed the Roman destruction of 'Druidic altars' in this way.

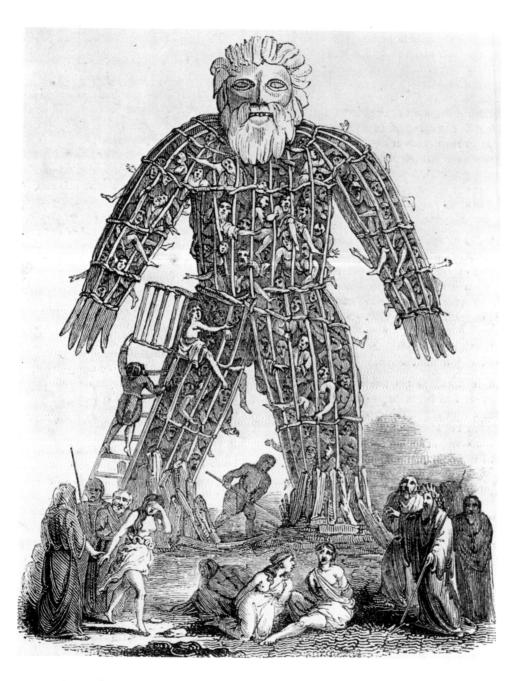

A visualisation of Caesar's 'wicker man'. It was claimed human sacrifices were put in this and burnt alive.

The Sheela-na-gig, frequently found in Ireland and sometimes in Britain.
This image is from Kilpeck in Herefordshire and is thought to be symbolic of
the pre-Christian concept of a mother goddess, who creates and destroys
with a Kali-like aspect (indicative of common European roots).

Many Celtic deities, like their Indo-European Hindu counterparts, are depicted in Buddha-like postures, as on this enamel from Email. The figures are similar to those on the Gundestrup Cauldron.

Winston Churchill being installed into the Albion Lodge of the
Ancient Order of Druids at Blenheim Palace, 15 August 1908.

Modern Druids? This English
group, claiming descent from
the eighteenth-century
'revivalists' are seen going to
commemorate a solstice at
Tower Hill, London, in 1964.

the Danube, which takes its name from the goddess Danu. Here, we are in the land in which the Celts are recognized to have originated; the headwaters of the Danube, the Rhine and the Rhône. And here we find that the Upper Danube, with its tributaries and sub-tributaries is a region full of Celtic names, as is the valley of the upper Rhine and also the Rhône. The Seine takes its name from the Celtic goddess Sequana. In England the Severn takes its name from Sabrann, which is the name of another Celtic goddess also found in the name of a Bedfordshire stream and in the old name for the River Lee in Ireland. The Boyne in Ireland is named from a goddess, Boann, the consort of The Dagda. And the Shannon named from the goddess Sinainn.

Dr Anne Ross has argued:

> The names of such rivers as the Dee (*Deva*), the Clyde (*Clòta*, cf. Gaullish *Clutoida*), the Severn (*Sabrina*) and perhaps the Wharfe (? *Verbeia*) as well as the Braint of Anglesey and the Brent of Middlesex (from *Brigantia*), would apparently reflect the same association of a river with a goddess as is attested for Gaul, and in the case of Ireland this suggestion is strongly supported by textual material. Not only do rivers have goddess names, but Irish cult legends occur which purport to account for the naming of such rivers.

MacCulloch maintains that:

> ... there is little doubt that the Celts, in their onward progress, named river after river by the name of the same divinity, believing that each new river was a part of his or her kingdom ... The mother-river was that which watered a whole region, just as in the Hindu sacred books the waters are mothers, sources of fertility ... the Celts regarded rivers as bestowers of life, health, and plenty, and offered them rich gifts and sacrifices.

Several times Celtic gods are depicted with female companions. The Gaulish god Sucellus, who carries a hammer in his left hand, is depicted in one relief found near Metz with Nantosuelta. The name Sucellus means 'he who strikes with good effect'. Nantosuelta has been translated as 'winding river'. So when patriarchy replaced the 'mother goddess' concept, to retain a continuity the new male gods had to consort with the old female river goddesses. A raven, the Celtic symbol of death and battle, perches at their feet. Sucellus and Nantosuelta appear in other monuments and other remains from the Celtic world. According to Dillon and Chadwick, the 'divine couple' is a typical motif with Luxovius and Brixia and Bormo and Damona also being represented. The marriage of a 'chieftain god' with a 'mother goddess' has been seen as assuring the people of protection and fertility. According to Dillon and Chadwick:

> Here again we are reminded of Hinduism, in which the god has a female companion, his *sakti*, or source of power. Thus Indra has a spouse Saci, Shiva has Ua, Vishnu has Sri-Laksmi.

After Christianity achieved its dominance in the Celtic world, the Celtic gods were relegated to dwell in the hills. In Irish, the word *sídhe* means mound or hill and denoted the final dwelling places of the Dé Danaan, the Immortals, after their defeat by the Milesians. The ancient gods, thus driven underground, were relegated in folk memory as *aes sídhe*, the people of the hills, or in later folklore as simply fairies. The word *sídhe* is now the modern Irish word for fairies. The most famous is the banshee (*bean sídhe*), the woman of the fairies whose wail and shriek portends a death, in later Irish folklore. Each god was allotted a *sídhe* or hill in Ireland by The Dagda, another proof of his rôle as 'father of the gods', before he gave up his leadership of the gods.

The Romans, and their Greek apologists, have reported that the main aspect of Celtic religious belief revolves around human sacrifice. We will discuss this matter in detail in the following chapter on Druidic ritual.

It is interesting to ask, bearing in mind the Celtic belief in immortality, and the happy rural spirit that pervades their mythology, what the Celts feared most in this world. It was, says Arrian, quoting Ptolemy, son of Lagus, a question which occurred to Alexander the Great of Macedon when he met the Celts on the banks of the Danube in 335/334 BC. 'We fear only that the sky will fall on our heads', replied the Celtic chieftains solemnly. Arrian comments that Alexander thought the Celts had a ludicrously high opinion of themselves. But there are two ways of interpreting the Celtic answer. Firstly, that the Celts were using a ritual formula to emphasize their good intentions for the treaty then being negotiated. The words were in fact a form of oath which was still found in the Irish law tracts a millennium later, committing the individual's corporeal integrity to keep a bargain but also invoking natural elements. 'We will keep faith unless the sky fall and crush us, or the earth open and swallow us or the sea rise and overwhelm us.' When Conchobhar Mac Nessa of Ulster sent off to rescue the captives and booty taken by Medb he declared that he would achieve his aim 'unless the heavens fell, the earth burst open or the sea engulfed all things'. The other argument is that it was merely an expression of fear of the 'end of the world', just as it is a fear often expressed in this modern age, for the Druids, as Strabo points out, taught that 'fire and water must one day prevail'. After all, Alexander was asking what they feared most and to express one's fear of the end of the world is natural enough. The war goddess Badb prophesied the end of the world after the battle of Magh Tuireadh, which has been noticed to resemble the Pythia's prophecy of doom in the *Voluspa*.

It has been the purpose of this chapter simply to discuss the Celtic religious origin myths, their gods and goddesses. Because we know so little about the detail of that religion it is pointless to speculate further. The concept of immortality of the soul, the idea that the soul had its abode in the head, hence the veneration of the head, and the idea that, indeed, all things were possessed of an indwelling spirit, are subjects that we will take up in the following chapters.

[7]

The Rituals of the Druids

CLASSICAL writers, alluding to Druidic ritual, seem to dwell on human sacrifice, a subject which we will discuss shortly. Pliny is the only writer who tells us about Druids climbing oaks when the moon was auspicious, ritually cutting mistletoe and sacrificing white bulls. Varro mentions the Druidic 'fire-walking ceremony'. It is to insular Celtic sources, particularly Irish, that we must turn to discover other rituals. Let us, then, attempt to delineate the rituals in a Druid's life.

According to Irish sources, the Druids had a form of baptism. Baptism is now popularly associated with the Christian faith, symbolizing purification from sin. The word is, of course, of Greek origin – *baptizien* – meaning 'to dip'. But the religious rite of initiation by symbolic purification through the use of water is to be found in a wide variety of religions throughout the world. The *Vedas* indicate that water is the symbol of Hindu purity and the texts include detailed purity rituals. Ritual bathing in the Ganges at Benares, Shiva's city, is an example. Joseph Campbell observed:

> . . . the people bathe in the Ganges. It's a constant, as it were, baptism rite; going in and absorbing the virtue of this miraculous gift of the universe, the waters of the Ganges. The Ganges actually is a goddess, Ganga, and this flowing water is the grace that comes to us from the power of the female power.

But water initiation is to be found in religions from as far afield as Manchu, Japan and Meso-America. It also appears in the *Koran* of Islam, in Hindu, Buddhist and Jainist texts as well as in Christianity. In pagan Rome we find that the religions of Isis, Dionysus and Mithras all had a water baptism in which it was believed that the rite of confessing sins followed by symbolic purification by sanctified water would wash away all the misdeeds of the believer and change his or her life for the better.

Some scholars have been openly sceptical about the references to the Druids baptismal rite, arguing that it was probably a Christian concept written down by those Christian scribes who recorded the early traditions. The idea was that these scribes were merely ascribing to the Druids a parody of their own rites. As baptism was not confined to Christianity it is certainly reasonable to accept the evidence of pagan Celtic or Druidic baptism.

The Irish Druidic baptism was called *baisteadh geinntlidhe*, which appears to mean 'the rain wedge of protection'. There is an old Irish proverb, which might even date from this time, *gan bheo, gan baistedach* – without life, without baptism. When the Red Branch hero Conall Cernach was born, 'Druids came to baptise the child' and they sang a ritual over him. Ailill Ollamh of Munster was 'baptised in Druidic streams' while Druidic baptism is also mentioned in the case of the three sons of Conall Derg. Sir John Rhŷs, in his *Lectures on the origin and growth of religion as illustrated by Celtic heathendom* (1888), pointed to a Druidic baptism of the Welsh hero Gwri of the Golden Hair, demonstrating that this Druidic baptism was not confined to Ireland. It seems likely that ritual purification was widespread through the Celtic world as it was among other Indo-European societies.

Was there, however, a ritual initiation into the ranks of the Druids? In 'The Spoils of Annwyn' Gwydion, the son of Don, is said to have gone to Caer Sidi, a synonym for the Otherworld, and undergone a strange ritual which made him a prophetic poet and the best bard in the world. Does the tradition imply an initiation? 'The Chair of Taliesin' refers to a purification in a cauldron, 'the cauldron of inspiration', for one seeking initiation into the mysteries.

As we have already discussed, the veneration of water, particularly in the form of rivers, was clearly a major factor in pre-Christian Celtic religion. In looking upon the Danube as the great 'mother goddess' the Celts had developed a concept of water veneration so ingrained in their folk-consciousness that Christianity could not overturn it but had to adapt it for its own uses; hence the preponderance of Holy Wells in the Celtic countries. In fact it was Pope Gregory in AD 601 who told the missionaries of the church not to destroy the pre-Christian sites of worship but to bless and convert them 'from worship of devils to the service of the true God'. We find Colmcille doing just that in blessing a Druid well in the land of the Picts. It was this reference in Adomnán's *Life of Colmcille* which Dr Whitley Stokes missed when he maintained that there was only one passage which connected Druids with well-worship and that was to be found in Tirechán's *Life of St Patrick*. Tirechán relates how Patrick came to the well of Findmaige, 'which is called Slán' (health), and found Druids making offerings to it 'as gifts to the gods'. He says they 'worshipped the well as a god'.

Insular Celtic literature indicates that the ancient Celts believed that the wells were formed by deities. In Gaul, Grannos, a god of healing and solar worship, who, according to Dio Cassius, was invoked by the emperor Aurelius Antonius (AD 211–217), was associated with well-worship. An interesting point here is that the emperor's nickname was 'Caracalla', derived from the long, hooded Celtic cloak which he introduced as a Roman fashion. Grannos was usually paired with the goddess Sirona (the name means 'star'), and his own name seems to be cognate with the Old Irish word *grian* meaning sun. Another Gaulish god associated with wells was Borvo, also Bormo or Bormanus. The name seems to denote seething or turbulent waters and survives in several place names. He appears with his divine consort Damona which means 'divine cow'.

A fascinating myth in respect of the supernatural qualities of wells is told in the story of The Dagda and his consort Boann. In other versions of this story, The Dagda is replaced by Nechtan, who seems to be an early water god, for the name implies to 'wash' in sacred water, to be 'clean', 'pure' or 'white'. We might well, in fact, be looking at a sobriquet of The Dagda, for Nuada was also called Nuada Necht. The Dagda or Nechtan had a well which was called the Well of Segais (also called Conlaí's Well). Nine hazel trees of wisdom grew over the well and the hazel nuts, described as rich crimson in colour, dropped into the well causing bubbles of mystic inspiration. Only The Dagda/Nechtan and his three cup-bearers were allowed to go to the well to draw water. But his young wife Boann disobeyed the taboo (*geis*). The waters rose up, pursued and drowned her. Their course formed the river named after her – the Boann or Boyne.

A similar tale is told of Sionan, daughter of the ocean god Lir's son Lodan. She went to the Well of Knowledge even though it was forbidden. The water rose from the well and chased her westward forming the great river which was named after her, Sionan (Shannon).

It could well be that the same origin story was told about the Danube.

The veneration of both wells and rivers, which has strong parallels with Hindu worship, has, as we have seen, caused Professor Bradley of Reading University to argue that the Thames (*tamesis* – the dark or sluggish river) occupied the same place among the British Celts that the Ganges now occupied with Hindus. Certainly many items, skulls, swords, shields and other items, which have been deemed votive offerings, have been found in the Thames, especially in the London area.

The Welsh *Mabinogion* contains a story of Owain, son of Urien, a warrior at Arthur's court, who sets out to revenge Cymon, slain by a Black Warrior. During his quest, he comes to a well by a tall tree. A marble slab bounds the well and on this is a silver bowl. If water is taken from the well in the bowl and cast on the slab it produces a peal of thunder and a furious storm which, when it ends, is followed by a multitude of birds singing in the tree. Then the black clad warrior arrives and a single combat must follow. A mysterious young girl, obviously a Druidess, in the Welsh sense, helps him overcome the black warrior and claim his wife, 'The Lady of the Fountain', for his own. In late Arthurian saga we also have the famous tale of 'The Lady of the Lake' which implies another indwelling water spirit.

A case can certainly be argued for the Druids, or pre-Christian Celtic priests, performing rituals at wells or river sources. The evidence provided by votive offerings found in such places is overwhelming.

Publius Terentius Varro (b. 82 BC), who was a Narbonese Gaul who wrote in Latin, mentions that the Druids practised walking on fire at some of their festivals, walking slowly over a bed of burning coals, which they were able to accomplish, he adds, by aid of a certain ointment which they had put on the soles of their feet. Varro's work, unfortunately, has been lost and is quoted only in extracts. We know that he wrote a work called *Bellum Sequanicum*, on the war against the Celtic Sequani. The point that Varro makes is repeated by John Toland in his *Critical History of the Celtic Religion* (1740). Talking of Ireland, Toland says:

> It was customary for the Lord of the place, or his son, or some other person of distinction, to take the entrails of the sacrificed animal in his hands, and walking barefoot over the coals thrice, after the flames had ceased, to carry them straight to the Druid, who waited in a white skin at the altar. If the nobleman escaped harmless, it was reckoned a good omen, welcomed with loud acclamations; but if he received any hurt, it was deemed unlucky both in the community and himself.

But more importantly, Toland claims that he had actually seen a similar custom carried out in Ireland in his day with people running across burning coals or embers. According to Lewis Spence: 'The *Gabha-Bheil*, or trial by Beli [Bilé] a later Irish ceremony, compelled a suspected person to pass three times with bare feet through a fire as proof of innocence . . .'

Joyce observed that 'many curious fire-customs are still, or were until very lately, prevalent in some parts of the country' but he goes on to warn that 'the detailed descriptions of sun and fire worship in Ireland, given by some writers of the last century, and their speculations about "bovine cultus", "porcine cultus", "Crom the god of fire or of the winds" and suchlike, as well as the pictures of divination by Irish Druids from the blood of victims, are all the dreams of persons who never undertook the labour of investigating the matter by reference to the ancient authentic literature of the country.'

However, we do know that 'fire-walking' is a ritual practised in many parts of the world. Fire played a central rôle in primal religious experiences and obsession with fire is of very ancient origin. Professor John E. Pfeiffer, in *The Emergence of Man* (1969), points out:

> Fire may be a stimulant as potent as drugs in arousing visions and previsions, and as such would have served the purposes of priests and priestesses, the cultural descendants of the fire bearers of *homo erectus* times.
>
> Fire, like tools, had a double impact. It kept predators and the cold away, and at the same time drew people closer together. It

served material needs, and at the same time helped create a new way of life and a new kind of evolution.

Following one's birth, the Irish Druids, at least, saw a person's life divided into two halves of three periods each. *Cormac's Glossary* puts these six ages of Man into *colonna áis* or 'columns of age'. The first half of life was 1) *náidenacht* (infancy); 2) *macdacht* (childhood); 3) *gillacht* (puberty). The next three stages were 1) *hóclachus* (manhood); 2) *sendacht* (old age) 3) *díblidecht* (senility).

Druids had rituals for the funeral of a departed person. In Ireland there was a feast, *fled co-lige*, followed by funeral games, *cluiche caintech*. The whole was a form of celebration because, as Philostratus pointed out, the ancient Celts celebrated the rebirth of the dead one in the Otherworld. It was a custom to wash the body and then wrap it in a *racholl*, a shroud, or winding sheet. The body was watched or waked for one or more nights. Depending on the rank of the person, this could be as long as twelve nights. St Patrick was waked for this period as was Brian Boru. According to Dr Joyce: 'among the pagan Irish, seven nights and days was the usual time for great persons'. The body was then placed on a bier or *fuat* which was afterwards destroyed to prevent evil spirits using it. When Christianity took control, the ceremony was accompanied by lamentations or the *caoine*, commonly anglicized as keening. Often a ritual or requiem was sung over the grave called *écnaire* and often accompanied by the *lámh-comairt* or clapping of hands. It is recorded that at the death of Mogneid, the Druid Dergdamhsa chanted the ritual over his body and then delivered a funeral oration. This elegy was called the *nuall-guba*, or lamentation of sorrow, often called an *Amra*. Dallan Forgall's *Amra* for Colmcille has long been celebrated and, according to Joyce, is one of the most difficult pieces of Irish prose in existence.

In pre-Christian times the body was usually brought to the grave in a covering of *strophais* or green bushy branches of birch. According to *Cormac's Glossary* the Druids used a *fé* or rod of aspen, with an Ogham inscription cut on it, with which they measured the graves. It was regarded with horror and no one touched it except the person whose job it was to measure the grave.

Caesar claimed it was a custom among the Gauls to cremate the body of a chief and, at the same time, burn his prisoners and favourite animals. In this we are reminded of the Hindu custom which evolved into *Sati* (from the Sanskrit 'devoted wife'), in which the widow followed her husband to the funeral pyre. It was officially abolished in India in 1829 in those areas under British control. There is no confirmation of this tradition among the insular Celts, and it certainly does not accord with the funeral rituals of the ancient Irish.

However, there is one reference to something similar being carried out. In the reign of Eochaidh Muigmedoin (*c.*AD 358–366), the High King led a punitive expedition into Munster. The victory over the Munstermen was dearly bought for the king's son Fiachra died of his wounds. During his burial, the fifty captives taken from Munster were assembled at the grave and slaughtered. The account is given in the *Leabhar na Nuachonghbala* (Book of Leinster), but a slightly different one is given in the *Leabhar Buidhe Lecain* (Yellow Book of Lecan) in which the captives, being marched towards Tara, find the wounded Fiachra left temporarily alone with them, and turn on him and bury him alive before escaping. The slaying of animals might certainly have been a custom. Ailill of Connacht asks on his death bed 'that his grave should be dug, that his lamentation might be chanted, and his quadrupeds might be slain'.

Among the pre-Christian burials in Ireland, a dead warrior of note, or a king, was buried standing upright with his weapons. Sometimes the body was placed in a sitting position but, more usually, the body was laid flat. Cremations have also been found. After Christianity only burial by the method of lying flat was approved of by the new religion.

Giraldus Cambrensis (*c.*AD 1146–1220) in his *Expurgatio Hibernica*, an account of the conquest of Ireland, describes a ritual during the inauguration of a king in a northern Irish kingdom which could well be a survival from Druidic times. He speaks of the ritual slaughter of a mare. The king-elect eats its flesh, drinks and bathes in a broth made from the carcass. It is obviously a ritual union through which the king seeks fertility for himself and his kingdom. Now Giraldus has been accused of painting the Irish in a barbaric light and some have been inclined to dismiss this ritual. However, the ritual of the horse sacrifice is significant because it appears in Hindu writings as the *asvamedha* and could, therefore, be a development from the same Indo-European symbolism.

The most famous Druidic ritual, thanks to the writings of Pliny the Elder, is the cutting of mistletoe from a sacred oak with a sickle on the sixth day of the moon and the sacrifice of two white bulls afterwards. Pliny is the only source for this ritual and we must beware because a similar ritual has been recorded in Egypt whereby the Pharaoh used a sickle to cut a sheaf of corn and sacrifice a white ox to Min, the god of fecundity, during the summer month of Pachons. Did Pliny mix his Egyptians with his Druids or is it possible that it is merely a parallel rite associated with fertility? There is another parallel whereby Romans offered up two white oxen in sacrifice at the Capitol in Rome to the god Jupiter.

Pliny adds that the Celts 'call the mistletoe (*viscum*) by a name which in their language means "all healing".' As mistletoe was not a plant indigenous to Ireland and not known there until the eighteenth century, we cannot call on Old Irish to check the veracity of this statement. In modern Irish mistletoe is known as *Drualus* (*Druidh lus*, Druid's weed). In Welsh it is called *uchelwydd* or *uchelfar*, in Breton the word is *uhelvarr* and in Cornish *ughelvar*. This predisposes one to believe that the Gaulish word would have been a similar compound for they all mean 'high branch', mistletoe usually being seen high above the ground though not on top of trees. So doubt is cast on Pliny's report on the meaning of the name. 'They believe that the mistletoe, taken in drink, imparts fecundity to barren animals and that it is an antidote for all poisons', says Pliny. Yet in the herbal traditions mistletoe is known as a nervine as well as an antispasmodic, tonic and narcotic. Pliny is the only source for this ritual and no other Classical writer speaks of it nor do we find it in native Celtic tradition.

However, we do find reference to mistletoe in Nordic tradition. In Norse mythology, Balder, son of Odin and the god of light, was slain by his rival Hodr. Frigga, Balder's mother, had bound all things by oath not to harm him but she accidentally omited the mistletoe. Hodr was armed with a mistletoe twig, by which Balder was slain. There is a significance in this that has a tenuous link with a Celtic perception. Mistletoe is neither this nor that; it is neither shrub nor tree. As a plant it neither grows from the ground nor falls to it. We find ourselves thinking of 'a man not born of woman' and 'pigs that never were farrowed' and are thus free from normal limitations; thus the mistletoe might be seen as a means whereby one is freed from the restrictions of convention.

How were the Druids able to exert their authority? This is an obvious question. In Christian times, priests used the rituals of excommunication and religious interdict as a means of making people obey. In the patriarchal society of Rome, supernatural sponsorship of the state laws was conjured by the authorities so that no citizen transgressed them without fear of retaliation from a divine power. Indeed, the philosophy of the 'divine right of kings', which caused Charles I of England such a problem, seemed to have its European roots in Rome. Numa Pompilius, the second legendary king of Rome (715–673 BC), devised his law system on the advice of the goddess Egeria, giving divine authority to his law.

In Celtic terms, however, we gather from Irish sources that the *geis* (*geasa* – a prohibition or taboo) was the prime power placed in the hands of the Druids, both male and female, to give authority to their edicts. The problem of accepting authority was more likely to arise in Celtic society than it was in Roman society. The Celts had a tendency to natural anarchy. Professor Markle has observed:

> Only the Druidic religion could unify peoples scattered all over the continent of Europe and the British Isles. So, as all contracts and agreements were liable to be disputed by somebody or other, these were placed under the direct protection of the divinities, with the Druidic priests officially safeguarding their application. This is why there were so many oaths sworn to sanctify treaties, and consequently, why there were so many divine 'curses' dealt out to those who broke their oaths and contravened those treaties.

Druids could pronounce the *glam dicín* or the *geis* to assert their authority. The *geis* was primarily a prohibition placed on a particular person and since it influenced the whole fate of that person it was not imposed lightly. Anyone transgressing a *geis* was exposed to the rejection of his society and placed outside the social order. Transgression could bring shame and outlawry and it could also bring a painful death. The power of the *geis* was above human and divine jurisdiction and brushed aside all previous rulings, establishing a new order through the wishes of the person controlling it.

When Setanta was given the name Cúchulainn (Hound of Culann) he was also given a *geis* never to eat the flesh of a dog. Trapped by his enemies, he broke the *geis* and this inevitably lead to his death.

Fergus Mac Roth's *geis* was the prohibition never to refuse an invitation to a feast and on this fact turned the tragedy of the fate of the sons of Usna. Conaire Mór was subjected to a whole series of complicated and independent *geasa*.

The *glam dicín*, like the *geis*, was only invoked by Druids and was a satirical incantation directed against a particular person which imposed an obligation. In short, it was a curse which could be pronounced for infringement of divine or human laws, treason or murder. Its pronouncement was feared as its victims had put upon them a sense of shame, sickness and death. The person subjected to the *glam dicín* was rejected by all levels of Celtic society.

Another method of exerting authority, available to all members of Celtic society, was the ritual fast – the *troscad*. As a legal form of redressing a grievance, this act emerged in the Brehon law system. That it was an ancient ritual can be demonstrated by the fact that it bears almost complete resemblance to the ancient Hindu custom of *dharna*. This custom is not only found in the Laws of Manu but as *prayopavesana* ('waiting for death') it occurs in ancient Vedic sources. Dr Joyce saw the *troscad* as 'identical with the eastern custom, and no doubt it was believed in pagan times to be attended by similar supernatural effects'; that is, that if the one fasted against ignores the person fasting then they would suffer fearful supernatural penalties. The *troscad* was the means of compelling justice and establishing one's rights. Under law, the person wishing to compel justice had to notify the person they were complaining against and then would sit before their door and remain without food until the wrongdoer accepted the administration or arbitration of justice. 'He who disregards the faster shall not be dealt with by God nor man . . . he forfeits his legal rights to anything according to the decision of the Brehon.'

The *troscad* is referred to in the Irish sagas as well as laws and when Christianity displaced the pagan religion, the *troscad* continued. We find St Caimin fasting against Guaire the Hospitable, St Ronan fasting against Diarmuid, even Patrick himself fasting against several persons to compel them to justice. Some people even fasted against the saints themselves to get them to give justice and wives also fasted against their erring husbands.

It is fascinating, as well as sad, that in the long centuries of England's sorry relationship with Ireland, the Irish have continued a tradition of the *troscad* which has become the political hunger strike. One of the most notable Irish political hunger strikes was that of the Lord Mayor of Cork, Terence MacSwiney, also an elected Member of Parliament, who was arrested by the English administration in Cork City Hall and forcibly removed from Ireland to London's Brixton Prison. He died in Brixton on 24 October 1920, on the seventy-fourth day of his hunger strike. He was, of course, not the first Irish political prisoner to die on hunger strike during this period. Thomas Ashe died as a result of forcible feeding on 25 September 1917. Mac-Swiney's sacrifice was said to have inspired Mahatma Gandhi to revive the custom of *dharna* in India as a moral political weapon. In recent times, and perhaps better known, came the hunger strikes in Long Kesh prison camp in Northern Ireland, when in 1981, ten Irish political prisoners died on hunger strike in an attempt to force the administration to restore their rights as political prisoners, taken away from them in 1974. Among them was Bobby Sands, elected Member of the British Parliament, and Kieran Doherty, elected Member of the Irish Parliament. But these ten Irish prisoners were not the first to resort to the continuing tradition of the *troscad* in an attempt to assert their rights during the current struggle in the north of Ireland, nor the first to die on hunger strike. Frank Stagg, for example, died after a sixty day hunger strike in Wakefield Prison on 12 February 1976, trying to compel the reinstatement of recognition of special status withdrawn in 1974. The *troscad* was never entered into lightly and always with full knowledge of the seriousness of the final intent.

The *troscad* in ancient times was the effective means of someone of lesser social position compelling justice from someone of higher social position. Thus Druids could fast against a king, or even a man or woman in the lower order of society could fast against their chieftain.

The circle of prosperity seems to be a survival of another Druidical ritual. The daily course of the sun, bringing about the alternation of light and darkness and the succession of the seasons, was the most immediate example of the natural order of the universe. In old Irish the universe was seen as something circular and the words for universe, *cruinne* and *roth*, signified that concept. The circle of the universe served as the *modus operandi* for prosperity and increase, both spiritually and physically. To imitate the course of the sun, to go right-handed, was to perform a ritual to bring beneficial results. Martin, in his *Description of the Western Islands of Scotland*, noticed that this rite occurred very frequently among the people there in the early eighteenth century. Fire was carried *deiseal* or righthand-wise around houses, corn, cattle or people to ensure a beneficial result. In the early days of Christianity, it was recorded that women, after child bearing, would have a similar circle of fire described around them and then around their infants before they allowed them Christian baptism. Similar processions of moving *deiseal*, or right-handed, around healing wells, sacred stones, cairns or churches have also been noted and among Celtic fishermen one began a journey by sea by rowing the boat 'sunwise', up until recent times. Indeed, to go *tuaithbel*, or lefthand-wise, in the contrary direction, would be a violation of the order of the universe and bring harm.

We will be examining some other rituals connected with divination later but at this point we should mention one divination ritual connected with the election of a High King of Ireland in the pagan period. The *Leabhar na hUidri* or the Book of the Dun Cow, compiled under the direction of Macl Muire Mac Ceileachair (d. 1106 AD) at Clonmacnoise, refers to the *tabhfheis* or bull feast associated with the election of a High King. A Druid would eat the flesh of a slain bull and drink its blood. He was then put to sleep by four other Druids, and the person of whom he dreamt would be the future High King. If he lied about his dream then the gods would destroy him. Now the widespread cult of the bull throughout the Celtic world would, I believe, make this particular ritual one most likely to have been used by all the Celts. Certainly, in the Western Isles of Scotland, a similar means of general divination was used even into recent times.

From insular Celtic sources, particularly folklore, as well as its rich literature, we can observe several other rituals which could well be survivals of pre-Christian Celtic worship. The most important of these will be examined as we consider 'The Wisdom of the Druids'.

But before we leave the subject of rites and rituals, we should deal with the most controversial rite ascribed to the Druids: the practice of human sacrifice. The question of whether the Celts did or did not practise such sacrifice has been the subject of much controversy between scholars during the last two centuries.

A Greek poet named Sopater of Paphos, in Cyprus, born in the time of Alexander the Great and living to mention Ptolemy II

(285–246 BC), writes that the Celts of Galatia sacrificed their prisoners to their gods by burning them after a victory. This reference survives in the work of the Greek author Athenaeus of Naucratis (c.AD 200). Diodorus Siculus, the Greek historian (c.60–30 BC) also speaks of the execution of prisoners by the Galatian Celts:

> The Galatian general returning from the pursuit, assembled the prisoners and carried out an act of extreme barbarity and utter insolence. He took those who were most handsome and in the strength and flower of their youth, and having crowned them, sacrificed them to the gods, if indeed any god could receive such offerings.

These references to the slaughter of prisoners have to be treated for what they are. There is not an army in the world in any historical epoch who has not been guilty of slaughtering prisoners after a battle. We must also remember the high degree of hysteria with which the Greeks regarded the Galatian Celts, especially after the invasion of Greece in 290 BC. Pausanias, (fl. c.AD 160), the Greek traveller and geographer, goes on record to accuse the Celts of practising cannibalism after their defeat of the Greek armies of Athens, Pocis, Aetiolia and Thessaly. He further implies that this was normal Celtic behaviour. According to Caesar, and he is always a questionable source, during the Roman siege of the Celtic hill fort of Alesia (Alias Ste Reine), a Celtic chieftain, Critognatus, proposed that the starving city hold out by eating its own dead. This was an extreme resort. The Celts were eventually forced to surrender Alesia and Vercingetorix, their king, was taken as captive to Rome, to be sacrificed to the Roman god of war, Mars.

Thus we have to be careful as to what is propaganda and what is truth. So far as the Celts eating the Greeks during their invasion in 290 BC, the story falls into the 'bogeymen' propaganda that is always spread in such circumstances, such as the fabricated stories of German atrocities in Belgium at the opening of the Great War in 1914. As Rudyard Kipling, a leading disseminator of the stories, cynically told an audience of Scottish university students after the war, the first use that the first man made of the gift of language was to lie about his neighbours.

The first contentious mention of human sacrifice as a deliberate act of religious worship by the Celts is made by Caesar and Strabo, apparently quoting Poseidonios as a source.

According to Strabo: 'They used to strike a man, whom they had devoted to death, in the back with a knife, and then divine from his death-throes; but they did not sacrifice without a Druid.' He goes further:

We are told of still other kinds of sacrifices; for example, they would shoot victims to death with arrows, or impale them in temples, or, having built a colossus of straw and wood, throw into the colossus cattle and animals of all sorts and human beings, and then make a burnt offering of the whole thing.

Even if we accept this at face value, there is nothing to suggest that the Druids were responsible for the sacrifice, only that their presence during it was essential. It has been pointed out that Strabo gives the Druids the position as judges and it can be argued that their presence was probably that of officials to check procedure and prevent miscarriage of the law.

Diodorus actually differentiates between the Druids and the seers who divine by human sacrifice. He says that on great occasions the *vates* nominate a person as a sacrifice and, after plunging a dagger into him, they read the future from the manner of his fall and the twitching of his limbs and the flow of blood. He adds that it was not the custom to make the sacrifice without a Druid, for it was a saying that offerings acceptable to the gods had to be made through those acquainted with their nature. He concludes that in internal wars among the Celts both sides would obey the Druids. Even when two armies were about to open battle, if a Druid stepped between them they would be forced to desist.

Caesar emphasizes that it was upon occasions of danger, whether public or private, that the Celts of Gaul immolated human victims, *or vowed to do so* (my italics), employing the Druids as to the conducting of these sacrifices. He adds that in order to appease the gods, a life must be paid. 'Others make use of colossal figures composed of twigs which they fill with living men and set on fire.' Caesar adds a new twist to this, when he says that the victims were preferably criminals but if the supply failed then the innocent were used. This passage corresponds in general very closely with those by Strabo and

Diodorus and it may be safely assumed that he, too, was using the same source.

Caesar's contemporary, Marcus Tullius Cicero (106–43 BC) in his oration in 64 BC, *Pro Fonteio*, mentions the prevalence of human sacrifice among the Gaulish Celts as if it were a well-known fact at the time. But whether this was merely something he had picked up from Poseidonius, the source of Strabo, Diodorus and Caesar, is a moot point.

Certainly, Pomponius Mela of Tingentera (near Gibraltar) c.AD 43, who wrote in that year *De Chorographia*, the earliest surviving Latin work on geography, which gives information on the Druids not found elsewhere, reports that the Celts had once made human sacrifices but that they were now a thing of the past. 'At one time they believed a man to be highly pleasing as a sacrifice to the gods.' However, Mela does not refer to the Druids as being in any way connected with sacrifices. But he says of the Celts: 'They have, further, their eloquence and their Druids, teachers of wisdom, who profess to know the greatness and shape of the earth and the universe, and the motion of the heavens and of the stars and what is the will of the gods.' Mela certainly borrows some material from Caesar, such as the passage: 'One of their dogmas has become widely known so they may the more readily go to wars; namely that souls are everlasting, and that among the shades there is another life.'

Marcus Annaeus Lucanus, Lucan, (AD 39–65) from Cordoba, a grandson of Seneca the Elder, is concerned to support Rome's imperial policies and justifies the repression of the Druids because of the 'barbaric rites and a forbidding mode of worship in deep groves'. In this he seems to be hinting at the ritual of human sacrifice.

Gaius Suetonius Tranquillus (b. c.AD 70) in his *Lives of the Caesars*, speaking of Claudius' reign, mentions that the religion of the Druids was 'cruel and savage' and thus hints at human sacrifice, like Lucan, but again without actually stating so.

We have a clearer reference from Tacitus who speaks of human sacrifices in Mona (Anglesey). He says that when Suetonius attacked Anglesey, the Druids 'lifting up their hands to heaven, and pouring forth maledictions, awed the Romans by the unfamiliar sight'.

After the conquest: 'A force was next set up over the conquered, and their groves devoted to cruel superstitions were cut down. They deemed it a duty, indeed, to cover their altars with the blood of captives, and to consult their deities through human entrails.'

Petronius Arbiter (d. AD 65) is quoted by Marius Servius Honoratus (c. fifth century AD) on the rite of the emissary sacrifice, whereby a person is chosen to be sacrificed to the gods. In ancient Greece, where of course sacrifice was practised, the victim was called *pharmakos*, a scapegoat. Petronius refers to this custom in Marseilles:

> Whenever an epidemic broke out at Marseilles, one of the poor of the town offered himself to save his fellow citizens. For a whole year he had to be fed with choice goods at the town's expense. When the time came, crowned with leaves and wearing consecrated clothes, he was led through the whole town; he was heaped with imprecations, so that all the ills of the city were concentrated upon his head, and then he was thrown into the sea.

While Marseilles was a Greek colony, founded in the sixth century BC, and this practice was undoubtedly a Greek custom, it has also been argued that Marseilles was on the Gaulish seaboard and that it was probably a Celtic custom. Lactantius Placidus, giving a commentary on the work of the Celtic writer, Caecilius Statius, from the Cisalpine Gaulish town of Mediolanum (Milan), talks of a similar custom which he attributes to his fellow Celts. Statius was brought to Rome as a slave c.223/222 BC, following the Roman invasion of the Celtic territory. Freed, he became the chief Latin comic dramatist of his day. According to Placidus' comments on Statius:

> The Gauls had a custom of sacrificing a human being to purify their city. They selected one of the poorest citizens, loaded him with privileges and thereby persuaded him to sell himself as victim. During the whole year he was fed with choice food at the town's expenses, then when the accustomed day arrived, he was made to wander through the entire city; finally he was stoned to death by the people outside the walls.

The passage is so similar to the comment on the Massiliot custom that it seems obvious that they both have a common source. But was it Greek or Celtic?

If such a basic philosophy as the need to propitiate their gods through human sacrifice had such prevalence among the Celtic peoples, one might expect some mention of it to emerge in the extensive Celtic literature, especially as these traditions were set down by Christianized Celts who would seize the chance to impugn their pagan past and revile the Druidic traditions. O'Curry in his *Manners and Customs of the Ancient Irish*, maintained: 'in no tale or legend of the Irish Druids which has come down to our time, is there any mention of their ever having offered human sacrifices'. There is, however, one specific reference to human sacrifice as a religious rite but not connected with Druidical observation. But it is one reference in the whole corpus of Celtic literature and even its veracity is questionable as it is open to interpretation.

This sole reference to human sacrifice as a specific religious rite in general practice comes from the twelfth century compilation of Irish place-names, the *Dindshenchas* (sometimes given as *Dinnsenchus*), recording traditions much older than the period it survives from. The *Dindshenchas* was recorded by a Christian scribe, of course, and mentions human sacrifice only twice in the account of the naming of Tailltenn and Magh Slecht. The first reference is to Patrick preaching at Tailltenn and arguing against the 'burning of the first born progeny', while the second reference is to the worship of the idol Cromm Cruach at Magh Slecht.

Cromm Cruach (sometimes Crom Cróich) was an early golden idol who was reported to have twelve stone gods to serve him and who was worshipped by the king Tigernmas (Lord of Death) on Magh Slécht (Plain of Cutting/Slaughter). To Cromm Cruach human sacrifices were offered in the form of 'the firstlings of every issue, and the chief scions of every clan.' This concept of the 'first born' as sacrifices seems more in keeping with Hebrew Biblical tradition, via Christianity, than Celtic custom. Importantly, as already pointed out, the concept of primogeniture, which stresses the importance of the first-born male, or, indeed, female, was lacking in the Celtic social order. A foreign concept has been introduced which places the whole validity of the Cromm Cruach story under question. We are told that for Cromm Cruach 'they would kill their piteous wretched offspring with much wailing and peril, to pour their blood around Cromm Cruach. Milk and honey' (again this seems more a Biblical analogy than a pre-Christian Celtic one) 'they would ask from the idol in return for sacrificing one third of their healthy issue. Great was the horror and the fear of the idol. To him noble Gaels would prostrate themselves. From the worship of the idol with many slaughters, the plain is called Magh Slécht.' (*Slecht*, cutting, hewing, slaughter.)

But this story is, in fact, presented in the form that Tigernmas and his idol were a social aberration and were soon overthrown by the Druids.

In the *Leabhar na Nuachonghbala* (Book of Leinster), there is a prose account of the idol and the death of Tigernmas with a multitude of his people while in the act of frenzied worshipping, an echo of the fate of Sodom and Gomorrah which might have seized the imagination of the Christian writers. But there is not a word about human sacrifice in this particular account, neither was it mentioned by the later writers such as Seathrún Céitinn, Ruaraidh Ó Flaithbheartaigh (Roderick O'Flaherty) or in the reference given in the *Annales Ríoghachta Éireann* (Annals of the Four Masters). Also, earlier in the ninth century AD, when the *Tripartite Life of St Patrick* claimed it was Patrick who overthrew the idol, rather than the Druids, no mention of human sacrifice is made. In fact, in Patrick's own *Confession*, his biography, in which he strongly criticizes pagan practices, there is no reference to human sacrifice. Nor does any of the early Celtic saints *Lives* mention such a rite. It seems obvious that the prejudice of the Christians had no genuine 'human sacrifice' material at all to seize upon.

There are a couple of other references which might well imply the existence of human sacrifice but as a very ancient custom long since abandoned by the end of the first millennium BC. This custom, however, is to be found in most early European societies. These references are connected with the ancient superstition that sprinkling the blood of some human victim on the foundations of a building, about to be erected, provides for its safety and stability. This custom has been found in Hindu culture, among the Greeks, Slavs and Scandinavians. In a *Life of Colmcille*, it is recorded that one of his disciples, Odran, a British Celt, offered to die so that his sacrifice and burial would scare away the demons that infested Iona. There are oral traditions relating to this, to the effect that Odran was buried under the foundations of Colmcille's church. According to Alexander Carmichael's *Carmina Gadelica* (1900), there are oral traditions found throughout the Hebrides of persons killed and buried, or even buried alive, under the foundations of newly erected buildings to ensure stability. But is this a tradition from the Celtic or the Scandinavian traditions, which were also prevalent among the Western Islands?

This custom is certainly reflected in *Historia Brittonum* by Nennius, the Welsh historian writing c.AD 829, which records that when Vortigern decided to build Dinas Emrys he consulted his Druids who told him that in order for the structure to last forever, a child, who had no father, should be sacrificed and his blood sprinkled on the foundations. Such a child was found. But the boy had great wisdom and argued the morality of the sacrifice with the Druids so successfully that he was released. The boy was Merlin. This story actually corresponds closely with an ancient Irish tale, 'The Courtship of Bécuma', copied into the fifteenth century AD *Book of Fermoy* from an earlier source. In this story a blight comes to the country because of a great crime committed by a woman. The Druids say that the only way to remove the blight is to sacrifice a child, the son of a couple who would have certain characteristics. The child's blood should be sprinkled on the doorposts of Tara. The child is found and about to be killed when a wondrous cow appears and is slain instead. The doorposts are sprinkled with its blood and the blight removed. There are also certain similarities between this and the Greek story of Iphigeneia, the sister of Orestes, whom Agamemnon was forced to sacrifice on the order of the seer Calchas. Artemis substitutes a deer for her on the sacrificial altar.

There is one other oblique Irish reference to this concept. In the *Sanas Chormaic* (Cormac's Glossary), written by Cormac Mac Cuileannáin of Cashel (d. AD 836), Emain Macha, the great palace of the kings of Ulster, received part of its name due to the sacrifice of a man at the time of its building. The fanciful etymology gives *em* or *ema* (blood), *ain* or *uin* (one), 'because the blood of one man was shed at the time of its erection'.

Of all the Classical writers, it is Pomponius Mela who seems the most accurate in recording that any tradition of human sacrifice among the Celts had ended long before the time he was writing, that is c.AD 46. Indeed, while there is much material on the rites and superstitions of the pagan Irish there is hardly anything, apart from the story of Cromm Cruach. This might be argued as supporting a claim of a human sacrifice tradition but the story actually shows Cromm Cruach as an aberration to the norms of society.

Even Mrs Chadwick, in her study *The Celts*, while inclined to believe the Romans, has to admit: 'There is little direct archaeological evidence relevant to Celtic sacrifice . . .' In her attempt to find something, she refers to the evidence of the bodies preserved in a bog in Denmark but while she has to admit that they are 'beyond the boundaries of the Celtic world proper' she still tries to link them up with the motifs on the Gundestrup cauldron. She has the scholastic grace to say that human sacrifices are '*apparently* represented on the bowl from Gundestrup'.

> The much more plentiful archaeological evidence, corroborated by classical literary references to various offerings of inanimate objects, often of considerable value, in rivers, lakes, sacred groves and the like, and the possibility of animal sacrifice, suggest that human sacrifice among the Celts, although of great ritual significance, may have been practised, appear commonly at time of communal danger or stress, rather than as part of regular ritual observance.

This comment by Mrs Chadwick makes many conceptual leaps. Why the offering of inanimate objects should lead one to believe that the people who made them also practised human sacrifice escapes one, as does the reason why human sacrifice should be of great ritual significance when there was no native literary or archaeological evidence to support it. And how is it that it was commonly practised at the time of communal danger when the only authority for such a statement is the sole and questionable opinion of Caesar? Mrs Chadwick's comments rely on an acceptance that the enemies of the Celts were accurate in their observations.

Indeed, as Jean Louis Brunaux states in *The Celtic Gauls*:

> Archaeological clues relating to the question of human sacrifice have for a long time been scarce and equivocal. The presence in graves of skeletons without a skull or the strange position of some burials with hands behind the back as though tied, have indeed been cited, but no formal proof of sacrifice as opposed to exceptional funereal customs has been identified.

The excavations at Gournay-sur-Aronde in France show some eighty skeletons of bodies that had apparently been divided into quarters.

If the deaths were violent, no trace has been left on the remains. Brunaux seems to imply that this was a funeral practice after people had died naturally. Similarly, the excavation at Ribemont-sur-Ancre in 1982 showed bones meticulously arranged belonging to some 200 individuals. But these excavations, along with those at Mirebeau and Saint-Maur, are more likely to be of Celtic cemeteries rather than evidence of sacrifices.

The argument that archaeology has finally produced evidence of human sacrifice is based on the discovery of 'Lindow Man'. On Friday 1 August 1984, workers engaged in peat cutting on Lindow Moss, near Wilmslow, on the southern outskirts of Manchester, found a well-preserved human leg. The police supervised the search for further remains and a complete head and torso were found. Radio carbon dating eventually placed the body to AD 50–100. The British Museum were called in and in 1986 produced a preliminary study, *The Body in the Bog*. In 1989, the leading Celtic scholar, Dr Anne Ross, together with Dr Don Robins, of the Institute of Archaeology at the University of London, published a book, *The Life and Death of a Druid Prince*.

The facts were that the body was that of a man of about 25/30 years who was in fairly good health apart from a mild osteo-arthritis. He wore a fox-fur amulet on his arm. The skull had been fractured at the crown and the jaw broken. The neck had been dislocated, consistent with hanging. There were lacerations on the preserved skin tissue. A post-mortem showed that the man had been hit twice from behind with an instrument such as an axe which probably rendered him unconscious. He was then garroted by a knotted cord of animal sinew which had cut into the skin. At the same time, a sharp blade had been plunged into his jugular vein. Then he had been dropped into the bog.

Now how had these facts then led to the identification by Drs Ross and Robins that this was a ritual human sacrifice? And further, that the victim was a 'Druid Prince'? Indeed, the conjectures get more imaginative. The fur amulet caused the authors to suggest that the man's name was Lovernios, that is 'fox' from the Gaulish *lovernios*, cognate with the Welsh *llwynog*, Breton *louarn* and Cornish *lowarn*.

But what is the basis for such conjectures? The basis is that the 'human sacrifice' report of the Romans is accepted without question. The authors argue:

Their (the Celts) penchant for human sacrifice shocked even the Romans, inured as they were to the horrors and carnage of the amphitheatre. Surrender to an enemy never figured largely in the Celtic order of battle. Prisoners of war, as we learn from Julius Caesar, were usually sacrificed to the gods. Caesar reports how captives were burnt in giant wicker cages . . .

Caesar, with due respect to him, says nothing of the kind. On the subject of sacrifices he says that criminals were chosen in the first place. References to Celts not taking prisoners of war, found in other Classical writings, could well have been simply a warning to Greek or Roman soldiers not to contemplate surrender and making them fight without quarter. But that's as maybe. And, as we have seen, the 'wicker man' report was not even an original one by Caesar but a rehash of Poseidonios.

The authors, Ross and Robins, refer to the traditions found in Scotland. 'It is in Scotland that the clearest traces of human sacrifice in connection with Beltain have been noted. This evidence is supported by Welsh oral lore and there is more than a hint of it in Ireland. In all cases the victim was chosen by means of the burnt piece of festival bannock.' Now this is departing a little from what the evidence actually shows, which I have cited above. The introduction of a burnt bannock into the proceedings is simply to reinforce the authors' arguments, because traces of a burnt bannock were found in the stomach of Lindow man. Indeed, at no time do the authors present their exact sources or evidence for the statement.

Also surprising is the statement:

The Celts believed in capital punishment, but they turned it into a religious act, making an execution into a sacrifice . . . Captives were vowed to the gods before battle, and for this reason could not be sold or given away. They had to be offered. Human beings were sacrificed in order to propitiate the god of blight and crop failure.

Presumably this is the authors' own imaginative interpretation of Caesar's remark that the sacrifices among the Gauls were usually of criminals.

Again, the authors are simply accepting the authority of the Roman general and their own interpretations of what he meant.

In contravention to this statement we find the Celtic law systems are opposed to capital punishment and to slavery in the form understood by Greece and Rome. Again one has to ask, what is the evidence for the statement 'the Celts believed in capital punishment', other than the throwaway line by Caesar? Laurence Ginnell in his study *The Brehon Laws* (1894) comes to a contrary statement: 'There is ample evidence of various kinds that the whole public feeling of Ireland was opposed to capital punishment; and still more was it opposed to the taking of the law into one's own hands without the decision of a court.' This is not to say that there was no capital punishment at all. 'At this day no one is put to death for his intentional crimes as long as *eric*-fine is obtained', says the commentary on the *Senchus Mór*. Dr Joyce explains 'the idea of awarding death as a judicial punishment for homicide, even when it amounted to murder, does not seem to have ever taken hold of the public mind in Ireland.' Indeed, Edmund Spenser and Sir John Davies, and other early English settlers in sixteenth and seventeenth century Ireland, commentating on the *eric*-fine for homicide instead of capital punishment, denounced it as 'contrary to God's laws and man's'.

According to Dr Joyce: 'There is no record of any human sacrifice in connection with the Irish Druids; and there are good grounds for believing that direct human sacrifice was not practised at all in Ireland . . .'

The Life and Death of a Druid Prince is a polemic, but too loaded with conceptual leaps of imagination to be acceptable as proven fact. Although as Dr I.M. Stead of the British Museum comments, 'The archaeologist would be hard put to produce a more convincing example' (of human sacrifice), more convincing examples do need to be found before we can truly come to the conclusions drawn by the authors.

The deduction one is really drawn to is that the idea of widespread human sacrifice among the Celts was mere Roman propaganda to support their imperial power in their invasion of Celtic lands and destruction of the Druids.

Additionally we can argue that we have more evidence of human sacrifice occurring widely both in Greek and Roman civilizations. Unlike Celtic literary tradition, Greek literature is full of traces of human sacrifice customs, particularly the slaughter of young virgins before a battle. The best known historical example is the mass ritual sacrifice of Persian prisoners before Salamis in 480 BC. Among the Romans there are many specific references to human sacrifices, notably in 228 BC and during the Second Punic War to propitiate wrathful war deities. Livy himself records that the Romans made human sacrifices after the defeat of Cannae in 216 BC. Among the sacrifices to appease the gods, two Celts were buried alive under the Forum Boarium. During the lifetime of Plutarch (AD 46–c.120) human sacrifices were still being made. In the time of the late Republic and early Empire, children were sacrificed in rites to conjure the spirits of the dead. During the reign of Claudius, foreign captives were being buried alive at Rome to ameliorate the gods of war. Prisoners of war, like the Numidian king, Jugartha, and the Celtic leader Vercingetorix, with their families, were held for long periods – six years in the case of Vercingetorix – in the deep underground prison of the Tullanium below the Capitol before finally being ceremonially sacrificed in honour of Mars. Even Roman patricians, such as the followers of Lucius Sergius Catilina (d. 62 BC), were ritually slaughtered here. During the second and third centuries AD, Tatian, Tertullian and Minucius Felix reported that human sacrifices were being carried out during the festival of Latini.

Above all, when examining Roman sensitivities, one has to remember the violent and bloodthirsty culture of the Roman 'circus'. The spectacle of prisoners and slaves fighting to the death before enthusiastic spectators had been recorded in Rome from the third century BC. By the time of the emperor Marcus Ulpius Traianus (Trajan – AD 98–117), a time when it is recorded that the Roman empire was at its 'greatest', Trajan himself could put five thousand pairs of gladiators into the arena and force them to fight to the death. As an 'interval' to the proceedings, tens of thousands of criminals were led into the arena and ritually slaughtered for the further entertainment of the masses. It was Decimus Junius Juvenalis, the satirical poet Juvenal, writing during this period, who wrote the famous statement: 'The people who have conquered the world have only two interests – bread and circuses.'

In the early empire, during the course of a single day in the Circus Maximus, three hundred prisoners had to fight each other to death; twelve hundred men and women, condemned by law, were slaughtered, most of them killed by wild animals, and, as a special feature, it was announced that twenty girls would be forced to copulate with wild beasts. Slaughter of, and by, wild animals was a particular feature of Roman 'entertainment'. When Titus Flavius Vespasianus (AD 79–81), who became emperor on the death of his father Vespasian, finished the Colosseum begun by his father, a total of nine thousand wild animals were killed in fights with men and women (*venationes*) to mark the 'grand opening'. The number of men and women slaughtered is not recorded.

Even when Flavius Valerius Constantinus Augustus (*c.*AD 285– 337) became emperor and a Christian, allowing Christians total freedom of rights within the empire, in AD 313, he allowed the continuance of the bloodthirsty spectacles. Even Pope Dionysius (AD 259– 268) is recorded as owning gladiators and attending the games. Ironically, it was not until the fifth century, when Rome was invaded by those they called 'barbarians', that those same 'barbarians' put an end to the bloody and violent spectacles.

Bearing this in mind one has to look at the Romans' expression of profound disgust and distaste for human sacrifice, as applied to the Druids, as rather meaningless and an act of high political cynicism.

Finally, we have to agree with the conclusion of Doctor Brunaux:

In the present state of research, knowledge of human sacrifice rests upon the texts that have a tendency to distort the reality of the facts and to exaggerate their frequency in order to make them more sensational. In this area, despite important discoveries, archaeology has nothing new to contribute. The absence of conclusive evidence, despite more and more numerous excavations, tends to confirm the hypothesis that the practice was rare. The ancient ethnographers had not actually witnessed any of these deeds with which they reproach the Celts. While exploring Gaul, like Poseidonios, they can only have seen skulls nailed above doors of houses and sanctuaries, for which there is some archaeological proof.

The Wisdom of the Druids

Druidic Schools

IT was Julius Caesar who spoke of the length of study involved
in becoming a Druid. In some cases the pupils would spend as
many as twenty years, so he says, under their teachers. He also
implies that there were great schools of Druidic learning in Britain.
Pomponius Mela, writing after the Roman proscription of the
Druids, talks of the Druids meeting to instruct their pupils 'in secret
either in a cave or secluded valley'. There is certainly enough evidence
to show that the Druidic caste was in charge of Celtic education. So
far as Gaul was concerned, Camille Jullian observes from the evidence that the Druids 'gathered round them the young men of Gallic
families and taught them all that they knew or believed concerning
the world, the human soul, and the gods. A few of these scholars
stayed with their masters until they had reached the age of twenty
years; but it is clear that those who were to become priests received
the lion's share of attention.' Jullian believed that Caesar was in
error when he maintained that one had to study twenty years to be
a Druid and that he really meant that pupils studied until the age
of twenty. Jullian's contention is not supported by insular Celtic
sources.

It is from Ireland that we have at least more tangible evidence of
a tradition of Druidic, or Bardic schools. Dr Douglas Hyde, in his
Literary History of Ireland, points out that side by side with the
monastic schools of Ireland there flourished the more traditional
'bardic' institutions. 'These were almost certainly a continuation of
the schools of the Druids, and represented something far more
antique than even the very earliest schools of the Christians, but
unlike them they were not centred in any fixed locality nor in a
cluster of houses, but seemed to have been peripatetic.' Dr Hyde
suggests these Druidic, or bardic, schools were initially centred

around a personality and pupils went where their teacher was pleased to wander. He believed that this was the system until the sixth century AD.

However, James Bonwick, in *Irish Druids*, cites the *Annales Ríogh-achta Éireann* (Annals of the Four Masters) as referring to a great school called Mur Ollamhan, the City of the Learned, existing in 927 BC. This, of course, is in the realm of legend. The important thing is the existence of such a long tradition of a fixed Druidic school. Giraldus Cambrensis claimed that at Kildare, Brigit built her community on the site of an older community of female Druids which was a school where they taught. There are, in fact, references to many such schools in Irish mythology. Indeed, Cúchulainn studied at a Druidic school under Cathbad the Druid. This demonstrates an early tradition of such schools.

The bardic schools, as a separate institution to ecclesiastical schools, lasted until the smashing of the Irish intelligentsia in the seventeenth century AD. From these schools, the poets, historians, the Brehons (judges), doctors and other professional people graduated. The education in these 'lay' schools ran parallel to education in the monastic or ecclesiastical schools. Ireland, unlike most of her European neighbours, such as England, therefore had an educational tradition outside the ecclesiastical foundations. The chief professor of such lay schools was known as a *druimcli* (ridge pole – that is, the support of a house), while his ecclesiastical equivalent was called a *fer-leginn* (man of learning) who had to be appointed under an abbot.

We hear that the lay schools were firmly established by the time of the convention of Druim Cett (Co. Derry) in AD 574 when laws were passed for their regulation. Any of them which were institutions without a fixed location were awarded permanent sites financed by the local clan assemblies. According to Seathrún Céitinn, the person who devised a new scheme of lay schools was Dallán Forgaill (*c.*AD 540–590), then *ard-ollamh* or chief bard of Ireland. The most famous of his surviving poems is *Amra Cholium Chilli*, the eulogy of the saint who also attended the assembly at Druim Cett. There was to be a chief school in each of the five provinces and a number of minor colleges under them. All those persons who required education within the society could obtain it.

Dr Hyde argued:

That the Bardic schools ... were really a continuation of the Druidic schools, and embodied much that was purely pagan in their *curricula* is, I think, amply shown by the curious fragments of metrical text books preserved in the *Books of Leinster* and *Ballymote*, in a *ms* in Trinity College, and in a *ms* in the Bodleian, all four of which have been recently admirably edited by Thurneysen as a continuous text.

Rudolf Thurneysen's work was published in the *Irische Texte* series edited by Ernst Windisch and Whitley Stokes, Leipzig, 1884–1905. The curricula shows that a scholar attending certain courses had to learn certain mystical incantations called the *tenmlaida*, *imbas forosnai* and *dichetal do chennaub na tuaithe* during one of his years of study, and learn the *cétnaid* in another. Yet another incantation, which has been mentioned before, was the *glam dicín*. These are listed as poetic methods of divination to find a thief, to achieve a long life or, with the *glam dicín*, to satirize and punish anyone who refused to pay the poet. But in pagan times it had been used as a method of exerting a Druid's authority. Dr Hyde observes:

These instances that I have mentioned occurring in the book of poets' instructions, are evidently remains of magic incantations and terrifying magic ceremonies, taken over from the schools and times of the Druids, and carried on into the Christian era, for nobody, I imagine, could contend that they had their origin after Ireland had been Christianized.

By the fifteenth century these Bardic schools were being run by certain families such as the Ó Cleirigh (O'Clery) family, who were driven out of Connacht, and the Ó Conratha (Mulconry) families of Roscommon and Clare. The Ó Cléirigh family ran three famous schools in Donegal renowned for studies in history, literature and poetry.

According to Edward Campion's *Historie of Ireland* (1571) there were still native colleges specializing in law and medicine in his day:

They speake Latine like a vulgar tongue, learned in their common schools of leach-craft and law, whereat they begin (as) children, and go on sixteene or twenty yeares, conning by roate the Aphorismes of Hypocrates and the Civill Institutions, and a few other parings of these two faculties.

But this notion that Latin was used as a language of instruction and that learning was 'by rote' or transmitted orally, without books, has been dismissed by Professor Francis Shaw, in his paper 'Irish Medical Men and Philosophers' in *Seven Centuries of Irish Learning 1000–1700* , edited by Dr Brían Ó Cuív (1971). He points out: 'The notion that at the end of the sixteenth century Latin was the language of the Irish medical schools is irreconcilable with the evidence of the Irish manuscripts.' Most medical books were written in the Irish language. As we will discuss later, the oldest surviving medical books in Irish date from the early fourteenth century and constitute the largest collection of medical manuscript literature, prior to 1800, surviving in any one language.

In 1615, commissioners appointed by James I of England to inquire into the state of education in Ireland ordered the closure of the schools, but it was not until the late seventeenth century, in the wake of the English conquests, that most of the ancient lay schools were suppressed. This followed the closure of the monastic schools. These ecclesiastical schools had already been under attack in 1310 when a law was passed in Ireland forbidding religious orders in Ireland to admit anyone who was not English. Another statute in 1380 again expressly forbade monasteries in Ireland to accept any Irish students. The suppression of the monasteries from 1539 saw the Irish flocking to the Continent for their education and to the Irish Colleges which had been established in Paris, Louvain, Rome and elsewhere. This destruction of native Irish learning, compounded by the Penal Laws of William III, saw the rise of a new educational phenomenon – the Irish Hedge School. During the late seventeenth and early eighteenth centuries, the Irish teachers were compelled to teach the children secretly and usually out of doors in some secluded spot, often in the shelter of a hedge – hence the name. One pupil was placed at a vantage point to give warning of the approach of English soldiers or informers, when the class would be disbanded at a word. The teacher, living on the hospitality of the people, that which they could afford in order to give their children some education, often increased his earnings by turning his hand to farm work as he moved from place to place. The artist, George Holmes, in *Sketches of some of the Southern Counties of Ireland collected during a tour in 1797*, could write of Co. Kerry: 'Amongst the uncultivated part of the Country, many may be met with who are all good Latin scholars, yet do not speak a word of English. Greek is also taught in the mountainous parts by such itinerant teachers.'

Eventually, as the Penal Laws were ignored or less strictly enforced, the teacher would gather his pupils in a barn or a cabin. It was not until the nineteenth century that the restrictions were eased and Irish people could openly enjoy education again.

We learn from the Brehon law system of Ireland that both bardic schools and ecclesiastical schools adopted certain similar ideas which could be a common inheritance, as Dr Hyde stated, of the former Druidical schools. The 'Sequel to the *Crith Gabhlach*' talks of the 'Seven Degrees of Wisdom'. 'The degrees of wisdom of the church correspond with the degrees of the poets and of the *féine* or story tellers: but wisdom is the mother of each profession of them, and it is from her hand they all drink.' The highest degree of all took twelve years of study.

After elementary teaching, by the second year, the first degree in a bardic school was *fochluc*, 'because his art is slender as his youth', like a sprig of *fochlacán*, brooklime. By the third year the student had risen to *mac fuirmid*, 'so called because he "is set" (*fuirmithir*) to learn an art'. By the fourth year the student was *dos* 'from his similarity to a *dos* – a young tree'. In the fifth year he had reached the degree of *cana* and in the sixth year became a *cli* (*cleith* is a pillar of a house). After seven to nine years of study, the student could qualify as *anruth*, 'noble stream'. At the end of the twelfth year of study, provided the candidate had passed all the tests he could achieve the highest degree of *ollamh* or professor.

The degree system in the ecclesiastical schools was similar. The *ollamh* was the title of the highest degree in any art or profession. It could apply to a builder, goldsmith, physician, lawyer or even judge.

The position of Chief Poet of Ireland survived until after the Anglo-Norman conquests. On state occasions the Chief Poet wore a special cloak, elaborately ornamented and called a *tugen*, or *taiden* and sometimes *stuige*. According to *Cormac's Glossary*:

The *tuigen* is derived from *tuige-en*, the *tuige* or covering [of the feathers] of a bird (*én*): for it is of feathers of birds, white or many coloured that the poets' mantle from their girdle downwards is made, and of the necks of drakes and of their crests from their girdle upwards to their necks.

The Chief Poet, and indeed, all poets, carried a *craebh-ciuil*, a small branch on which were suspended a number of diminutive bells, which tinkled when shaken. The *ollamh* carried a golden branch, the *anruth* a silver one, while all others carried branches of bronze.

The traditions show us that pre-Christian Celtic society had in place a sophisticated educational system long before the start of the Christian epoch.

Druidic Books

'It is said,' wrote Julius Caesar of the Druids, 'that they commit to memory immense amounts of poetry, and so some of them continue their studies for twenty years. They consider it improper to commit their studies to writing, although they use the Greek alphabet for almost everything else . . .'

A superficial interpretation or misreading of this now famous quotation, has led even the most serious scholars to sometimes express the idea that the pre-Christian Celts were illiterate. It is well known that Irish and Welsh surviving texts date from the Christian period, when it was considered that the Druidic religious proscription on committing Celtic knowledge to writing no longer mattered. Irish then became Europe's third written language after Greek and Latin.

When we discuss the philosophy of the Druids, in our next section, we shall be dealing with the Druidic concept of Truth as the supreme power, which we find as a basic Indo-European thought. We should, at this stage, simply mention, as a reason for the Druidic prohibition on writing, that the teaching was that Truth was the Word and the Word was sacred and divine and not to be profaned. The Celts believed in the magic power of the Word. 'Truth is the foundation of speech and all Words are founded upon Truth'. The Druids believed that 'by Truth the earth endures'. But how far did this religious proscription, which Caesar speaks of, apply?

A closer reading of Caesar shows us clearly that it is only Druidic knowledge (the 'Word') that is prohibited from literary form and that the Celts – in this particular instance, the Continental Celts – were using Greek letters. We should add that they used Etruscan and Latin letters as well. The proof of this is gathered from the early Celtic inscriptions, particularly those found in northern Italy (Cisalpine Gaul) and in Spain. Inscriptions on memorial stones dating between the fourth and second centuries BC, such as Briona, Todi and Saignon have been studied in *Lepontica*, by Dr Michel Lejeune (Paris, 1971). The Celtic funeral inscriptions, manufacturer's markings on pottery and other goods are sufficient to demonstrate some degree of literacy. Moreover, for many years the Calendar of Coligny, dated to the first century BC, was regarded as the most extensive document in the Gaulish Celtic language. However, in 1983 the leaden tablet, the Larzac inscription, previously referred to, was discovered, and in 1992 a bronze tablet was found in northern Spain. These have provided scholars with lengthier and more fascinating texts. So there was, as Caesar remarked, already literacy in the Celtic languages.

One point that many also forget is the fact that following the Roman conquests of the Celtic lands, many Celts started to write in the language of the conqueror. Presumably these Celts, unless they had totally rejected the pagan Celtic religion, believed that the Druidic proscription on committing knowledge to writing did not extend to literary expression in other languages. The passage of time has caused these writers to be accepted as Latin authors – just as many Irish, Scottish or Welsh writers, because they write in English, are thought to be English writers. Indeed, in the first century BC there rose a whole 'Celtic literary school', mainly identified with writers from Cisalpine Gaul. Celts from Iberia, Provence (The Province) and later from Gaul proper, soon added to Latin literature. Dr H.D. Rankin in his *Celts and the Classical World* (1987), has touched briefly upon those Celts who wrote in Latin.

The most important question is whether any writing relating to Celtic history, philosophy, law and other matters escaped the Druidic proscription.

According to Dr Joyce: 'The Gaulish Druids prohibited their disciples from committing to writing any part of their lore, regarding this as an unhallowed practice. There is no mention of any such prohibition among Irish Druids.'

Certainly in the Irish sagas the Druids read and write in a distinctive Irish alphabet – Ogham. In Irish mythology the invention of the alphabet is ascribed to Ogma, not only god of eloquence and learning but, significantly, of the Druids. However, the bulk of surviving Ogham inscriptions date from the Christian period, that is the fifth and sixth centuries AD. There are 369 inscriptions, the bulk in Ireland, but many in Wales and Scotland, with a few in Cornwall and the Isle of Man and some in what is now England. The most easterly Ogham inscription was recorded at the site of Silchester, which was the tribal capital of the Celtic Atrebates. The spread of these inscriptions, from a concentration in Munster (significantly the area of primal origin in Irish tradition) eastward is accorded to the movement of Irish Christian missionary teachers. When, in 1390, Maghnus Ó Duibhgeánnáin compiled the *Book of Ballymote*, which included a copy of the *Leabhar na gCeart* (Books of Rights), he included a treatise on Ogham with an alphabet key. The alphabet itself consists of short lines drawn to, or crossing, a base line. Ogham has been claimed as the Druidic alphabet in popular fantasy and more often 'The Tree Alphabet', for each Irish letter takes the name of a tree: eg, A – *ailim* (elm); B – *beithe* (birch); C – *coll* (hazel) and so on.

Because all remains date from the Christian period, it had been argued that Ogham was not devised until that time and that it was based on the Latin alphabet. Others, like Dr Barry Fell of Harvard, see Ogham inscriptions practically everywhere – both in Spain and even in America, and date such 'inscriptions' to 500 BC! We can be assured, however, that Ogham does not survive from before the fifth century AD. But it is pertinent to ask whether it could have existed before that date.

Mention of the use of Ogham frequently occurs in the ancient Irish myths. In the *Immrain Brain* or Voyage of Bran, the surviving text of which is dated to the eighth century AD but with the story clearly of pre-Christian origin, Bran son of Febal is said to have written down fifty or sixty quatrains of poetry in Ogham. In the *Táin Bó Cuailnge*, Cúchulainn writes warnings and challenges to his enemies in Ogham. Druids put down magic incantations and spells in Ogham. In the story of Midir the Proud, a Druid named Dalan informs Eochaidh Airemh that his wife Étain has been carried off to

Brí Leith. He is able to write in Ogham. There is clearly a literary tradition being demonstrated.

More importantly, in the story of Baile Mac Buain we are told of a library of 'rods of the Filí' on which ancient stories and sagas are inscribed. The Ogham was cut on bark or on wands of hazel and aspen. These libraries or Tech Screpta are also mentioned in the *Leabhar na Nuachonghbala*, The Book of Leinster, compiled about 1150 AD by Fionn Mac Gormain of Glendalough. Certainly such libraries existed from the sixth century AD, following the introduction of Christianity, but did the Tech Screpta of Ireland exist in pagan times?

A clue exists in the *Leabhar Buidhe Lecain* (Yellow Book of Lecan), compiled about 1400 by Giolla Iosa Mór Mac Firbis, containing many earlier texts such as another copy of *Leabhar na gCeart* (Book of Rights), a political treatise on the constitutions of the Irish kingdoms, compiled, it is said, in the fifth century AD by Benignus. The work records that Patrick, in his missionary zeal, burnt 180 books of the Druids. This destruction of books by the zealous Patrick, adds Mac Firbis, 'set the converted Christians to work in all parts, until in the end all the remains of the Druidic superstition were utterly destroyed'. Mac Firbis writes approvingly as a Christian. His work contains much early material copied from the period in which the books were said to have been destroyed. Therefore we can be fairly certain that Mac Firbis was copying contemporary sources. In corroboration of which, in Murchu Moccu Machteni's seventh century AD *Life of Patrick*, and repeated in the ninth century AD *Tripartite Life*, we hear of Patrick contesting with the Druids at Tara before the High King Laoghaire. The king proposes that one of Patrick's Christian books and a Druidical book be thrown into some water as an ordeal. After a while, the books would be taken out of the water and whichever book remained readable, in which the water had not run, the owner of that book would be declared the purveyor of truth.

The Irish Christian sources are fairly clear that books existed in Ireland before the arrival of Christianity and that Christian missionaries caused these 'pagan works' to be burnt. If this is so, then it was an utterly senseless destruction. Supporting evidence for the existence of books in Ireland before the arrival of Christianity comes from a Christian writer of the third and fourth centuries AD –

Aethicus of Istria. Aethicus wrote a *Cosmography of the World (Cosmographia Aethici Istrii)*, part of which was inserted by Orosius Paulus in his *History Against the Pagans* composed in seven books about AD 417. It is stated that Aethicus sailed from Iberia and 'he hastened to Ireland and remained here some time examining their books'. Aethicus calls these books *ideomochos*, implying that the literature was particular to Ireland and quite new and strange to him. He speaks of the *volumina* of the Irish as a noteworthy feature of the country. If Aethicus was examining libraries in Ireland in the third or fourth centuries AD then clearly we have independent confirmation of later Irish Christian writers' and numerous saga references to the existence of such libraries.

Many pre-Christian poets and their work are still remembered in later Irish literature. We have already discussed the three extant poems of Amairgen the Druid. But there are works by others such as Feirceirtné, who is credited with the authorship of *Uraicept na nÉigeas* (Primer of the Learned), a grammatical treatise. Feirceirtné contended with Neidé for the position of chief poet of Ireland. His work begins: 'This is the Book of Feirceirtné. Its place Emain Macha; its time the reign of Conchobhar Mac Nessa: its person Feirtceirtné the *filé*; its cause to bring ignorant people to knowledge.' Feirceirtné is also the author of a poem on the death of Cú Roí and the *Leabhar Gabhála* ascribes another poem to him about the High King Ollamh Fodhla. As well as Neidé, we hear of his father, Adhna, as yet another famous poet and scholar.

Athairné is described as an insolent satirist from the Hill of Howth. It is Athairné, Neidé and Feirtceirtné who are said to have compiled the code of laws, the *Breithne Neimhidh* which are embodied in the Brehon laws.

We have a copy of *Audacht Morainn* (Morann's Will), an important text which is ascribed to Morann, a judge, who lived at the close of the first century AD. Indeed, there are references to several writers from the first and second centuries AD, whose works are mentioned by later writers and sometimes quoted (short poems or prose fragments). The names of Feradach, Modan, Ciothruadh and Fingin are among them. To the third century AD, the century to which the semi-legendary Cormac Mac Art, Fionn Mac Cumhail, Oisín, Fearghus and Caoilte are dated, quantities of poems and prose pieces are credited.

Is it possible that instead of being committed to oral tradition, these texts were set down on the 'rods of the Fili' and kept in the various Tech Scretpa until burnt by enthusiastic Christian missionaries? The Ogham inscriptions which survive only do so because they were carved on stone. It is obvious that the wooden wands, if they had existed, would have been more easily burnt or, if they survived the Christian zealots, that they would have perished by decay over the years. And an interesting point is that the Ogham inscriptions which did survive are shown to be an archaic form of 'literary Irish'; archaic even at the time that the inscriptions were made. This correlates to the fact that the language of the Irish law books, whose first recorded codification, according to the *Annals of Ulster*, was in the year AD 438, was written in a similar archaic form known as the *Bérla Féini*. This archaic form seems to be proof that the text was handed down for many centuries without alteration. As the language of the people changed, the ancient texts did not. They were, presumably, handed down in a strictly memorized oral tradition from ancient times until the point where they were committed to writing. As Myles Dillon and Nora Chadwick have both observed:

> Ireland possessed a greater wealth of carefully preserved oral tradition from the earliest period of our era than any other people in Europe north of the Alps. For this reason the foundation of her early history from traditional materials is of general interest far beyond her geographical and political area, and second only to that of the ancient Greek and Roman world.

A tremendous literature and learning has been handed down to us from Ireland. But, even so, we can still lament the apparent destruction of the Druidical books by the zealot Christian missionaries which was clearly a crime against knowledge.

Druids as Philosophers

The word 'priest' was never applied to Druids by any Classical writer but many Greeks and Romans used the term 'philosopher' to describe them. Dio Chrysostom, in fact, makes a clear distinction between a 'Druid' and a 'priest'.

What was the philosophy of the Druids? Can we salvage any of their basic tenets? Nora Chadwick has observed, in her study *The Druids*, that: 'The outstanding feature of Druidical teaching may be summed up as natural philosophy and natural science – the nature of the physical universe and its relationship to mankind.' Diodorus Siculus states: 'The Druid joined to the study of nature that of moral philosophy, asserting that the human soul is indestructible, and also the universe, but that some time or other, fire and water will prevail.'

Much has been discussed about Druidic moral philosophy. If one was to attempt to extract that philosophy from the sources one can only point to the summary of Diogenes Laertius that the Druids' chief maxim was that the people should 'worship the gods, do no evil and exercise courage'. To summarize, from various sources, the Druids taught that one should live in harmony with nature, accepting that pain and death are not evils but part of the divine plan and that the only evil is moral weakness. From the Old Irish texts one gathers that the Druids were concerned, above all things, with Truth and preached '*An Fhírinne in aghaidh an tSaoil*' (The Truth against the world). Professor Myles Dillon argues that 'this notion of Truth as the highest principle and sustaining power of creation pervades the [Irish] literature.'

Dillon observes:

In Ireland too we have stories in which an Act of Truth has magical power. (It is not a question of virtue being rewarded: it is the magical power of Truth itself.) Many of you will know the story of the child Cormac at Tara, who heard the king Lugaid Mac Con, give a false judgment, when he awarded the sheep who had trespassed on the queen's garden as forfeit for their trespass. At once the courthouse began to fall and slide down-hill. Cormac said: 'No! That is a false judgment. The woad will grow again in the garden. Only the sheep's wool, which will also grow again, is forfeit for the woad!' And all people cried out: 'This is the Truth'. At once the court-house was stayed in its fall. Lugaid Mac Con had to leave Tara, and Cormac later became king.

In fact, with regard to Cormac again, he was later given a cup which shattered into pieces if three lies were told over it and reformed if three truths were told. But perhaps the clearest indication of the power of Truth can be found in the *audacht* or will of the famous Brehon, Morann Mac Cairbre, who left instructions for the High King, Feradach Finn Fachtnach (AD 95–117) which are recorded in *Leabhar na Nuachonghbala* (Book of Leinster):

> Let him magnify the truth, it will magnify him.
> Let him strengthen truth, it will strengthen him.
> Let him guard truth, it will guard him.
> Let him exalt truth, it will exalt him.
> For so long as he guards truth, good shall not fail him and his rule shall not perish
> For it is through the ruler's truth that great clans are governed.
> Through the ruler's truth massive mortalities are averted from men.
> Through the ruler's truth mighty armies of invaders are drawn back into enemy territory.
> Through the ruler's truth every law is glorious and every vessel full in his lands.
> Through the ruler's truth all the land is fruitful and every child born worthy.
> Through the ruler's truth there is abundance of tall corn.

Several linguistic concepts of this idea of Truth survive. One fascinating point is that the Old Irish word for truth is also the basis for linguistic concepts of holiness, righteousness, faithfulness, for religion and, above all, for justice. Even in modern Irish one can say: '*Tá sé/sí in áit na fhírinne anois*' to express that a man/woman is dead. This literally means 'he/she is in the place of Truth now'. This is clearly a teaching of the Druids because we find an exact parallel in Persian-Iranian Parseeism. The *Avesta* is the sacred book of the Parsees dating from the third or fourth centuries AD, and collected from the ancient writings and traditions of the religious teacher and prophet of ancient Persia, Zoroaster, more popularly known as Zara-thustra (*c.*628–*c.*551 BC). In the *Avesta*, *Asa*, or Truth, is the name of the Otherworld or the Paradise to which all hope to attain. In the Hindu *Vedas* we find that Truth (*rta*) is a land in the highest state of paradise and the source of the sacred Ganges. We are also reminded of the mystical pool of Segais which became the source of the Boyne and also the Shannon, into which the hazel-nuts of Truth and Wisdom fell, and were eaten by Fintan the salmon, from whose taste Fionn Mac Cumhail learnt his wisdom. What I believe we are seeing are traces of a once common Indo-European belief.

Professor Dillon pointed out that one finds, in 'Morann's Will', a distinct echo of the Hindu *Upanishads*, a collection of treatises on the nature of man and the universe forming part of the Vedic writings. Here again is an example, I believe, of the remarkable development from a common Indo-European root. Dillon shows that Hindu culture has the same concept of the magical power of Truth. The heroine, Sita, pursued in the forest by a wicked hunter, declares she loves Rama, the seventh incarnation of the deity Vishnu. 'By this Truth may I be delivered!' she cries and the hunter falls dead. The Act of Truth, *satyakriya*, occurs frequently in Hindu literature. The same notion of Truth can be found in some of the surviving teachings of Heracleitus of Ephesus (*c.*540–480 BC), in which he puts forward a tenet of what became the Stoic school of philosophy, that nature or the universe was controlled by *logos*, the Word or reason, which was Truth and synonymous with godhead. Whatever happened was in accordance with this Truth and the aim of men and women was to live in harmony with it. The concept was retained by Stoics and Stoic Platonists, such as Philo Judaeus (*c.*30 BC–45 AD), an Alexandrian Hellenized Jew, whose work influenced the early Christians. The *Gospel of St John* was written in about AD 100 and, unlike the Synoptic Gospels, is a unified composition by one author. This author shows clearly that he was influenced by the ideas of Philo or other Stoic Platonists with his very opening sentence: 'In the beginning was the Word (*logos*), and the Word (*logos*) was with God, and the Word (*logos*) was God.'

Augustine of Hippo, in *Confessions*, admits that he found this very concept in the books of the Platonists.

So we return to the basic Indo-European idea of Truth being the Word and synonym for divinity. For the Druids and Brahmins, the life-giving principle and sustaining power was the Word or Truth, the ultimate cause of all being. The *Vedas* say that 'by means of Truth the earth endures'. That early Indo-European concept found its echo in Heraclitus' philosophy and arrived in the Christian *New Testament* via the Stoics and Platonists. Thus we also find in many Celtic myths the idea of some retribution for the person not speaking the truth. Usually, blemishes would appear. That idea permeates many European cultures; the famous modern survival of the ancient idea being found in the children's tale *Le aventure di Pinocchio* (1883) written by the Italian 'Collodi', Carlo Lorenzini (1826–1890). In this tale the nose of Pinocchio grows larger every time Pinocchio tells a lie.

A further demonstration of the importance of the Word is seen in the concept that the naming of things brings them into being. We are told that Ra, the great sun god and first Egyptian deity to appear out of the primal Chaos, created himself by calling out his own name. Until something is named it remains unknown, without place or purpose. To Christians, a newborn baby remains without a soul and cannot hope to enter the kingdom of God unless it has been baptized with a name. Therefore the Word is one of divine power. In Old Irish, as well as Modern Irish, we find that *ainm* was not only the word for name but for soul (as opposed to body) and life. The comparison occurs in Welsh with the words *enwi*, *enaid* and *einioes* being evolved from the common word. For the ancient Celts, along with other Indo-European societies, the world was created by the Word, from the process of the development of language.

We have already observed that the Celts evolved a doctrine of immortality of the soul and were one of the first European peoples to do so. Ammianus Marcellinus observed: 'With grand contempt for the mortal lot they professed the immortality of the soul'. And Lucan, in his poem *Pharsalia*, addressed the Druids thus: 'It is you who say that the shades of the dead seek not the silent land of Erebus and the pale halls of Pluto; rather, you tell us that the same spirit has a body again elsewhere, and that death, if what you sing is true, is but the mid-point of a long life.'

The Alexandrian School were divided as to whether the Celts had developed their doctrine themselves or whether they had borrowed the concept from the Greeks, notably from Pythagoras.

The Greek Alexander Cornelius Polyhistor (*c.*105 BC), was the main source on Pythagoras and his material was used by Diogenes Laertius, Pliny the Elder and Stephanus of Byzantium. Polyhistor wrote a tract on the philosophy of Pythagoras, *De Symbolis Pythagoricis*, in which he claimed to be using 'Pythagorean note books' handed down from the Pythagoreans of the fourth century BC. There is some scholastic argument as to whether Polyhistor's sources were genuine. However, Polyhistor, writing at the same time as Timagenes, was using sources that seem older than Poseidonius. And his work provided at least one of the sources for Clement of Alexandria, an Athenian born c.AD 150, who became head of the Catechetical School of Alexandria. He died c.AD 211–216. Clement's source is confirmed by the fact that Cyril of Alexandria, archbishop in AD 412–444, quotes identical passages used by Clement in *Contra Julianum*, and states categorically that they come from Polyhistor's book on Pythagoras.

Pythagoras, in the sixth century BC, taught a doctrine of reincarnation or transmigration of the soul. He claimed to have been the Trojan Euphorbus, slain at Troy, in a previous reincarnation.

According to Diodorus Siculus it was Polyhistor who first makes mention that 'the Pythagorean doctrine prevails among the Gauls' in which the immortality of the soul was taught. Timagenes also seems to have taught the same idea and Ammianus Marcellinus, using Timagenes as his authority, says: 'The Druids, men of loftier intellect, and united to the intimate fraternity of the followers of Pythagoras, were absorbed by investigations into matters secret and sublime, and unmindful of human affairs, declared souls to be immortal.'

Strabo says: 'The Druids and others joined to the study of nature that of moral philosophy, asserting that the human soul is indestructible, and also the universe, but that some time or other, fire and water will prevail.' Caesar's cynical soldier's remark that this doctrine accounted for the Celts' bravery in battle is also echoed by Lucan.

Hippolytus (c.AD 170–c.236), an important Christian author writing in Greek but of whose work only fragments remain, claimed that the Druids had adopted the teachings of Pythagoras through the intermediacy of Zalmoxis of Thrace, who had been his slave. According to Herodotus (c.490 – c.425 BC), a Greek from Halicarnassus, sometimes referred to as 'the father of history', Zalmoxis was the philosopher's slave during the time Pythagoras lived on Samos. Hippolytus says that Zalmoxis ultimately returned to Thrace with wealth and prestige, and promised his people immortality by this new teaching and became regarded as their god.

The Druids among the Celts having profoundly examined the Pythagorean philosophy, Zalmoxis, a Thracian by race, the slave of Pythagoras, having become for them the founder of this discipline, he after the death of Pythagoras, having made his way there, became the founder of this philosophy for them. The Celts honour the Druids as prophets and prognosticators because they foretell matters by the ciphers and numbers according to the Pythagorean skill . . . The Druids also practise magic arts however.

There is one problem here. Hippolytus obviously knew that Thrace had been occupied by the Celts. Cambaules and a Celtic army had moved into Thrace in 298 BC. The Celts settled the country for a while. The last king of Thrace to bear a distinctive Celtic name ruled in 193 BC. But Pythagoras lived in the sixth century BC, long before the Celts had reached Thrace. So how far can we trust the tradition of Zalmoxis? Was he a Celt or was he a Thracian? While Hippolytus does not make it entirely clear what the source of his statement was, nevertheless Diogenes Laertius and later Clement of Alexandria quote passages similar to those of Hippolytus.

It is Clement who puts the proverbial cat among the pigeons by saying that it was not the Druids who accepted Pythagoras' doctrine of immortality of the soul, but Pythagoras who had accepted the Druids' doctrine. Clement cites Polyhistor as his source. 'Alexander (Polyhistor) desires to state that . . . Pythagoras was one of those who hearkened to the Celts (Galatae) and the Brahmins.'

Diogenes Laertius contradicts this: 'There are some who say that the study of philosophy had its beginning among the barbarians . . . It was from the Greeks that philosophy took its rise; its very name refuses to be translated into foreign speech.' As an interesting digression, it can be noted that the sources for the words meaning philosopher in all the Celtic languages today mean literally 'man of wisdom'. So it would appear that the concept of 'lover of wisdom', which is the Greek derivation, is paralleled by the Celtic. However, Welsh has an older term, *athroniaeth*, based on the root *athro* meaning teacher. But perhaps more interesting is the fact that in Old Irish are found other words for philosopher; *cailleóir*, whose basis means auguring or star divination and which is used in Scots Gaelic in the form *càileadar* to mean philosopher or star-gazer; while a further Old Irish term *feallsamhacht* survives in Manx as *fallosgyssagh* which means an astrologer. We shall discuss these linguistic concepts later.

Diogenes Laertius cites his main authority on the Druids as Sotion. Sotion, writing in the second century BC, is therefore the earliest surviving authority on the idea that the ancient Greeks took their doctrine of immortality of the soul from the Celts. Diogenes Laertius also cites the anonymous writer of the second century BC, whose work *Magicus* was wrongly ascribed to Aristotle. Kendrick has pointed out that such works, written long before the Romans conquered Gaul, showed that the Druids had a great reputation as philosophers outside the Celtic world and that this must have been a long established reputation.

The Pythagorean link with the Druids has been romanticized by the claim that a Druid named Abaris travelled to Athens and discoursed with Pythagoras. An examination of the first reference to this in Strabo's work has been translated as:

> He came not clad in skins like a Scythian, but with a bow in his hand, a quiver hanging on his shoulders, a plaid wrapped about his body, a gilded belt encircling his loins, and trousers reaching down from the waist to the soles of his feet. He was easy in his address; agreeable in his conversation; active in his dispatch and secret in his management of great affairs; quick in judging of present accuracies, and ready to take his part in any sudden emergency; provident withal in guarding against futility; diligent in the quest of wisdom; fond of friendship; trusting very little to fortune, yet having the entire confidence of others, and trusted with everything for his prudence. He spoke Greek with a fluency that you would have thought that he had been bred up in the Lyceum; and conversed all his life with the academy of Athens.

Now Abaris is described as a Hyperborean. A Hyperborean, 'a dweller beyond the north wind', was a member of a fabulous people believed by the Greeks to exist in the inaccessible north. They were worshippers of Apollo who was thought to dwell some of the year with them. Those who were particularly favoured by the gods might become immortal and live with the Hyperboreans. The original sources do not make Abaris a Celt or, more particularly, a Druid. It was John Wood in 1747 who stated 'the Britons and Hyperboreans were one and the same people ...' His authority was, apparently, Hecateus of Miletus who identified the Hyperboreans as dwelling in the British Isles.

Reverend Henry Rowlands, however, in *Mona Antiqua Restaur-*

ata, 1723, had already claimed Abaris, with a rather extravagant linguistic justification, as a Welsh Druid named 'ap Rees'. Then John Toland, in his *A Critical History of the Celtic religion & etc* decided to hail Abaris as a Scottish Gael, in spite of the fact that Scottish Gaels did not exist at this time, and it was Toland who decided to authenticate his description by translating the Greek *chlamys* as 'plaid'. Finally, John Wood, the architect of Bath, in *Choir Gaure, Vulgarly called Stonehenge, on Salisbury Plain Described, Restored and Explained*, 1747, gives an account of a mythical Celtic Briton called Bladud; a king, whom he makes synonymous with Aquila and Abaris. After his stay in Greece, Wood has Abaris returning to Britain where he creates the Druid order. In fact, Abaris the Hyperborean, whose visit to Greece was, according to Greek tradition, long remembered, became the English antiquarians' equivalent of the French antiquarians' Druid, Chyndonax of Dijon, imaginatively conjured to present a picture of an ancient Druidic philosopher and sage. There is no Classical reference to Abaris and Pythagoras meeting. But we will return to Abaris later.

In reality, just how close was the teaching of the Celtic Druids to that of Pythagoras? The first thing we must remember is that Pythagoras wrote nothing which has survived nor, indeed, is he known to have written anything. He is a figure of mystery and legend with the traditions for his life as contrary as any pre-Christian Irish philosopher or king. Heraclitus regarded him as a fraud while Xenophanes mocked his teachings on immortality. From later writers we hear that Pythagoras taught that the soul is immortal, a fallen divinity imprisoned in a body. The soul, by its actions, determined how it would be reincarnated, in human, animal or even plant form. Empedocles, a follower of Pythagoras, claimed to have been reincarnated from a bush. Pythagoras himself declared he recognized a friend's voice in the howling of a puppy dog which was being beaten, according to Xenophanes. Pythagoras maintained that the soul could at last obtain its release from worldly cares by keeping itself pure, which entailed an austere regime of silence, self-examination and abstention (mainly from eating flesh and beans). This theory of the transmigration of souls (*metempsychosis*) was alien to Greek philosophical tradition at this time. The belief was, however, widespread in India where it was believed that due to its *karma* a soul transmigrated from one life to another in a never-ending cycle which could only be broken in Nirvana. The belief still exists in Hinduism, Jainism and Buddhism. Nirvana is a state of supreme bliss which, once achieved, liberates from the repeating cycle of death and rebirth. Nirvana is attainable through moral discipline and the practice of Yoga, a spiritual discipline to attain higher consciousness, liberation from ignorance and suffering, and rebirth. In fact, Alexander Pope, writing on the Druids comments sardonically:

> Go, like the Indian, in another life,
> Except thy dog, thy bottle and thy wife.

The basis of the Celtic idea of immortality of the soul was that death was but a changing of place and life went on with all its forms and goods in *another* world, a world of the dead, the fabulous Otherworld. When people died in that world, however, their souls were reborn in this. Thus a constant exchange of souls took place between the two worlds; death in this world took a soul to the Otherworld, death in that world brought a soul to this. Philostratus of Tyana (*c.*AD 170–249) observed correctly that the Celts celebrated birth with mourning for the death in the Otherworld, and regarded death with joy for the birth in the Otherworld. One Classical writer observed that so firm was their belief in rebirth in the Otherworld that some Celts were quite happy to accept promissory notes for debts to be repaid in the Otherworld. The source is Valerius Maximus in the early first century AD, who says of the Celts that 'they lent sums of money to each other which are repayable in the next world, so firmly are they convinced that the souls of men are immortal'.

Pre-Christian Celtic graves, throughout the Celtic world, are filled with personal belongings, weapons, food and drink and other items to give the departed a good start in the Otherworld. The grave of a forty-year-old Celtic chieftain, buried around 550 BC, at Hochdorf, at the edge of the Black Forest in Southern Germany, is one of the best examples of such pomp and circumstance. Discovered in 1968, the chieftain, six feet tall, was dressed in robes of silk, richly embroidered and a hat of birch-bark. Gold brooches fastened his cloak. He wore a gold bracelet, a wide leather belt with a gold band, a gold dagger of exquisite craftsmanship, and his shoes were decorated with gold. He lay on a great bronze couch. Significantly, a great cauldron stood nearby in which there was four hundred litres of fermented honey-mead, alongside nine drinking horns, one of which was able to hold nine litres. His grave goods included weapons, cooking and eating utensils, knives, a four-wheeled wagon made of ash, elm and maple, and many tapestries. There were also iron nail-clippers, wooden comb, fishing hooks and other items. Thus did the Celts prepare their illustrious dead for the journey to the Otherworld. What is clear from all the evidence is that the Celts believed that life in the Otherworld was essentially the same as life in this world. Lucan in *Pharsalia* actually maintains that the Celts believed that their souls remained in control of their bodies in the Otherworld.

What is interesting is that Virgil (Publius Vergilius Maro – 70– 19 BC) in his *Aeneid* presents some ideas about a life after death which bear a strong resemblance to the Celtic belief. This is put into perspective when we realize that Virgil was born at Andes, near Mantua, in Cisalpine Gaul, and was of a Celtic family. His works show his intense love of his native land and Dr Rankin has commented: 'We need not deny Celtic influences in the background of Virgil's life.' Therefore Virgil grew up with a knowledge of the Celtic culture which still existed all around him.

In *The Celtic Empire*, I have put forward the notion that the Celts did not borrow their philosophy from the Greeks nor did the Greeks borrow from the Celts. The evolution of the doctrine of immortality of the soul could simply be one of parallel development or, more reasonably, it can be argued that the similarities of the doctrines of the Druids and Pythagoras are so superficial that they do not really exist. Professor Piggott has also come to the conclusion that the philosophy 'is not in fact Pythagorean in content at all'. After all, the Pythagorean belief was in the transmigration of souls through all living things in this world. The Celtic belief was in two parallel worlds and the rebirth of the soul in human bodies from one world to the other. It could therefore be argued that the Celtic and Pythagorean doctrines were mutually exclusive. There is, of course, some evidence in insular Celtic literature that souls could migrate through various births. In Irish texts, Fintan survives the Deluge by changing into a salmon while in the Welsh texts Gwion Bach is a favourite example used by the transmigration lobby, for he is reincarnated as a hare, fish, bird and a grain of wheat which is then swallowed by a chicken before he is eventually reborn as Taliesin.

But one must be careful to differentiate transmigration of souls from simple shape changing. The ability to shape change is not to be confused with the idea that the human being was part of a one-ness with nature, believing in the consciousness of all things. Trees, fountains, even weapons and implements were but fragments of a cosmic whole. Stones, being 'old beyond time' were possessed of an indwelling spirit. Thus could the Lia Fáil (Stone of Destiny) roar with joy when it felt the touch of a righteous ruler's foot. Caladcholg, the sword of Fergus, with its magic propensity, had its equivalent in Welsh, Caladwlch, which, through the corruption of Latin phonetics, has become the world famous Excalibur. Conaire Mór also had a sword which could sing. The god Ogma took the sword of Tethra, the Fomorii king, having killed him at the second Battle of Magh Tuireadh. This sword, Orna, could speak and recite its deeds of valour. Lugh had a spear, Luin, which roared at the approach of a battle and once cast did not return without slaying the foe. He left it on a battlefield where it was claimed by the hero Celtchair. It twisted and writhed in the hands of Celtchair before a combat and if it did not taste blood it would turn on its holder, unless immersed in a cauldron of venom. Ochain, the 'moaner', the shield of Conchobhar Mac Nessa, would moan warnings when its bearer was in danger. Manannán Mac Lir had a boat which could navigate across the sea by itself. Other inanimate objects were possessed of the power of reason and the ability to emit warnings.

The theme of death and rebirth is a consistent thread throughout Celtic mythological sagas and tales. The theme of warrior resurrection can be found in both the Second Branch of the Mabinogion and in the story of the battle between the Tuatha Dé Danaan and the Fomorii in which bodies cast into magic cauldrons return to life. On the Gundestrup Cauldron is a scene of a god accompanying a group of warriors where he is dipping one of them in such a cauldron. The rest are symbolically carrying a tree – perhaps the *crann beatha* or tree of life?

On one night of the year the Otherworld became visible to mankind. This was the feast of Samhain (31 October 1 November), when the gates to the Otherworld were opened and the inhabitants could set out to wreak vengeance on those living in this world who had wronged them. The ancient belief survived into Christianity in a transmuted form as Hallowe'en, the evening of All Hallows, with

All Hallows or All Saints' Day being on 1 November. The modern idea is that it is the night when witches and demons and spirits from Hell set out to ensnare unsuspecting souls.

Portrayals of the Otherworld among the Celts range from the dark, brooding purgatory of the Fomorii islands to the sunny, pleasant lands of the Land of Youth or Land of Promise.

If we can accept the authority of observations by Athenaeus (fl. AD 200), quoting Poseidonius, so little fear of death did some Gaulish Celts feel that they actually sold their lives to pay their debts and provide money for their families. The matter is referred to in a glossary attributed to Lactantius Placidus, a grammarian of the sixth century AD, who says it was a Gaulish custom to sell their lives for money, and, after a year of feasting, the Celt was then ceremonially executed. Such extremism is not confirmed in any other source and certainly not in Celtic sources. However, the idea of a voluntary sacrifice by someone whose belief in an afterlife is so strong is not beyond the realms of possibility, and even happens in the modern world. One recalls the self-immolation of Buddhist monks in Vietnam in protest at the American involvement. But if this occurred in the ancient Celtic world it did so only as an isolated gesture and certainly not as the common 'Gaulish custom' that Lactantius Placidus maintained it was.

The closeness of Hindu law, customs and other matters to the Irish, has been seen as evidence for supporting the Indo-European hypothesis. The parallels in both cultures seem to prove the common cultural origin of both peoples. Dillon and Chadwick have accepted the Druids and Brahmins as sharing a common Indo-European origin. The possibility of the doctrine of immortality of the soul as being a common 'Aryan' idea, taken from the Russian steppes in the third millennium BC, and spreading through the Indo-European settlements, has also been argued. The *Vedas* show that the goal of Hinduism, Buddhism and Jainism alike was release from perpetual death and rebirth. It seems very likely that the Druidic immortality of the soul was indeed a development from a common Indo-European idea, which developed with its own particular cultural attributes parallel to the Hindu philosophies and certainly to the *metempyschosis* of Pythagoras.

One thing which is agreed upon even among the Greeks and Romans is that the Druids were admired for the sincerity of their belief and teaching. Diodorus Siculus observes: 'They are of much sincerity and integrity, far from the craft and knavery of men among us, contented with homely fare, strangers to excess and luxury.' And Strabo confirms this with his comment that 'the Druids are considered the most just of men'. The philosophy of the Celts, as instructed by the Druids, was certainly a moral system based on distinguishing right (*fas*) from wrong (*nefas*), what was lawful (*dleathach*) and unlawful (*neamhdhleathach*), and it was impressed on people by the series of taboos (*geasa*) which we have already discussed. In this, there is again much to be compared with developments in Hindu religion.

Puns and riddles were much in evidence in the Insular Celtic literatures, as, indeed, riddles play an important part in many ancient cultures. Classical writers, sometimes in perplexity, speak of the Druids teaching by way of riddles. We hear of a contest between Marbán, 'chief prophet of heaven and earth', and Dael Duiled, chief *ollamh* of Leinster. From the story of 'The Wooding of Ailbe' several riddles are recorded.

What is sweeter than mead? – Intimate conversation.
What is blacker than the raven? – Death.
What is whiter than snow? – Truth.
What is swifter than the wind? – Thought.
What is sharper than the sword? – Understanding.
What is lighter than a spark? – The mind of a woman between
two men.

I do not think we can leave a discussion on the philosophy of the Druids without referring to the fact that the Celts produced some of the most fascinating early Christian philosophers. These philosophers range from the Gaulish Celt, Hilary of Poitiers (*c*.AD 315–*c*.367), considered one of the most outstanding theologians of the early Christian Church, who wrote, among other discourses, *De Trinitate* (on the Trinity), to Eriugena (*c*.AD 810–*c*.880), sometimes called Johannes Scotus, John the Irishman, who is considered the most considerable philosopher of the Western world between Augustine of Hippo and Thomas Aquinas.

But between these two remarkable Celtic philosophers there appears another who, significantly, was accused by his enemies of attempting to revive the 'Natural Philosophy of the Druids'.

The philosopher in question was Pelagius (c.AD 354–420). He was a Celt who usually had the appellation 'Brito', which would mean he was British although one contemporary writer sneered that he 'was full of Irish porridge', which has caused some scholars to consider that he was an Irishman. Heinrich Zimmer thought so in his study *Pelagius in Ireland* (Berlin, 1901). The name is considered to be a Hellenized form of the Celtic name 'Morgan', meaning sea-begotten. His contemporary, a man who knew him personally, Eusebius Hieronymous (St Jerome), described him as a thoughtful, grave, and stolid man. Pelagius does not appear to have been an ordained priest but was *veluti monarchus*, one who followed the discipline of the monastery. He was initially respected for the wisdom of his pronouncements.

Pelagius went to Rome in about AD 380. He was distressed by the laxity of moral standards which he found among the Christians there and blamed it squarely on the doctrine expounded in the writings of Augustine of Hippo, which maintained that everything was preordained and that Man was polluted and sinful because he took on the original sin of Adam. Further, God had already ordained this therefore Man had no free will in the matter. Pelagius believed that both men and women could take the initial and fundamental step towards their salvation, using their own efforts and not accepting things as preordained. Pelagius believed that Augustine's theories imperilled the entire moral law. If men and women were not responsible for their good and evil deeds, there was nothing to restrain them from an indulgence in sin on the basis that it was preordained anyway. In Pelagius' earliest known writing, about AD 405, one philosophy became clear: 'If I ought, I can.'

Pelagius left Rome, avoiding the sack by Alaric's Visigoths in AD 410. He journeyed together with a colleague who supported his philosophies, one Coelestius who was referred to in one text as an Irishman. Pelagius left Coelestius in Carthage while he went on to Palestine. Augustine had been angered by the criticism of his work and a friend of his, Osorius Paulus, a deacon of Milan, was persuaded to 'test the waters' by accusing Pelagius' friend, Coelestius, of heresy. A synod under Auretius of Carthage met and considered seven accusations of heretical belief.

These were that: Adam would have died even if he had not sinned;

Adam's sin injured only himself; newborn children were in the same spiritual condition as Adam before his fall; the whole human race was not responsible for Adam's fall; obeying the laws gives entrance into heaven as well as the Gospels and church ritual; even before the coming of Christ men and women were without sin and able to pass to the Otherworld; and that infants unbaptized in the Christian Faith could still have eternal life.

It is interesting here that while the ancient Celts certainly had a word for culpability or responsibility they did not seem to have a clear concept of the Christian idea of sin. In both Old Irish and Welsh the word for sin, *pecad* (Irish), and *pechod* (Welsh), is borrowed from the Latin *peccatum*, and is always used in its Christian sense as opposed to the Old Irish *cin* or *lochtach* meaning guilt or culpability, or the Welsh *euogrwydd*. The new concept of the Christian idea of sin seems very alien to the Celtic world and, I believe, this is underscored by the Pelagian arguments. In the Celtic Church, confession of sin was not obligatory and any confessing that was needed was made to a chosen 'soul friend'. According to Father Joseph MacVeigh in *Renewing the Irish Church* (1993): 'The soul-friend (*anam chara*) who acted as a spiritual guide and counsellor – not confessor – to young monks and converts was part of Druidic practice.' So sin and the need to confess it was something new to Celtic perceptions.

The idea of the soul-friend, or spiritual guide, was a concept used in pre-Christian Celtic society, and the rôle was usually filled by a druid. It is, perhaps, also significant that in early Celtic Christian society, the position of soul-friend was filled by women. There are many examples; Ita of Cluan Credill was the soul-friend of Brendan. Columbanus had a woman soul-friend. But in later life, as he spent more time in France and Italy and was influenced by Roman perceptions, he ordered that males could only confide in male soul-friends.

Leslie Hardinge has pointed out the close similarities between Druid and early Celtic Christian 'saints':

In their social position and political influence the powerful saints were, on occasion, seemingly the successors of the druids. Druidism and Christianity were superficially similar. Both had seasons in which fires were ceremonially extinguished, and were then relighted from a symbolic flame. Both baptised infants, at which time the child's name was bestowed on it. Both claimed to work magical cures, to predict events, and to transfer diseases from human beings to plants or other objects. Both were teachers of youth and counsellors of kings. Like the druid, the Christian soul-friend might banish a sinner. Both cursed their enemies, and, as [St] Senan once exclaimed, 'Stronger is the spell that I have brought with me, and better is my lore'.

We have no record of Coelestius' defence at his hearing before Auretius of Carthage. He was adjudged guilty of the seven charges brought against him.

Coelestius was condemned and excommunicated for believing in the ideas propounded by Pelagius. With this success, Augustine and his supporters began their attack on Pelagius himself. In AD 415 he had been living in Palestine and was respected and well-liked. He was well-known and seemed to be a personal friend of St Jerome, then living in Bethlehem, who had a knowledge of Celtic, having lived in Gaul, and knew enough of the language to compare the Celtic spoken in Galatia, where he also travelled, with the particular Gaulish dialect of the Treveri. Augustine himself wrote to St Jerome a tract known as *De peccatorum meritis* (On the merit of sin) warning against Pelagius. Then Osorius arrived in Jerusalem, flushed from his success in prosecuting Coelestius. St Jerome swung to the side of Augustine and accused Pelagius before a Council presided over by John of Jerusalem in June, AD 415. St Jerome now seemed shocked by Pelagius' teaching that men and women could become without sin if they desired to be so. But the prosecution broke down. Undaunted, Augustine pressed on. In December, AD 415, another synod was held at Diospolis (Lydda) with fourteen bishops in attendance, and Heros of Arles and Lazarus of Aix prosecuting. But the synod again found Pelagius not guilty of heresy.

Augustine was obviously furious. Pelagius had now been cleared by two church investigations. And now Pelagius issued his treatise *De Libero Arbitrio* (On Free Will) to explain his views. The essential of all his teaching was that man had freedom of will. However, Augustine finally convinced the bishops at Carthage and Milevius to charge Pelagius once more. They appealed to Pope Innocent I who was flattered that the African bishops – who, so far, had taken very little notice of the dictates of Rome – were now appealing to its bishop for a decision as supreme arbiter. He declared Pelagius guilty.

Innocent's successor, Zosimus, immediately overturned this ruling, declaring Pelagius innocent of heresy, having studied his works, especially his *Libellus Fidei* (Statement of Faith). Outraged, Augustus and his supporters renewed their campaign against Pelagius. This time they decided to bypass theological authority and appeal to political authority. On 30 April, AD 418, at Ravenna, the emperor Honorius (AD 395–423) was persuaded to preempt the theological question by making a political proscription against Pelagius, confiscating all his goods. Zosimus, as bishop of Rome, had little choice but to follow the 'hint' given by the emperor. He now reluctantly denounced Pelagius as well.

Significantly, there was a lot of opposition within the Church against this move. Augustine and his followers did not sweep all before them. Even among the Italian bishops some nineteen of them refused to condemned Pelagius and these were led by Julian of Eclanum in Apulia. The Eastern Church did not make a denunciation of Pelagius until the synod of Ephesus in AD 431. The Celtic Church was considered riddled with 'Pelagian heresy' almost to the end of its days. Certainly, the second Council of Orange in AD 592 made a reaffirmation of the condemnation of Pelagianism as a movement which implied that it still had a strong following among the Celts.

By AD 420 no more is heard of Pelagius himself although his friend Coelestius emerged in AD 428 at Constantinople seeking aid from the bishop Nestorus. What happened to this remarkable philosopher is not known.

Now if Pelagius was truly echoing the philosophy of the Druids, and this is not unlikely, for he was undoubtedly a man of his culture and teaching its social concepts within the framework of the new religion, and it was this point which caused Augustine and his followers to denounce them as an attempt to revive the 'Natural Philosophy of the Druids', we must ask – what was this philosophy?

The essence of Pelagianism was that men and women were responsible for all their acts and that though there were several governing outside factors, the final choice was their own. There is, and can be, no sin where the will is not absolutely free; where one is not able to choose between good or evil. (*Si necessitatis est, peccatum non est; si voluntatis, vitari potest.*)

Pelagius taught that we are born characterless (*non pleni*) and with no bias towards good or evil. To distinguish good from evil, one has to be taught (*ut sine virtute, ita et sine vitio*). He argued that, unlike Augustine's teaching, we are not already damned by Adam's sin save in so far that it gives us an example from our ancestors of evil which can influence or mislead us (*non propagine sed exemplo*). The power of choice, which reaffirms the freedom of will, means that in each choice in life, at each moment of life, no matter what has happened previously to the individual, he or she is able to choose between good or evil.

Perhaps significantly, Pelagius used a triad – *posse, velle, esse*. 'We distinguish three things; the ability, the will, the act. The ability is in Nature, and must be referred to as God, who has bestowed this on his creature, Man. The other two, the will and the act, must be referred to mankind because they flow from the fountain of free will.' In *Libellus Fidei*, Pelagius reiterates that 'free will exists generally in all mankind'. He maintained that 'it is the human will which takes the initiative and is the determining factor in the salvation of the individual, whether men and women use their lives for good or evil'. Augustine of Hippo argued that the will belonged to God and not man; that whether someone was good or evil had already been ordained and that only God's will gave the initiative of enabling the human will to accept and use the aid and grace of the Holy Spirit.

It could be argued that to deny 'divine influence' in this matter Pelagius was suggesting that the Christian doctrine of 'Grace' was superseded by that of 'Nature', although he does not appear to have carried this rationalization through to the logical conclusion, which would have been a denial of 'atonement', so central to Christian belief. Western Christianity was emphasizing, at this time, the supernatural character of Christianity as an agency in the subjective world, developing a doctrine of 'sin' and 'Grace'. Pelagius, and indeed the Celtic Church, which had more in common with the eastern Orthodox Church and early Greek Christians like John Chrysostom and Origen, was jealous to maintain the human freedom of will, loathed to make 'sin' a Natural power, and was developing the doctrine of Trinity, incarnation and the supernatural character of Christianity in an objective world.

Concurrently with Pelagius, there were several Celtic philosophers writing tracts which are now all lumped together as 'Pelagian'. But they seem to indicate a shared, or common, set of philosophies, especially social philosophy, which, I believe, gives credence to the view that Pelagius was espousing a pre-Christian Celtic philosophy. Works written by an anonymous British Celtic writer, labelled by scholars as the 'Sicilian Briton', because they appear to be written in Sicily, have been called 'Pelagian'. In *Tractatus de Divitiis* – a tract on wealth – in which the writer used a triad teaching on *divitiae*, *paupertas*, *satis*, the Celt claimed that mankind was divided between wealth, poverty and sufficiency. He argued: 'Overthrow the rich man and you will not find a poor man . . . for the few rich are the cause of the many poor'. Heady revolutionary stuff in fifth century AD Italy but perfectly acceptable to the egalitarian Celts, with their lack of the concept of absolute private property, their lack of the concept of primogeniture and electoral methods of officialdom, including kingship.

A British Celtic bishop Fastidius, writing *De Vita Christiana* (The Christian Life) about AD 411, also argued:

> Do you think yourself Christian if you oppress the poor? . . . If you enrich yourself by making others poor? If you wring your food from others' tears? A Christian is a man who . . . never allows a poor man to be oppressed when he is by . . . whose doors are open to all, whose table every poor man knows, whose food is offered to all.

These were the teachings which caused such concern to the orthodoxy of Rome and still, in spite of the philosophical revisionism of the Church away from the predestination arguments of Augustine, cause Pelagius to be regarded as a heretic. It is, I believe, a supportable argument that Pelagius had not evolved a new philosophy but was a representative of Celtic culture whose philosophy was already established before Christianity by none other than the Druids and what Rome saw as the teachings of Pelagius winning converts in Ireland and Britain was no more than the Celts abiding by their own social and cultural order. They were especially worried when Ireland began to export its philosophers during the so-called 'Dark Ages'. As Heiric of Auxerre (*c.*AD 876) observed: 'Ireland, despising the dangers of the sea, is migrating almost *en masse* with her crowd of philosophers to our shores . . .'

I certainly do not think it a coincidence that when Eriugena (which means 'Irish born') wrote his first known treatise in AD 850, *De*

Praedestinatione, he embarrassed his sponsors who claimed that it appeared to revive certain aspects of Pelagianism. This was seen in Eriugena's refutation of the work of the Saxon monk, poet and philosopher, Gottschalk of Orbais (*c.*AD 803–*c.*869). Gottschalk in his own *De Praedestinatione* had reaffirmed some teachings of Augustine, that Christ's powers of redemption were limited and only the elect would be chosen for paradise, and that who was chosen was already predestined. In denying this predestination, Eriugena's work was condemned by two synods, in AD 855 and 859. It is also significant that in *Periphyseon, or the Division of Nature* (written *c.*AD 864–866), Eriugena felt more at home with quoting Greek or Eastern Orthodox Christian philosophers than with Western (Roman) philosophers. The Greek Christian Fathers, as we have seen, were more compatible in their thinking with the Celtic Church than the Roman Church Fathers. For Eriugena, as for Pelagians, reason is by nature superior to authority and has greater dignity. Any authority is weak unless it can be supported by reason, by a logic founded in truth, in which case such reason does not require the support of authority. Eriugena seems to be echoing the Druidic aphorism: 'The Truth against the world!'

Eriugena was not condemned by Rome and is still regarded as the most considerable philosopher in the Western World between Augustine of Hippo and Thomas Aquinas. Bertrand Russell, in *A History of Western Philosophy* (1946) sums up his analysis of Eriugena by saying 'his independence of mind ... is astonishing in the ninth century.'

> His Neoplatonic outlook may perhaps have been common in Ireland, as it was among the Greek Fathers of the fourth and fifth centuries. It may be that, if we knew more about Irish Christianity from the fifth to ninth century, we should find him less surprising ...

Alas, Russell had little knowledge of the tremendous wealth of Irish sources for this period and he still writes with the unfortunate, prejudiced view of an Englishman who sees little of worth among the Celts. He even claims 'St Patrick *was an Englishman*', ignoring that he was a British Celt. He works out a theory that during the Dark Ages European scholars went to Ireland to escape the Huns, Goths and Vandals, taught there and this was why Ireland became a centre of learning. This is a perverse way of looking at things. It ignores the facts of history. Students from Europe flocked to the long established colleges of learning in Ireland to study under Irish professors. There is no record of foreign scholars in Ireland during this period except as students. Irish teachers and missionaries were also leaving Ireland during this time to establish churches, monasteries and centres of learning in Europe to educate and reconvert it to Christianity. In this respect, Russell, in spite of his acclaim as one of the most important thinkers of the twentieth century, merely becomes a prisoner of his culture, presuming nothing of worth could come from the 'barbaric Irish'.

Russell observes of Eriugena that the patriarchy of Christianity had entered his thought, without actually being spelt out:

> His view of creation as timeless is, of course, also heretical and compels him to say that the account in Genesis is allegorical. Paradise and the fall are not to be taken literally. Like all pantheists he has difficulties about sin. He holds that man was originally without sin, and when he was without sin he was without distinction of sex. This, of course, contradicts the statement 'male and female created he them'. According to John (Eriugena) it was only as a result of sin that human beings were divided into male and female. Woman embodies man's sensuous and fallen nature. In the end, distinction of sex will again disappear, and we shall have a purely spiritual body. Sin consists in misdirected will, in falsely supposing something good which is not so. Its punishment is natural, it consists in discovering the vanity of sinful desires. But punishment is not eternal. Like Origen, John (Eriugena) holds that even the devils will be saved at last, though later than other people.

In Pelagius, the 'Sicilian Briton', Fastidius and other 'Pelagian' writers, some echo, and perhaps a strong echo at that, of the philosophies of the Druids might well be discovered. But the observer might now contend that surely there is a contradiction in their philosophical approach here. We know that the Celts were renowned for their auguries; their divination by bird flight and other means; their foretelling of the future. Celtic mythology and folklore is full of Druids who proclaim the fate of individuals, and the attempt of those individuals to escape from that fate is usually the very path by which they eventually meet it. This seems contradictory to the basic idea enshrined in the philosophy expounded by Pelagius and his ilk which might be summed up by the lines from the poet W.E. Henley (1849–1903):

> I am the captain of my soul
> The master of my fate

The matter is not so black and white. There are two arguments. The most reasonable argument, and the most simple, is that in dealing with a Europe-wide civilization over a millennium and a half, various strands of philosophical outlook could and would emerge. It is probably more accurate to speak of Druidic philosophies rather than Druidic philosophy; those who accepted Fate or Predestination and those who did not. However, nothing is ever clear-cut; more serious astrologers, for example, will argue that astrology does not have to be an argument for predestination, but simply that a knowledge of astrological influences at various times presents people with choice. And choice is what the Pelagian approach is most concerned with.

Druids as Judges

According to the *Annals of Ulster*, after countless centuries of oral transmission and practice, the High King, Laoghaire (428–463 AD), decided to appoint a commission of nine eminent persons to study, revise and commit the laws of Ireland to writing. The ancient chroniclers claim that it was Ollamh Fódhla, a High King in the eighth century BC, who first gave the Irish their law system. Among the nine men were three Christian leaders, one of whom was Patrick. The committee took three years to study the Fénechas, or laws of the land tiller, which we now popularly call the Brehon laws, the word deriving from *breitheamh*, a judge. The Brehons, in pre-Christian times, were Druids.

One of the most important functions of the Druids noticed by both Strabo and Caesar was that of judges in the Celtic law courts. Strabo mentions that they were entrusted with all legal decisions, both in private and public cases. 'The Druids,' he says, 'are considered the most just of men.' Caesar maintains that the Druids' prestige as judges was paramount in Celtic society and confirms that they were sole judges in all public and private cases and that there was no appeal against their decisions. He adds that at the great Druidical assembly in the territory of the Carnutes in Gaul (Chartres), people attended from all parts of the region bringing disputes for submission to the Druids' arbitration. Ferdinand Lot has pointed out that this implied both a degree of judicial and political unity among the Celtic tribes of Gaul. Caesar adds that in 52 BC *Vergobret* was elected chief magistrate and judge of the Aedui 'by the Druids, according to usages of the state'. *Vergobret* is a title, a job description rather than a name, deriving from *vergo* (effective), *breto* (judgement), cognate with the Old Irish term *brethach*, from which *breitheamh* or Brehon derives.

The Druids' ability to go on to a battlefield between two opposing armies and stop them, implies that the Druids had the authority as 'international judges'. Diodorus Siculus attests to this. 'Often when the combatants are ranged face to face, and swords drawn and spears bristling, these men come between the armies and stay the battle, just as wild beasts are sometimes held spellbound.' And Strabo adds of the Druids, 'they even arbitrated in cases of war and made the opponents stop when they were about to line up for battle'.

This rôle of the Druids as international arbiters and ambassadors is confirmed from several sources. We have already mentioned the rôle of female ambassadors (Druidesses) in negotiating a treaty between the Celtic Volcae and the Carthaginian general Hannibal. We know that, about 197/196 BC, citizens of Lampsacos arrived in the Greek colony of Marseilles seeking an alliance. The Massiliots used the influences of the Celts of Gaul with the Celts of Galatia, in this particular instance the Tolistoboii of the Sangarios valley, to persuade the Galatians not to aid Antiochos III of Syria against the Lampsacenians. This is astonishing when one considers the distances in the ancient world. According to Henri Hubert it showed 'that the Greeks of Marseilles and of Lampsacos knew that they would find among Celtic peoples living very far apart a sense of oneness.'

But what created that sense of 'oneness'? Hubert is in no doubt:

This solidarity of the Celtic peoples, even when distant from one another, is sufficiently explained by the sense of kinship, of common origin, acting in a fairly restricted world, all the parts of which were in communication. But the Celts had at least one institution which could effectively bind them together, namely the Druids, a priestly class expressly entrusted with the preservation of traditions. The Druids were not an institution of the small Celtic peoples, of the tribes, of the *civitates*; they were a kind of inter-national institution within the Celtic world . . .

In other words, the word of the Druid as arbiter of the law had equal weight in Galatia, Gaul, Britain or Ireland and even kings had to succumb to the rule of that law.

Certainly Dio Chrysostom indicates that the legal authority of a Druid was above that of a king when he says 'the kings were not permitted to adopt or plan any course, so that in fact it was these (Druids) who ruled and the kings became their subordinates and instruments of their judgements.'

The brief, though explicit, references by these Classical writers also imply that the Celtic peoples had developed a sophisticated law system which applied to them all wherever they were found and that the Druids controlled this legal system.

The question is, can this be substantiated by Celtic records and traditions?

The simple answer is: yes.

There survives codification of two Celtic legal systems from which we may learn much: the Irish Brehon Law system and the Welsh Laws of Hywel Dda. A comparison of the two systems indicates a Common Celtic law at some period, for both systems have developed from identical basic principles. As well as Irish and Welsh systems there survive references to other Celtic legal systems. Geoffrey of Monmouth mentions the legendary Molmutine Law of Cornwall which was concerned with the protection of the weak against oppres-sion. Between AD 858–862 Domnuil I of Alba (Scotland) had the ancient laws of Dàl Riada, obviously a version of the Brehon Laws, promulgated at Forteviot and Fortriu and, later, when the kingdom of Alba incorporated that of the Strathclyde Britons and the Cum-brians, it was important that a legal code be drawn up to reconcile any discrepancy between the law systems of the Goidelic and

Brythonic Celts. A document, the *Leges inter Bretonnes et Scotos*, dates from the eleventh century and includes terms which are similar to those found in both the Brehon Laws and the Laws of Hywel Dda. According to Professor Kenneth Jackson: 'This may imply the existence of a common Brittonic legal tradition of considerable antiquity.'

As the Irish system is the oldest surviving complete codified legal system in Europe with its roots in ancient Indo-European custom and not in Roman law, and is therefore the oldest surviving Celtic system of jurisprudence, and one in which the Druids are still mentioned, it is to Irish sources that we will turn to see what Druidic systems of justice have survived.

As mentioned at the opening of this chapter, we are told, in Irish sources, that in the year 714 BC Ollamh Fódhla, the High King, founded rule by legislature and drew up a system of law. He founded the great Féis Temhrach or Festival of Tara, which was held every three years and was where the laws were discussed and revised. Myth or not, it is as acceptable as the legends surrounding other lawgivers of the world. Manu, in Hindu legend, was the divinely inspired lawgiver who survived a flood and devised the laws which were then compiled between 200 BC and AD 200. Moses, the other divinely inspired lawgiver, is said to have produced a law system for the Hebrews in the thirteenth century BC. The Greeks are said to have passed from a system of individual vengeance to a codified system when Draco, in 621 BC, was given extraordinary power to codify the laws of Athens for the first time, and devised new laws. Demades (*c*.380–319 BC) commented that the code was written in blood rather than ink, for it was a harsh code with the death penalty prescribed for many crimes, not only homicide (hence the word *draconian* coming into English). Administration of the law was by the *archons*, an appointed council, and it was Solon (*c*.640–558 BC), an *archon*, who tried to modify Draco's system and make it more humane, although his reforms were overturned by Pisistratus (*c*.612–527 BC), one of the great tyrants (*tyrannos*, king) of Athens.

The Romans had their own divine lawgiver in the person of Numa Pompilius, the legendary successor to Romulus (715–673 BC) who received counsel from the goddess Egeria. His laws were thought to have been eventually codified in 450 BC on twelve tablets, knowledge of which was restricted to patrician priests.

In Ireland, however we view the tradition of Ollamh Fódhla, the Féis Temhrach was certainly an assembly where legislation was regularly enacted down into historical times, as demonstrated by Dr Joyce. Perhaps the most famous legal gathering was in 697 AD when Adomnán, abbot of Iona (624–704 AD), introduced his 'Law of Innocents', a sort of proto-Geneva Convention, which forbade injury to the elderly, women and children and the clergy – indeed, any non-combatants – in wartime. This law became binding not only in Ireland but among the kingdoms of the Picts and Scots and its enactment was witnessed by fifty-one kings and chieftains and forty leading churchmen.

According to the Irish sources, the laws and their administration were in the hands of the *filí*, who were undoubtedly Druids. Again, if the Druids were the intellectual caste, the *filí*, or poets, were merely a section of that caste whose name implied a 'job description'. John Davies, James I's attorney general in Ireland, wrote an essay on the Irish law system in which he says that from 'the time that Amergin (Amairgain) of the white knee, the poet, delivered the first judgment in Erin, it was to the *files* or poets alone that belonged the right of pronouncing judgments . . .'

But according to the sources, during the time of Conchobhar Mac Nessa, the Ulster king, a dispute arose between two poets, Feirceirtné and Neidé, who argued their case in public. Neidé, a son of Adhna, chief Ollamh of Ireland, claimed the *tugen* or mantle of his father. Feirtceirtné, a bard of Cú Roí of Munster, challenged him. Their disputation is featured in 'The Dialogue of the Sages', the principal version of which is given in the *Book of Ballymote*, compiled by Maghnus Ó Duibhgeánnáin in 1390/91 from earlier texts. Conchobhar Mac Nessa of Ulster was attending the dispute and found that their language was so technical neither the king nor his chieftains could understand them. An assembly was called and it was agreed that the running of the judiciary would be taken out of the hands of the *filí* and given to special judges and that the legal profession would be open to all who could qualify. While we are still in the realms of legend, this story nevertheless must commemorate an historic event in Ireland by which the legal system was reformed. The traditions of Conchobhar Mac Nessa are clearly associated with a period before the birth of Christ, a period in the Iron Age, so we can be assured that the legal reforms occurred in an ancient period.

There arose a new class of judges who are now popularly called Brehons. According to *Cormac's Glossary* another name for a Brehon was *aignesa*. This word seems to derive from the term *aignes*, meaning to plead, or argue one's case. Dr Joyce points out: 'Several great lawyers are commemorated in the tradition, among whom, it is worthy of remark, some women are included.' So, once again, the remarkable place of women in ancient Celtic society is reaffirmed. The names of some of these judges, referred to in other sources as 'Druids', are known. Cennfaela, the Druid of Cormac Mac Art, in the third century AD, was reputed one of the most learned judges in Ireland. There are references to the office of *Aire Échta*, or chief magistrate, for each tribe. Aonghus Mac Airt was reported to have been elected to this office for the Dési. His main task, according to the Brehon Law, was to 'right the wrongs of his people as well as protecting the weak and poor'. We also have an instance in Irish tradition which confirms the observations of Diodorus Siculus and Strabo about the rôle Druids played in international law. We find that Finnchaemh, Druid to Dáithí of Connacht, was sent as an ambassador to Feredach of Alba to arbitrate over a dispute between the two kings. Also, we know the name of one of the most prominent women judges – Brigh, which name seems to imply authority, virtue and fortitude.

Cormac's Glossary points out that the judges, in giving judgement on a case, had to cite a *fasach*, a precedent or maxim to justify their decisions. Anyone refusing to accept a judgement was excluded from the society and 'shall not be paid by God or man'. This confirms what Caesar tells us when he observes that those who refused the Druids' judgement were ostracised. Martin, in his tour of the *Western Islands of Scotland* in 1695, found a man who had violated a covenant and was ostracized, a late survival of the custom of the ancient law. This ancient concept of ostracization, known in the Brehon laws as *dibert*, survives in modern Irish as *sligdhíbirt*, the word for ostracization meaning, literally, the way of banishment. '*Ar díbirt ort!*' would be a blunt way of telling one to 'get lost!' It was, of course, the Irish who gave the word 'boycott' to the English language as descriptive of an effective means of ostracization. In 1880 Captain Charles Cunningham Boycott (1832–1897) was an English agent for the estates of the Earl of Erne, at Lough Mask in Co. Mayo. He had become symbolic of the colonial English landowners and their agents who, just twenty-five years before had, due to insensitive policies and uncaring greed, let an artificially induced famine spread through Ireland causing a loss to its population in real terms of two-and-a-half millions between 1844–48. The Irish Land League, rejecting violence as a way of dealing with men like Boycott, decided to use the ancient Irish *dibert* or ostracization as a new social and political weapon. The word 'boycott' soon entered the English language following the success of the weapon.

In the fifth century AD, Roman Law, which, by virtue of its spread by means of the Roman Empire, became the basis of Western Law, was revised to take in the new Christian concepts. It was inevitable that the Brehon Law should also be revised when the country became Christian. This was done, as we have seen, by Laoghaire of Tara, who appointed his commission of nine eminent persons to study, revise and commit the laws to writing. It is a popular myth that it was St Patrick who ordered the laws to be codified. While Patrick is named as one of the three Christian advisers on the committee, with Benignus and Cáirnech, he had no authority to call for a codification of the laws. Three Brehons, Dubhtach Maccu Lugir, Rossa and Fergus are named as the legal advisers on the committee and Dubhtach is referred to in other sources as Laoghaire's Chief Druid. Laoghaire himself sat on the committee with Dara, king of Ulster and Corc, the king of Munster.

When the civil law of Ireland was codified into the *Senchus Mór* the law applied to all Ireland and was called the *Cáin Law* to distinguish it from the *Urradus Law* which was local law applying only to the province where it was in force. The criminal law of Ireland was set down afterwards in the *Book of Acaill*. Even in the fifth century the 'law' language, called the *Bérla Féini*, was already archaic and shows just how old the Brehon system was at that time. The codification produced no new laws but was made up of those already in use with the addition of Scriptural or Canon law. The introduction of the *Senchus Mór* says:

What did not clash with the word of God in the written Law and in the New Testament, and with the consciences of the believers, was confirmed in the laws of the Brehons by Patrick and by the ecclesiastics and the chieftains of Erin; and this is the *Senchus Mór*.

Both these law codes survive in their completest form in the *Leabhar na hUidre* (Book of the Dun Cow) dating from the eleventh and twelfth centuries.

The Brehon system is unique and what makes it one of the most fascinating ancient law codes in world jurisprudence is that the basis of the system was compensation for the victim or victim's family, not merely vengeance on the perpetrator. Compensation was more important and the provision of compensation by the transgressor was seen as punishment enough. The culprit or his family had to contribute to the society they had wronged.

The Brehon code survived in Ireland, in spite of regular attempts to suppress it by the English after the conquest, down to the seventeenth century. This is not to say that the laws remained in a static or ossified condition. As we have seem from the references to the Féis of Tara and that of Druim Ceatt, meetings were regularly held among the leading representatives of the country to discuss and agree new laws when the need for their enactment arose. At the end of the sixteenth century the English poet Edmund Spenser, one of the earliest English colonists in Munster, wrote in disgust that the Brehon system prevailed virtually undisturbed and that many English colonists in Ireland were turning to it for judgement rather than the imported English law. It was the English Attorney General of Ireland, under James I, Sir John Davies, who was the principal agent in bringing about the suppression of this unique legal system. According to Davies:

> There is no nation of people under the sun that doth love equal and indifferent justice better than the Irish, or will rest better satisfied with the execution thereof, although it be against themselves, as they may have protection and benefit of the law when upon just cause they do desire it.

But having made this observation, Sir John determined that the law the Irish should be made to 'love' must not be their own but that of their conquerors. He went on to denounce the Irish law in general, and the land laws in particular, being so different from the English system and therefore, according to him, absolutely barbarous. A programme to stamp out all traces of the Brehon system was commenced. According to the Master of the Court of Wards, Sir William

Parsons: 'We must change their (the Irish) course of government, apparel, manner of holding land, language and habit of life. It will otherwise be impossible to set up in them obedience to the laws and to the English empire.'

By the end of the seventeenth century, the Brehon system had almost been erased. By the end of the eighteenth century and certainly early nineteenth century, the general population in Ireland had become unaware that a written native law system had ever existed. Yet law manuscripts were preserved in spite of the punishments and persecutions of those found hiding them. Dr W.K. O'Sullivan, who edited and wrote the introduction to Eugene O'Curry's *On the Manners and Customs of the Ancient Irish* (1873) stated:

> During the first part of the eighteenth century the possession of an Irish book made the owner a suspect person, and was often the cause of his ruin. In some parts of the country the tradition of the danger incurred by having Irish manuscripts lived down to within my own memory; and I have seen Irish manuscripts which had been buried until the writing had almost faded, and the margins rotted away, to avoid the danger their discovery would entail at the visit of the local yeomanry.

But the Irish books and manuscripts did survive in spite of systematic burnings, burials and drownings. Ironically, many law books lay forgotten in public libraries and in private collections owned by the Anglo-Irish aristocracy.

Charles Graves (1812–1899), the grandfather of the famous poet Robert Graves, began a study of the Irish law system. Graves was a Dubliner, a graduate of Trinity College, and a Professor of Mathematics who became Anglican bishop of Limerick, Ardfert and Aghadoe. An expert on Ogham, he also became President of the Royal Irish Academy in 1860. It was in February 1852 that Graves petitioned the London Government to establish a commission to edit and translate the Brehon laws. He was supported in this by James Henthorn Todd (1805–1869), the founder of the Irish Archaeological Society and Regius Professor of Hebrew at Trinity. Surprisingly, the Government of the day appointed a Royal Commission on 11 November 1852, to direct, superintend and carry into effect the transcription, translation and publication of the *Ancient Laws and Institutes of Ireland*. Six volumes were published between 1865 and 1901.

Within Irish law we find more support for the Indo-European hypothesis and astonishingly close links between the Brehon system and the *Manavadharmasastra*, the Hindu Laws of Manu. Dillon and Chadwick also point out that the metres of the *Rigveda* are to be seen in the cadences of the Irish law, 'thus confirming the antiquity of Celtic tradition, and the common heritage of the Druid and Brahmin'. We have already mentioned some of the similarities.

The Welsh law system was codified at a much later period than that of the Irish. During the reign of Hywel Dda (910–950 AD), the Welsh ruler is said to have called upon his chief legal adviser, Blegywyrd ab Einon, Archdeacon of Llandaf, a man reputed to be of great learning and experience in the area of native Welsh law. Hywel wanted the laws that already existed to be set down in writing. The prefatory remarks to most of the law books agree in this essential, that Blegywyrd summoned an assembly of bishops and scholars, with six men from each of the local sub-divisions of the country (presumably elected civic leaders), to examine and discuss the laws for a period of forty days. Their recommendations were thus set down into a single code which applied to the entire Welsh kingdom. The majority of surviving Welsh law books date between AD 1200 and 1500. But, although Wales saw the reemergence of an independence state under Owain Glyn Dŵr for a brief decade at the start of the fifteenth century, the Welsh had been conquered by England at the end of the thirteenth century and the Acts of Annexation, later called 'Union', in 1536 and 1542, effectively suppressed the native law system. It was in 1841 that, ironically in view of the subject matter, the *English* Records Commission published a two volume study of the *Ancient Laws and Institutes of Wales*, edited and translated by Aneurin Owen.

Both legal systems point to a common Celtic root, although the Welsh system, because of the greater influence of Roman Law and later Roman Christianity, does not have the same amount of comparative references leading one to an Indo-European tradition as displayed in Irish law.

This is not the place to discuss the laws in detail. That would be the subject of a book in itself. But the point being made in this section is that the native Celtic tradition underscores the brief references of Classical writers which imply the existence of a sophisticated legal system among the ancient Celts whose administrators were, in those pre-Christian times, the Druids.

Druids as Historians

It perhaps goes without saying that the Druids, as the intellectual caste, were also the source of all the wit and wisdom, the poetry and literary endeavour and the history, genealogy and custom of the Celtic people. Some Classical writers seem to have separated the bards as a distinct group from the Druids but, as we have argued, this was not so. It is, however, from Timagenes that we first have a direct reference to the rôle of the Druids as the historians of the Celts. As previously mentioned, Timagenes was an Alexandrian, living circa the mid first century BC. He collected many traditions relating to the Celts and is cited as an authority on the Druids by both Diodorus Siculus and Ammianus Marcellinus. Not only does Timagenes say that the Druids were the authorities on Celtic history but he relates one of their teachings on the origin of the Celts which, as I have said previously, is not at odds with any modern view, archaeologically or historically, on early Celtic history.

Tacitus is able to tell us that in AD 69 the Druidic historians of Gaul had kept a knowledge of how the Cisalpine Gauls, led by Brennos, had, in c.390–387 BC, defeated the Roman army and sacked Rome, capturing the city but with the notable exception of the Capitoline Hill. Three hundred years after this event, the Druids of Gaul appear to be lamenting that their ancestors had not finished off the job instead of accepting payment of a tribute and withdrawing to leave the Romans to rebuild their city and create the empire which was now swallowing their civilization. For such detailed knowledge as this to have been handed down in oral form is fascinating but not surprising.

In Irish mythology, the Druids are clearly represented as the authorities to turn to for information and advice in respect of history and genealogy.

It is to the Roman historian Livy that we can turn to pick up some of the earliest Celtic historical traditions. This is because Livy

(59 BC–AD 17) came from a family who had colonized the Celtic areas of Cisalpine Gaul following the Roman conquest. He was born at Patavium (Padua) and grew up when Celtic was still the spoken language of the area. Doubtless, he encountered some of the traditional historians, our elusive Druid historians, and noted down some of their stories. In fact, it is accepted that one of Livy's sources was a Celt who was then writing in Latin and making no secret of his Celtic origin – this was Cornelius Nepos (c.100–25 BC) who boasted that his Celtic ancestors had been established in the Po Valley long before the capture of the Veii (396 BC). He was a member of the Insubre tribe and wrote a universal history, *Chronica*. In fact Nepos was only one of many Celts from Cisalpine Gaul who were making a name for themselves by writing in Latin, as I have already shown in *The Celtic Empire*. Today, we mistakenly think of them as Roman writers; poets like Catullus and historians like Trogus Pompeius (27 BC–AD 14), a Vocontii Celt from Transalpine Gaul, who wrote a universal history in forty-four books. Were these Celtic writers in Latin heirs to the Druidic traditions? I would argue, almost certainly.

There is no question that Livy was using Celtic traditions when he recorded the reasons for their early expansion into Cisalpine Gaul. He recounts that there was an excess population in Gaul so the king of the Bituriges ('kings of the world'), Ambicatos ('he who gives battle everywhere') ordered his nephews to take certain tribes and seek out new lands to settle. His nephew Sigovensos ('he who can conquer') went to what is now the central German plains while his nephew Bellovesos ('he who can kill') took his followers to northern Italy.

Much more research in this area needs to be done to see what other Celtic traditions can be observed in the Latin writings of the Cisalpine Gaulish *literati*. What is fascinating about Livy's history is that Camille Jullian has argued that it consists almost entirely of Celtic epics rather than Roman traditions. Livy mentions an extraordinary episode which he ascribes to a campaign by the Romans against the Celts in 345 BC, which is remarkably similar to an episode in the Irish epic the *Táin Bó Cuailnge*.

The form of old Irish sagas and epics was of prose narrative with verse used for dialogue. Professor Dillon points out: 'This prose-and-verse form is also the oldest Indian narrative form, and in Sanskrit we have examples which show how heroic epic grew out of a verse dialogue with the story left to the creative memory of the reciter, through a prose tale with dialogue in verse, into the verse epic of ancient India and Homer's *Iliad*.' That the form was also found in ancient Celtic tradition is confirmed, says Dillon, 'from the explanation put forward by Sir Ifor Williams of the *englynion* in the Welsh *Red Book of Hergest*. He says that those verse dialogues between Llywarch Hen and his sons, Gwen and Maen, belong to lost sagas, of which (I suggest) the prose part was perhaps never written down, but preserved only by oral tradition.'

By the time the Irish laws were codified, history was the prerogative of specially trained men and women. The *Senchus Mór* states that the historian or *ollamh* has to be specially learned in chronology, synchronism, antiquities and genealogy. He or she had to know at least 350 historical and romance tales by heart and be able to recite them word perfect at a moment's notice. They had to know the prerogatives, rights, duties, restrictions and tributes not only of the High King but all the provincial and petty kings. Indeed, the *Leabhar na gCeart* (Book of Rights) states: 'The learned historian who does not know the prerogatives and prohibitions of these kings, is not entitled to visitations or to sell his compositions.'

By this time, the profession had become one for men rather than women. Henri Hubert speaks of the Christian 'process of depriving woman of her powers which everywhere accompanied her loss of the privilege of conveying descent'.

The title of the male historian now became *seanchaí*, which in modern Irish still means a custodian of tradition, an historian and reciter of ancient lore, as well as a traditional story-teller. Each chieftain employed a *seanchaí* to keep his family genealogy, which became written from the start of the Christian period. Most of these pedigrees and family histories were scrupulously kept until the devastating English conquests of the seventeenth century when the native intelligentsia of Ireland and the ruling families were destroyed or driven into exile in Europe. Most of the written records were also destroyed although a few have survived. For example, the family pedigree of the MacCarthy Mór, descendants of the Eoghanacht kings of Munster, survived their exile in France which began with the Williamite conquest in 1691. They had their titles recognized by the French state, which accorded them titles as Duc de Clancarthy and Comte

MacCarthy Reagh de Toulouse. The current MacCarthy Mór is recognised by *Debretts* as having one of Europe's oldest verifiable pedigrees stretching back as 51st generation in unbroken male line descent from King Eoghan Mór (d. AD 192).

An interesting parallel emerges here in that we find in Hindu society a class of poets emerging called *sutas* or court poets who also acted as charioteers for the warriors. The charioteer in Hindu tradition was the intimate friend of the warrior and we find just such a relationship in Irish sagas, the best known being that of Cúchulainn and Loeg Mac Riangabra. In Irish saga, charioteers extolled the prowess of their warriors. The *Satapatha Brahmana* says that on the evening of the first day of the horse sacrifice the poets had to chant a praise poem in honour of the king or his warriors, usually praising his genealogy and deeds. Professor Dillon points out that praise poetry is found in the *Rigveda* termed *narasami*, 'praise of the warrior', and such praise poems are found in Irish sources, several in praise of Labraid Loingsech, the warrior ancestor of the Lagin (of Leinster). He points to a long poem of a kind known as *fursundud* (illumination) which traces a genealogy back to Adam. There are praise-poem genealogies surviving for the Eoghanacht kings of Munster. According to Professor Dillon:

> I suggest that these oldest Irish poems are true *narasasyah* (they date from a time before the classical Irish metres had developed, some of them before the use of rhyme), and that they were sung at the king's consecration, and on so solemn an occasion as the holding of the Feast of Tara by the High King.

Dillon recalls that when Joseph Vendryès gave a lecture to the French Academy in 1932 on 'The Courtly Poetry of Ireland and Wales', Sylvain Lévi, one of the great Sanskrit experts, was in the audience. He was so excited by Vendryès' lecture that he wrote him a letter (printed in *Revue Celtique*, Vol. L) saying that the Celtic poems were 'almost a chapter of the history of India under another name'.

One of the last in the tradition of the native Irish genealogists and historians was Dubhaltach Mac Firbisigh (1585–1670) whose family were chroniclers to the Ó Dubhda (O'Dowd) chieftains of Sligo. He compiled his famous *Genealogies of the Families of Ireland* in about 1650 but when Galway fell to Cromwell's soldiers, he fled to Dublin where he sought the protection of Sir James Ware. Sir James commissioned him to make translations into English of some ancient Irish annals. On Sir James' death, Mac Firbisigh was destitute and a refugee again. Travelling on the road between Sligo and Dublin he was killed by an English soldier.

Another famous Irish historian killed in the Cromwellian conquest was Seathrún Céitinn (c.1570–c.1649) whose principal work was *Foras Feasa ar Éirinn* (written in about 1629/31). Céitinn's work is very valuable in that he uses source books which were destroyed during the Cromwellian devastations. One passage is of particular interest for he describes, from a far earlier source, how the historians took on a rôle which we could identify today as that of proto war-correspondents:

> Every captain bore upon his standard his peculiar device or ensign, so that each distinct body of men could be easily distinguished from all others by those *seanchaí* whose duty it was to attend on the chieftains when about to contend in battle, and that these *seanchaí* might then have a full view of the achievement of the combatants, so as to be able to give a true account of their particular deeds of valour.

One would have little hesitation in accepting that this sort of practice could well have happened among the pre-Christian Celts.

In spite of the destructions of the English conquests, many Irish annals and chronicles survived, though anyone with sensitivity must shudder at the wealth that was destroyed. The value of that which has been lost can be judged against those works which, despite all odds, have survived. Scholars have reflected on the accuracy of the Irish annals. How can we be so sure that these ancient annals are accurate when there is so little in the way of corroborative comment on internal Irish affairs from foreign sources?

Dr Douglas Hyde, in his *Literary History of Ireland*, has stated:

> But despite the silence upon Irish affairs of ancient foreign writers, we have luckily another class of proof of the highest possible value, brought to light by the discoveries of modern science, and powerfully strengthening the credibility of our annals. This is nothing less than the record of natural phenomena. If we find, on calculating

backwards, as modern science has enabled us to do, that such events as the appearance of comets or the occurrence of eclipses are recorded to the day and hour by the annalists, we can know with something like certainty that these phenomena were recorded at the time of their appearance by writers who observed them, whose writings must have been actually consulted and seen by those later annalists, whose books we now possess. Nobody could think of saying of natural phenomena thus accurately recorded, as they might of mere historical narratives, that they were handed down by tradition only, and reduced to writing for the first time many centuries later. Now it so happens that the *Annals of Ulster*, annals which treat of Ireland and Irish history from about the year 444, but of which the written copy dates only from the fifteenth century, contain from the year 496 to 884, as many as 18 records of eclipses and comets which agree exactly even to the day and hour with the calculations of modern astronomers. How impossible it is to keep such records unless written memoranda are made of them by eye-witnesses, is shown by the fact that Bede, born himself in 675, in recording the great solar eclipse which took place only eleven years before his own birth is yet two days astray in his date; while, on the other hand, the Ulster annals give not only the correct day but the correct hour – thus showing that Cathal Maguire, their compiler, had access either to the original or to a copy of the original account of an eye witness.

We can say, with certainty, that the old oral records of the Irish Druids, relating to Irish history, were being transmitted into written form by the fifth century AD, although, as we have discussed in our examination of Druidic books, there is also good reason to believe in literacy before this period. However, the first name of an Irish historian which has survived to us is that of Sinlán Moccu Min (d. AD 607) who was abbot of the monastery at Bangor, which became one of the great Irish centres of education and where many European princes were sent for their learning, including some Anglo-Saxon princes and scions of wealthy families.

Sinlán had a copy of the *Chronikon* of Eusebius (*c.*AD 260–*c.*340), a bishop of Caesarea in Palestine. Eusebius's *Ecclesiastical History* had already earned him the title of the 'father of Church history'. The *Chronikon*, in two books, was an outline of world history, or rather the world as Eusebius knew it. It contained synchronical tables and lists of rulers to his own times. The original Greek text exists only in fragments but a Latin adaptation by St Jerome (c.AD 342–420) is the source that is regarded as important to any study of ancient history.

Sinlán made a copy of Eusebius' *Chronikon* but, and importantly, he made a parallel text chronicling Irish events from earliest times and dating them up to his own times. By this ancient record, Sinlán made the first known attempt of an Irish historian to fit Irish events into the framework of a universal chronology. Dr Eoin MacNeill has been inclined to make little of the work of Sinlán, presumably because it was espoused by his academic rival, Dr Joyce.

The same wealth of historic material has, alas, not survived in other Celtic literatures, although a tradition of historians does emerge in Wales. While Gildas (c.AD 500–d. c.570) wrote a first hand account of the devastations of the Anglo-Saxons in *De excidio et conquestu Britanniae* (Concerning the Ruin and Conquest of Britain) it is only history in retrospect. The first Welsh historian emerges as Nennius (fl. c.800) who appears to have been a disciple of Elfoddw, a bishop of Gwynedd who died in AD 809. Nennius wrote his Latin *Historia Brittonum* which is a primary source for British Celtic history. Individual scraps, pieces from the lives of saints, lead to the *Annales Cambriae* (c.AD 955), a Latin history of the British Celts, and to the thirteenth century compilation *Brut y Tywysogion* (Chronicle of the Princes). Also, in this tradition, mention must be made of Geoffrey of Monmouth (c.AD 1100–c. 1155) whose Latin *Historia regum Britanniae* (History of the Kings of Britain) has been, at one and the same time, both controversial and of considerable influence. Geoffrey claimed that he was no more than a translator of this work from a British Celtic language into Latin:

> Walter, Archdeacon of Oxford, a man skilled in the art of public speaking and well informed about the history of foreign countries, presented me with a certain very ancient book written in the British language. The book, attractively composed to form a consecutive and orderly narrative, set out all the deeds of these men, from Brutus, the first king of the Britons, down to Cadwallader the son of Cadwallo. At Walter's request I have taken the trouble to translate the book into Latin . . .

This has been dismissed as an outright lie by modern scholars because they cannot find a Welsh composition which could reasonably be looked upon as the original or groundwork to Geoffrey's history. This presupposes that any such Welsh book survived the ravages of both the ages and of the English. But Geoffrey speaks of 'the British language', which of course encompasses Cornish and Breton as well as Welsh. A copy of a poem in Latin hexameters by John of Cornwall dated 8 October 1474 survives in the Vatican library. John actually lived in the twelfth century and, from the manuscript, it is obvious that he was translating from an older Cornish work. In proof, the manuscript still carries glosses from Old Cornish, whose form has been dated to the tenth century, and the section bears a more than passing resemblance to 'The Prophecies of Merlin' section of Geoffrey's work. Indeed, the poem itself is called 'The Prophecy of Merlin'.

One episode in the fabulous and epic *Historia regum Britanniae* leaps out at the reader. Tacitus had referred to the Gaulish Druids' tradition in AD 69 of the history of the Celtic sack of Rome *c.*390/387 BC, led by the chieftain Brennos. In Geoffrey's text the sons of Dunwallo Molmutius are called Belinus and Brennius. They argue about the succession to the kingship of Britain. Belinus becomes king of Britain. The brothers are then eventually reconciled. Rome threatens the peace and Brennius marches an army to Rome, besieges it and plunders the city. The tradition corresponds with history, not, of course, in specifics but in basics. We are also told by Geoffrey that Brennius led an army of Senonian Gauls. The Senones were not a British Celtic tribe. So it is fascinating to notice that the Senones, a major Cisalpine Gaulish tribe, did take part in the historical sack of the city. The territory of the Senones was situated just north of Ancona, their capital being Senigallia (Senones Gallia or Gaul). After Rome's fall Brennius is said to have settled in Italy, that is there is no tradition of him after the fall of Rome. The bare facts are, in essence, correct. As with most mythologies, there are some recognizable facts in the traditions of the *Historia regum Britanniae*, and doubtless they were the result of centuries of Druidic oral historical tradition.

But what is particularly interesting about the basic facts of the sack of Rome by the Celts in the fourth century BC surviving in both the traditions of the Gaulish Celts of the first century AD and in the traditions of the British Celts of the twelfth century AD, is the very fact of their survival. The Celts who sacked Rome were Cisalpine Gauls, yet the historic traditions had not only made their way into Transalpine Gaul but into Celtic Britain and become inseparably linked with the histories of those disparate Celtic peoples. Here, surely, is another demonstration of how closely the Celtic world was united by the common bonds which the Druids, as a class, represented.

Druids as Poets and Musicians

Classical writers frequently remark on the Celtic love of poetry and music. Diodorus Siculus and Athenaeus, quoting Poseidonius, point to a class of professional minstrels. Diodorus says: 'They have also lyric poets whom they call bards. They sing to the accompaniment of instruments resembling lyres, sometimes a eulogy and sometimes a satire.' Now the Classic sources differentiate bard from Druid, although the native Celtic sources often do not make that distinction. Druids, as we have noted, in later Welsh literature were regarded as poets and musicians. Once again we return to our main contention that the Druids were an intellectual caste and therefore some of them undertook the rôle of poets and musicians, as demonstrated in insular Celtic sources.

We have, in the preceding chapters, dealt with some aspects of poetry which were, as records show, sung rather than recited. Athenaeus, quoting Poseidonius, shows just how quick-witted, and able to compose in an *extempore* manner, poets had to be. The reference is to a feast given by a Gaulish chieftain named Louernius (the fox).

> A Celtic poet who arrived too late met Louernius and composed a song magnifying his greatness and lamenting his own late arrival. Louernius was very pleased and asked for a bag of gold and threw it to the poet who ran beside his chariot. The poet picked it up and sang another song saying that the very tracks made by his chariot on the earth gave gold and largess to mankind.

It would be difficult to indulge in an examination of early Irish and Welsh poetry in a work strictly limited to Druids. However, one cannot pass over the subject without some reference to the fascinating evidence of epigrams used by early Celtic Christian poets which indicate that they were the inheritors of an early and ancient tradition of teaching by this method.

There is certainly some argument for imagining Zen Master perceptions in some of the writings of these Celtic Christians who had inherited such traditions from the Druids. Some verses would not be out of place in a volume of Zen poetry.

Siadhal Mac Feradach, known by his Latin appellation of Sedulius Scottus (c.AD 820–c.AD 880) was a remarkable Irish poet of whom it has been said that his voice echoes across the centuries as intensely human. Irish marginalia on a Greek text in the Royal Library of Dresden have been identified as being the work of Siadhal by Professor Ludwig Traube in his study *Sedulius Scottus* (Munich, 1906):

> *Téicht do Róim*
> *múr saído bec tobai;*
> *in rí con-daigi i fus*
> *maini mbera latt ni foghai.*

Frank O'Connor, who also believed the author was Siadhal Mac Feradach, translated the verse as follows:

> To go to Rome –
> Is little profit, endless pain;
> The Master that you see in Rome,
> You find at home, or seek in vain.

Professor James Carney agreed with Frank O'Connor that the quatrain 'may well have been composed by Sedulius'. He adds: 'Save for his priesthood and his humility, he falls very well into the pattern of the Irish bardic or court poet, successor to the Druid, and a constant element in Irish life from remote times until the seventeenth century.'

Another O'Connor translation from a ninth century AD Irish poem underscores this ancient form of almost *haiku* teaching which is called *Deibhidh*:

> Sad to see the sons of learning

> In everlasting hell-fire burning
> While he that never read a line
> Doth in eternal glory shine.

Professor Kuno Meyer translated a tenth century Irish poem in this form:

> Avoiding death
> takes too much time, and too much care,
> when at the very end of all,
> Death catches each one unaware.

This form of epigram poetry, or *Deibhidh* metre, also survived in Welsh, more specifically as the *englynion* as shown in these four-teenth century examples:

> No need for jealousy
> Because another likes me.
> Winds may shake a twig
> Only an axe disturbs the tree root.

And:

> No traitor, the salmon.
> He returns to his home.
> When you're tired of searching there
> You'll find the answer here.

Anthony Conran, in *The Penguin Book of Welsh Verse* (1967) commented that the *englynion* was fiendishly hard to translate into English. 'Without its articulation of rhyme and *cynghanedd* (too delicate a tracery to stand the equi-distancing tension of English stresses) its poetry usually evaporates.' Conran also saw the parallel between the *englynion* and the Japanese *haiku* form. The *haiku* consists of seventeen syllables while the *englynion* consists of thirty. The Irish have an equivalent of the *cynghanedd* in the *dán dírech*, a metrical system of multiple alliteration and rhyme within every line of the strict metre. Professor Carney believed that this form was an essential tradition of 'Druidic' teaching through verse.

Classical writers noted the Celtic use of lyres, drums, pipes and other instruments. On Celtic pottery dating back to the seventh century BC various instruments have been depicted, including a stringed instrument looking like a lyre. Trumpets were also in evidence and a magnificent example of one of them, a bronze trumpet, was found near Navan, Co.Armagh, which is now in the National Museum, Dublin. Both Greek and Roman observers also point out that vocal music was highly popular, as well as dancing. We find that the insular Celts held regular contests in music and poetry and there is no reason not to presume that such contests also occurred among the Continental Celts. Dancing figures can be observed on Celtic pottery dating back to the seventh century BC. Bronze dancing figures have been found at Neuvy-en-Sullias, in France.

Celtic mythology abounds with references to music and musicians and descriptions of the Otherworld are replete with such references. When Bran Mac Febal is tempted by a goddess into joining her in the Otherworld, she says: 'There is nothing rough nor harsh but only sweet music striking the ear'. A warrior comes to Cormac at Tara bearing a branch with three golden apples. When the branch is shaken it makes a sweet music which allows the wounded to fall peacefully asleep. The Dagda had a harpist whose music could cause people to laugh, weep or fall peacefully asleep. In the *Táin Bó Cuailnge* we have references to the harpers of Caínbile from *aes Ruaidh* who are described as 'men of great knowledge and prophecy and magic'.

What do we know of ancient Celtic music? Ireland again seems to have the oldest music records. But the oldest musical notation manuscripts only seem to survive with the Drummond Missal of the eleventh century AD and a twelfth century treatise on music which gives some philosophical approach to the subject. Irish music had already generally undergone several changes by the time we have notation records. According to Professor Aloys Fleischmann, in *Music in Ireland* (1952), a Gaulish ecclesiastical chant had been introduced in Ireland after the fifth century AD and the Roman chant had been introduced in the twelfth century with the Anglo-Norman invasion. So can anything remotely pre-Christian in musicological terms be observed in Ireland? Certainly as 'Western' music gradually evolved during the early medieval period under Latin Church influence, in Ireland, the cultural clash between native Celt and alien conqueror combined to deny this music a normal course of development so that Ireland did cling to many ancient forms of music, retaining also its pentatonic scale.

The Irish music critic, Fanny Feehan, believes that the *sean nós* form of singing which has survived, mainly in Conamara, has affinities with Indian music. In a paper entitled 'Suggested Links Between Eastern and Celtic Music' (1981), she recorded:

> In the area of vocal ornamentation East and West come close. I once played a Claddagh recording of Máire Aine (Ní Dhonnacha) singing 'Bárr an tSléibhe' for an Indian Professor of music who refused to believe, until I showed her the sleeve of the record, that it was an Irish song. She claimed, and demonstrated by singing to me, that the song bore a strange resemblance to an Indian (North) raga about a young girl being lured towards a mountain. The Professor was interested in the mode, the pitching of the voice, and certain notes which were characteristic of both the raga and 'Barr an tSléibhe'.

For the current writer this passage was reminiscent of a discussion back in 1970 with the Greek composer Christos Pittas, who played for the author a recording of a piece of Thracian folk music without explaining what it was. The author identified it as a piece of Conamara *sean nós* music, although identifying certain sounds that were not 'quite right'. The author was dumbfounded to learn of its real origins.

One remembers that the Irish composer Seán Ó Riada, (1931–1971), after studying serial music in Paris, returned to his native Ireland and began to rescue vestiges of the original folk music of Ireland which was then disintegrating into a form of Anglo-Irish balladry. According to Christos Pittas (in *Hibernia*, 4 February 1971):

> What Ó Riada achieved is the revelation of a living cultural tradition which, to most Europeans, was undiscovered and unknown. Some philosophers have tended to judge societies and countries by their musical traditions, and that Ireland has such a music, with such personality and depth, is indicative of a great culture.

One of the most ancient forms of Celtic music which still survives is the *marbhnaí* or 'death song', sometimes called the *caoine* (keening). Fanny Feehan noted that the *Marbhna Luimni*, said to be composed about 1635, was approaching the raga style of India and revolving around three or four notes. The comparison to the Indian raga is made time and again as well as comparison to the basic concept of jazz. There is a theme and then there is improvisation around the theme. The tune is never played exactly the same way twice no matter how well the player might know it. Both Irish and Indian audiences could not anticipate it but would know each small deviation from the main theme.

As the keepers of the intellectual and therefore artistic soul of the Celts, the bardic group of Druids developed a musical culture with forms stretching back millennia towards the hypothesized Indo-European root, which still today shows striking parallels with Hindu musical culture.

Druids as Physicians

Pliny was the first Classical writer to dwell on the Druids' reputation for medical knowledge. He speaks of eminent physicians in Gaul in the half century before the Roman conquest and suppression of the Druids. He says that they had such excellent reputations that many went to study with them. He lists the famous Crinias of Marseilles and Charmis from the same city. Astrology and medicine were combined in their art and Charmis made a fortune using this method of diagnosis.

James J. Tierney, the Latin scholar who edited the work of the Irish geographer, Dicuil (1967) has asserted: 'There can be little doubt that the medico-magical side of the Druids so prominent in Pliny's *Natural History* is the real historical basis of their power and influence, and that the rest is a mere ideological superstructure.'

That Celtic society was well advanced in medical practices was brought home to the current author when he was a boy visiting Brighton Museum, Sussex. One of the prize exhibits was what was called 'The Ovingdean Trephined Skull'. It was found in January, 1935, off the coast of Ovingdean, by a fisherman who trawled it in his nets. The skull had two large round holes deliberately cut into it over the brain. It was dated to the pre-Christian Celtic period. What is remarkable is that although the ancient surgeons had cut into this person's skull on two separate occasions, the healing of the bone around both holes indicated that the patient lived but eventually died of sepsis some weeks after the second operation. Similar skulls have been discovered in France. To perform a trephining operation with the patient surviving indicates an advanced degree of medical knowledge and is in keeping with what Pliny has to say of the 'genus vatum medicorumque' of Gaul.

Trephining is even acknowledged in ancient Irish records for we find it recorded, at the Battle of Magh Rath or Moira in AD 637, that a young Irish chieftain named Cennfaelad had his skull fractured by a sword blow. He was taken to the medical school of Tomregan and had the injured portion of the skull and a portion of his brain removed. On his recovery, it is said his wits were sharpened and he became a great scholar and the author of *Uraicept na n-eces* (Primer of Poets), a work still existing in copied form. Certain legal commentaries on the *Book of Acaill* are also ascribed to Cennfaelad who is credited with founding the famous bardic college at Derryloran, Co. Tyrone.

Druids appear as healers in many Irish and Welsh tales. And in the sagas we find both male and female physicians. Dian Cécht is the Irish god of medicine. And in the Brehon law tracts relating to medicine are 'The Judgments of Dian Cécht', which Professor Binchley dates stylistically as early as the sixth century AD. Thus even into the early Christian period the old pagan Irish god of medicine was invoked as a legal medical authority. Dian Cécht gave Nuada a silver hand after he had lost his real one in the first battle of Magh Tuireadh. But Dian Cécht's son Miach proved a better physician and gave Nuada a hand of flesh and blood. Among the stories we find Miach even doing an eye transplant. Dian Cécht slew his son in a fit of jealousy. Moreover, we find that Miach's sister Airmid, who helped guard the secret 'Well of Healing', was equally renowned for her prowess as a physician. She is credited with identifying the 365 herbs of healing. Bebinn and Modarn's daughter, Binn, appear as famous female physicians in other stories.

The Druidic physicians appear in native sources as being skilled with herbs as well as surgery and among their operations they perform Caesarean sections, amputations and brain surgery. In Irish mythology both Goll Mac Morna and Furbaide are born as the result of Caesarean operations.

We are told that a whole medical corps accompanied the army of Conchobhar Mac Nessa during the *Táin* wars under the direction of Fingín Fáithliaig. Each doctor had a bag full of medications called a *lés*. Another semi-legendary tale has a Munster chieftain named Tadhg Mac Cian wounded at the Battle of Crinna in AD 226. He is cured by a skillful Druidic physician who is also called Fingín Fáithliaig. Perhaps there is a confusion of the name. However, it may be significant that *fáithliaig* is a compound of *fáith*, a seer, and *liaig*, a leech, as in the English term for a doctor. The term is often used for a Druidic doctor in the ancient texts.

In pre-Christian times in most European societies, even those of Greece and Rome, little provision was made for the treatment of the ailing poor. The sick, feeble and elderly were often put to death as the ultimate remedy for their ills. These societies regarded disease as a curse inflicted by supernatural powers and sought to propitiate the malevolent deities rather than organize relief work. The Greeks, of course, did have an advanced medical knowledge. Hippocrates (*c*.460 BC – *c*.370 BC) of Cos is still remembered in modern medicine for the 'Hippocratic Oath' but nothing is known of his life and of the origin of the sixty medical treatises compiled between *c*.430 BC and 330 BC known as the *Hippocratic Corpus*, there is no evidence that Hippocrates wrote them. Alexandria became a leading medical centre in the third century BC at which Herophilus made use of drugs, and Erasitratus was not far from understanding the conception of blood circulation which was finally elucidated by William Harvey in 1628. And the works of Galen of Pergamum (AD 129–99) have formed the basis of most European medical lore with his name becoming the standard for medical perfection. Nevertheless, there was no system of medicine and health care in Greece that was, by law, available to all regardless of their position in society. It is now part of European cultural folklore that it was not until the Roman matron St Fabiola (d.*c*.AD 399) set up a hospice for the sick and needy at Porto near Rome that the first hospital in Europe was founded.

Such institutions were, however, already established in India. The *Charaka-Samhita* (Annals of Charake) tell us that Asoka (*c*.273–232 BC), the emperor of India who, sickened by war and the struggle for power, turned to Buddhism and professed non-violence, established the first hospitals for the ailing poor.

The Irish sources refer to the establishment of the first hospital in Ireland by the semi-legendary queen of Ireland, Macha Mong Ruadh (d.c.377 BC). She is said to have established a hospital called Bróin Bherg (the house of sorrow) at Emain Macha (Navan). Legend or not, we know that by the time of the Christian period, there were hospitals all over Ireland, some for sick people with general ailments and others serving specialist needs, such as leper hospitals. And when the law system came to be codified, it showed the existence of an advanced and sophisticated medical system. The existence of such a system was in no small way a result of Druidic ideas which had been noted by Pliny.

During the years of the 'Carolingian Renaissance' in the eighth and ninth centuries AD, Irish medical schools were famous throughout Europe, such as that of Tuaim Brecain (Tomregan, Co. Cavan) founded in the sixth century AD. This medical school was founded by the saintly physician Bracan Mac Findloga, a disciple of St Finian of Clonard. Medical schools are mentioned at Clonmacnoise, Cashel, Portumna, Clonard and Armagh. But these Christian medical schools were, as I say, the direct descendants of the Druidic ones.

Under the Brehon law the provision of sick maintenance, including curative treatment, attendance allowance and nourishing food was made available for everyone who needed it. The *Senchus Mór* states: 'All classes in the territory have the same right under the law of sick maintenance.' Expenses for the treatment of wounded people, those injured unlawfully, were paid out of the fines for injury made against the perpetrators of the deed. Indeed, it is made clear that whoever unjustly inflicted bodily injury on another would have to pay for that person's maintenance either in a hospital or in a private house. The 'Law of Torts' says that 'full sick maintenance (must be paid) to a worker injured for the sake of unnecessary profit . . .' Again one can see that the basic perception is in keeping with the philosophical attitudes of the early Celtic Christian writers such as Fastidius and the 'Sicilian Briton', who were dismissed as 'Pelagians' trying to revive 'Druidic philosophy'. Not only did the Brehon law insist that sick maintenance should be provided but that society should not let the dependants of a sick or injured man lack food or security until he recovered.

The Brehon law makes it clear that only qualified physicians could treat the sick and if 'quack' doctors, unqualified physicians, were founding practising then there were severe penalties. Dr Sophie Bryant in her outstanding work *Liberty, Order and Law under Native Irish Rule* (1923), comments: 'The Irish recognised that it was rather easy to deceive people who were ill and who, desperately seeking a cure, would grasp at any straw to secure it.'

On the other hand, qualified physicians were responsible for the treatment of their patient and should they, through negligence or ignorance, cause a patient's condition to worsen, they were responsible for compensation by law. Each physician undertook by law to maintain four medical students and train them. Dr James J. Walsh has pointed out: 'The provision for nursing in these hospitals is rather interesting because it included, at the same time, the training of the young men for the practice of medicine, and therefore resembled, in certain respects at least, our (modern) system of clinical teaching.' He continued:

> There is nothing in the world, as we have come to realise very well in modern times, equal to a custom of this kind for making practical physicians – that is, giving a good clinical knowledge of medicine: and at the same time there is nothing that is so good for the patients, because a physician is, as it were, on trial before these keen students, who are gradually gaining experience in medicine, and he is consequently obliged to put forth his best efforts to show his skill . . .

Importantly, it was recognized that the physician had to have time away from his practice to study new techniques and knowledge. The local clan had to make such provision for the physician that 'he might be preserved from being disturbed by the cares and anxieties of life and enabled to devote himself to the study and work of his profession'.

Each territory had to maintain a hospital. The law is exact on this. It should have four doors, be placed by a stream of running water, and be maintained free of charge or taxation by the local assembly. The existence of numerous hospitals in ancient Ireland is attested by the names of towns or places, such as An Spidéal (Spiddal, Spital etc.). The laws were very explicit on how these hospitals should be run.

Local physicians and their students would practise at the hospital. A full-time caretaker, or hospital manager in modern parlance, had to be employed who would be responsible for keeping away dogs, mentally sick people (who had their own institutions) or anyone liable to cause the sick and injured distress.

Irish annals contain many references to pestilence and diseases which, as in most early societies, were ascribed to malevolent demons. During the Christian period, Druids, whose rôle was now changed into wizards, were blamed by Christians for creating disease. *Annales Ríoghachta Éireann* (Annals of the Four Masters) states, under the year AD 986: 'Druidical or magical sickness was caused by demons in the east of Ireland which caused mortality of men plainly before people's eyes.' Adomnán in his *Life of Colmcille* also ascribes pestilence to the arrival of demons.

Macldor Ō Tinnri, 'the best physician in Ireland', has his death recorded in AD 860. His name is the first in a whole series of famous Irish Christian physicians in historical times. By the tenth century AD families of physicians are identified. The O'Callanans, O'Cassidys, O'Lees, O'Hickeys (*ichidhe* means 'healer') and O'Shiels, are identified as hereditary physicians. Jan Baptiste, Baron Van Helmont of Vilvoorde (1580–1644), the famous chemist, physiologist and physician, wrote in his *Confessio Authoris* (1648) that in his day Irish physicians were considered far better than any others in Europe because of their knowledge and training:

> These doctors obtain their medical knowledge chiefly from books belonging to particular families left them by their ancestors, in which are written down the symptoms of the several diseases, with the remedies annexed; which remedies are vernacular – the productions of their own country. Accordingly the Irish are better managed in sickness than the Italians, who have a physician in every village.

Typical of these Irish doctors, to whom Van Helmont refers, was his contemporary Niall Ó Glacan (c.1590–1655). He was from Donegal and trained in the old Irish tradition. He went to France in 1628 and was active treating cases of plague in the Clermont-Toulouse area, following which he wrote *Tractatus de Peste*, Toulouse, 1629. He became personal physician to the King of France Louis XIII, and professor of medicine at Toulouse University. After Louis XIII's death he took up an appointment as professor of medicine at Bologna and while there he wrote his famous medical study, *Cursus Medicus*.

Even after the English suppression of Irish medical schools and the destruction of the Irish intelligentsia in Ireland during the seventeenth century, Irish physicians still won fame in many countries in Europe to which they were forced to migrate. One of the most intriguing of these later medical personalities was Barry Edward O'Meara (1786–1836) who became personal physician to Napoleon during his exile on St Helena.

There is a wealth of medical texts which survive in the Irish language. Some of the texts are translations into Irish of works accredited to Hippocrates, and by Galen, Herophilus, Rhazes, Avicenna, Serapion, Dioscorides and others. Cormac Mac Duinnshléibhe (c.1420–1480), whose family were hereditary physicians to the Ó Domhnaill chieftains, was trained abroad in the new schools of 'Arabic' medicine. He translated several of the new texts into Irish. But the great bulk of the surviving texts are native Irish. The oldest surviving medical book in Ireland is dated AD 1352 and is in the Royal Irish Academy. This book is obviously a copy of a far older text. Older medical books exist and are housed in the British Museum. There are four medical tracts in *Leabhar Buidhe Lecain*, or the Yellow Book of Lecan. The majority of such texts date between the fourteenth and sixteenth centuries, such as the books of the O'Hickeys, O'Lees, O'Shiels and the 1512 *Book of Mac Anlega* (son of the doctor). These works constitute the largest collection of medical manuscript literature, prior to 1800, surviving in any one language. It is therefore, in the author's opinion, somewhat scandalous that no attempt has been made to systematically collate, edit and translate this wealth of medical knowledge which undoubtedly would cast a new light on knowledge of ancient Celtic medical practices. And who knows what 'forgotten knowledge' might turn up in these neglected texts?

One things is clear; the ancient Irish physicians had native names for all manner of medical conditions, which attests to a long native tradition of medicine.

It is interesting that the story concerning the *Book of the O'Lees*, compiled in 1443, has a parallel in Welsh myth. The book was said to have been given to O'Lee (the name comes from *liaig* meaning a leech or doctor) by Otherworld entities. In the story of the Meddygon Meddfai, three sons of a mortal male and an Otherworld spirit became the greatest physicians in Wales through her knowledge.

One fascinating exhortation in the *Book of the O'Hickeys*, 1352, is for doctors; 'more especially that they do their duty devotedly in cases where they received no pay on account of the poverty of the patients'. This is certainly in keeping with the perceptions seen in the fascinating system of native Irish laws on medical practice.

Although these great medical textbooks remain neglected, we can still observe treatments mentioned in other Irish sagas. One favourite treatment, which Dian Cécht gave in the second battle of Magh Tuireadh, was that of medicated baths. We find also that the Druid of Eremon of Leinster advized the preparation of a bath into which the milk of 159 white hornless cows was poured. An immersion in this helped heal wounded warriors. Fingin, the Druid physician of Conchobhar Mac Nessa, cured his wounded warriors by baths of medicinal herbs. *Cormac's Glossary* mentions that a medicated bath (*fothrucud*) was most often given for lepers (*doinnlóbru*).

A further development of the medicated bath was the hot-air bath, used in Ireland as a cure for rheumatism until recent years. The structure in which these baths were given was known as a *Tigh 'n alluis* or 'sweating house'. One such ancient structure survives on Inishmurray in Donegal Bay and several have been described in the last century particularly in the north of Ireland. They are small constructions of stone, five to seven feet long. A turf fire was kindled inside until the house was heated like an oven. The fire was removed. The patient, wrapped in a blanket, crept in and sat down on a bench. The door was closed up. The patient remained until in a profuse perspiration and then, on leaving, was plunged in cold water and then rubbed warm. The patient was then encouraged to meditate (*dercad*) to achieve *sitcháin* (a state of peace). It is not beyond the realm of possibility that this act, found in many cultures in the world as a religious action, had similar religious connotations in the Celtic world.

The fame of these baths found its way to the Continent. Professor Henry Hennessy observed in the *Kilkenny Archaeological Journal* for 1885/6: 'It is remarkable that what are called Turkish baths in

Ireland and Great Britain have been designated Roman-Irish baths in Germany and Bohemia. I saw baths designated '*Römische-Irische bäder*' at Prague and Nuremberg in 1879.' Such baths were also seen by Dr William J Walsh, the Archbishop of Dublin (1841–1921) at the turn of the century at Treves, Prague and Metz.

We know of the high degree of surgical skill which was possessed, already discussed earlier on the matter of trephining. We know that Irish surgeons knew how to close up wounds by stitching as in the case of Conchobhar Mac Nessa's head-wound which was sewn with gold thread. Irish physicians carried a stethoscope, a horn called a *gipne* or *gibne*, explained in *Cormac's Glossary* as *adarc lege* (physician's horn). A surgical probe (*fraig*) is also mentioned.

Sleeping draughts were given by Druids (*deoch suain*). Medieval Irish physicians, and their Druid ancestors, had also achieved a reputation outside of Ireland by the seventh century in medicinal botany. A few treatises have been translated on herbs and their medical qualities as applying to various diseases, by Whitley Stokes in *Revue Celtique* (ix, 224), and by Joseph O'Longan, (ms. in the Royal Irish Academy). O'Longan shows that astrological observations, as aids in medical prognosis, were universal among physicians. As well as curative herbs, the use of deadly poisons was also known. Cridenbél, the satirist, was poisoned *tre luib eccineol*, through the herb *eccineol*, not identified but obviously a deadly one. Ailill, the son of Laoghaire Lorc, was poisoned by Cobthacht Coel Breg.

A direct inheritance from Druidic knowledge was use of 'healing stones' which have survived in folklore. Colmcille is said to have used such a stone to work a cure while Martin, in his *Tour of the Western Islands of Scotland* in 1695, found 'healing stones' still commonly used there.

It is possible only to give a glimpse of this knowledge which has come down to us through Irish Celtic sources. The surviving evidence indicates that Pliny the Elder was absolutely correct when he acknowledged the prominence of the Druids as practitioners of medicine.

Druids as Seers

When Dio Chrysostom said that the Druids were 'well versed in the art of seers and prophets' he was simply stating general knowledge of his day. From the earliest Greek and Roman sources it was claimed that the Druids practised auguries, could foretell the future and 'interpret nature'. The reputation of the Druids as seers, prophets, diviners and augurers is confirmed by a Celtic writer of the first century BC. Trogus Pompeius was a Cisalpine Celt from the tribe of the Vocontii, so Justin, who wrote an abridgement of Trogus' *Historiae Philippicae*, informs us. Professor Horst Schmidt, the Celtic philologist, has pointed out that there are a number of Gaulish names commencing with the prefix *trog* and connects them with the Irish *trog/truag* and Welsh *tru* meaning 'miserable'. Trogus wrote in Latin, of course, but of his forty-four books of history only Justin's epitome survives. Trogus states, with some obvious personal pride and authority, 'the Gauls excel all others in the skill of augury'.

The Greeks and Romans wrote much about the methods of the Druids in foretelling the future. In the following section we will be considering their reputation as astronomers and astrologers. Other methods of augury ascribed to the Celts by the Classical writers include, searching for omens in the death throes of human sacrifices, in the entrails of sacrificial animals and in the flight of birds.

Both Strabo and Diodorus Siculus, obviously using the same source, that of Poseidonios, talk of divining from the death throes of human victims. Tacitus says: 'The Druids consult the gods in the palpitating entrails of men'. Indeed, those writers who mention human sacrifice seem to indicate that the purpose of such sacrifices was solely for the purpose of divination rather than propitiating the gods. Caesar also suggests that the Druids believed that they could only gain power over supernatural forces by the sacrifice of a human life. We have already considered this matter in our discussion on Druidic rituals.

Divination by observation of the entrails of sacrificial animals, from the size, shape, colour and markings of the liver and gall bladder was not confined to the Celts but widely practised by the Etruscans and Romans. Known as *haruspices*, these particular diviners had their own college in Rome and the art was known as the *Etrusca disciplina*, implying that its origin was among the Etruscans.

The use of animals as a means of divination is confirmed in Irish sources — particularly the use of the bull. We have already discussed the *tabhfheis* as a Druidic rite. The bull was especially venerated by the ancient Celts, presumably because of its strength, virility and belligerent qualities. At Gournay-sur-Abonde (Oise) there is ample evidence for the ritual slaughter of cattle. Bull sacrifice is recorded by Pliny who, in his famous passage on mistletoe, mentions the sacrifice of two white bulls by the Druids.

The cult of the bull was widespread in the Celtic world and images of Tarvos Trigaranus, the three-horned bull, are found in Gaul, Britain and Ireland. Bulls frequently appear in the Irish sagas. The best known is Donn Cuailnge or the Brown Bull of Cuailnge whose story is related in the great epic *Táin Bó Cuailnge*. There is also recorded a Gaulish proper name Donnotauros ('The Brown Bull').

Seathrún Céitinn, in his *Foras Feasa ar Éirinn* (History of Ireland), written with access to many Irish sources subsequently destroyed during the Cromwellian devastations, refers to the Druid custom of using the hides of sacrificial bulls for the purpose of divination. They made a construction of the quicken tree or rowan and spread the bull hide over it, the inside skyward to attract the necessary aura.

According to Lewis Spence: 'We possess a striking illustration of a survival of this Druidic rite in the Highlands and Islands of Scotland down to a late period in what is known as *taghairm*.' The word originally signified an 'echo' and has come to mean 'divination through the medium of demons' and is conjunct with the Old Irish *togairm*, an incantation. According to Spence, the seer wrapped himself in the hide of a newly slain bull and lay down by a waterfall, or at the foot of a precipice, and meditated (*dercad*). In due time the spirits visited him and informed him of what he wanted to know. The ceremony was observed by Martin in 1695 during his tour of the Western Isles. We could also point to the Welsh tale 'The Dream of Rhonabwy', in which Rhonabwy goes to sleep on the skin of a yellow heifer and has a vision of Arthur's last great battle.

Other animals were also sacrificed. When King Conaire and his retinue are in Da Derga's hostel, the king is moved by various ominous omens to ask his Druid, Fer Caille, to sacrifice a pig in order to discover what is about to happen. This is done and Fer Caille then tells of the impending destruction of the hostel.

Perhaps the most popularly known method of Druid augury is that clearly described by Diodorus Siculus, the prediction of the future from the flight of birds. Divining from the flight or behaviour of birds was also an ancient practice common to the Greeks and Romans. Indeed, the words *augury* and *auspices* were used interchangeably as divination from the habits of birds. Sacred chickens were carried by the Roman armies and when fed, if they ate ravenously, good was portended. Before the sea battle of Drepaum in 249 BC the chickens refused to eat and the Romans were defeated. Divination by watching the habits of birds became entrusted to a Roman college of augurs.

From the fact that both forms of divination attributed to the Druids were practised by the Greeks and Romans also, we may conclude that while the Druids had a reputation in this art, their forms of prophecy or divination were not peculiar to them but were forms shared commonly with other European cultures.

From native Celtic sources comes confirmation that bird augury was widely used. An Irish version of the *Historia Brittonum*, by the Welsh historian Nennius, includes an ancient poem which refers to six Druids who lived at Breagh-magh and who practised 'the watching of birds'. According to Giraldus Cambrensis, the Welsh prince, Gruffydd ap Rhys ap Tudor, in the early twelfth century, was able to cause the birds on Llangorse Lake, Brecknock, to sing because he was rightful ruler of Wales. It was also believed in Welsh folklore that 'descendants of a person who has eaten of the eagle's flesh shall be possessed of second sight to the ninth generation'.

John Toland, preparing his *History of the Druids*, recounts that in the year 1697 he was at Finglass near Dublin and came upon two Irish gentlemen who assured him that the business they were engaged in would turn out favourable because they had seen a raven with some white feathers in its plumage, but that they could not proceed until they had observed in which direction the bird would fly. An old manuscript in Trinity College, Dublin, mentioned by O'Curry, contains references to bird omens and their meanings such as the croaking of ravens, chirping of wrens, flight of crows. A raven croaked when St Cellach, bishop of Killlala, was about to be murdered. The croaking of the raven was deemed as a bad augury.

The name of the wren was given in *Cormac's Glossary* as *drui-en* – the bird of the Druids. Certainly an Irish name for the wren was *drean* and a *Life of St Moling* confirms the etymology of the *Glossary*. The wren has come down to us as a bird of some significance and on St Stephen's Day (26 December) in Ireland, Scotland and the Isle of Man, and even in parts of Essex and Devon, it was hunted and killed by local boys before being carried in procession through the village with the boys asking for a penny to bury it. They chanted a rhyme which has been recorded in each place the custom survived:

> The wren, the wren, the king of all birds
> St Stephen's day was killed in the furze,
> Although he be little his honour is great,
> So, good people, give us a treat.

As well as bird augury, other methods of divination appear in Celtic sources. The interpretation of dreams was a popular way of foretelling the future. The Druid Dubhdiadh interprets Domhnall's dream on the eve of the battle of Magh Rath (Moira) and foretells the defeat and death of Congal.

Another form of divination was called *coelbreni* or 'omen sticks' in which the Druids used sticks, in some cases wands of hazel inscribed with Ogham, which were cast upon the ground, their fall then being interpreted. It was from such a means that Dalan the Druid discovered the whereabouts of Étain after she had been abducted by Midir the Proud. Dalan made four rods of yew inscribed with Ogham and cast them down. This system of divination is still used in the East and particularly in parts of China, where it forms part of the I-Ching. A development of this theme occurs in some Welsh literature, where there are obscure references to a frame called a *peithynen* (in modern Welsh a ridge-tile) which some have called 'the Druid's wheel' or 'elucidator'. Sir John Daniel in *The Philosophy of Ancient Britain* (1927) carried an old illustration of this construction. According to Sir John the *peithynen* was a system of divination derived from staves of wood on which maxims were cut. It was worked into a wheel-like affair which, when spun, produced an answer. According to Edward Davies, in his *Celtic Researches* (1804), the poems popularly attributed to Llywarch Hen but dated to the ninth century AD contain references to the *peithynen*.

Taliesin, the sixth century poet, has been conjured both as a Druid and prophet. In a translation of one poem ascribed to him, he exclaims:

> I am Taliesin,
> Chief of the bards of the west.
> I am acquainted with every tree-branch
> In the cave of the arch-diviner.

Lewis Spence believes that this is a reference to the *peithynen* but it does require a little imagination to make the connection.

There appears confirmation of the wheel system from Irish sources from a tale in which we find the celebrated Munster Druid Mug Ruith of Dairbre apparently using this form of divination. According to the *Cóir Anmann*: 'Magh [Mug] Ruith signifies *Magus rotarum*, the magician of the wheels, for it is by wheels he used to make his *taiscéladh druidhechta* or magical observation.' But, as we have seen, Mug Ruith was a solar divinity and the wheel is a symbol of the sun. However, Mug Ruith's daughter, Tlachtga, according to a text quoted in O'Grady's *Silva Gadelica*, made a *roth ramhach* or rowing wheel for the purpose of divination.

The Irish historian Ruariadh Ó Flaithbheartaigh (Roderic O'Flaherty, 1629–1718), in his Latin history *Ogygia*, refers to Druids divining from the appearance of the roots of trees. And there is divination from the appearance of clouds. Indeed, the old Irish word *néladoir* (cloud diviner) became used in the medieval period for an astrologer. The Druid of Dáithí went to the top of Cnoc nan Druad (Hill of the Druid), now Mullaroe, in Skreen, Sligo, on the feast of Samhain, and remained all night until sunrise. When he returned he told the king that the clouds had foretold that he would make a conquering expedition to Alba, Britain and Gaul.

Fionn Mac Cumhail, whose thumb touched the salmon of knowledge, which was being cooked by the Druid Finegas, could henceforth suck that thumb and acquired the knowledge he required. It is a motif repeated in many of the tales of Fionn and rather an interesting form of divination.

In *Cormac's Glossary* and other works there are references to the three rites of prophecy. The *imbas forosnai*, *teinm laegda* and *dichetal do chennaib*. With the *imbas forosnai*, 'palm knowledge', the Druid chewed a piece of specially prepared meat and went into a state of meditation, placing the two palms of his hands on his cheeks. The *teinm laegda* was performed in a different manner but for the same purpose as prophecy. *Cormac's Glossary* states that Patrick had the *imbas forosnai* and the *teinm laegda* officially prohibited but he allowed the *dichetal do chennaib* because it did not involve any rite before the prophecy was pronounced.

This *dichetal do chennaib* is what Jack Kerouac (1922–1969), an American writer of Breton origin, would have called 'spontaneous prose' in which the *fili* recited his verses, according to the Brehon Laws, 'without having meditated or even thought of them before'.

But despite Patrick's ecclesiastical prohibition, the Brehon law states that one of the requirements of receiving the degree of *anruth* was that a person must master the three forms – the *imbas forosnai*, the *teinm laegda* and the *dichetal do chennaib*. In the eleventh century, Domhnall Uí Neill of Ulster called a council to assess the amount of reparation to a poet Erard Mac Cosse. Flann of Monasterboice, the chief Brehon, assessed the damages and said that these damages would stand for future poets providing they knew the three forms of prophecy. Thus these three forms were still in use six hundred years after Patrick was supposed to have proscribed them.

In both Irish and Welsh myth and saga, the art of foretelling the future is an essential part of the story. More often than not, it is to escape their fate, prophesied by the Druid, that leads the protagonists into adventures which inevitably lead them to the fate they seek to avoid. In some prophecies, such as the death of Diarmuid at the fortress of Banbán, the prophecy seems so unlikely that it cannot be fulfilled. But people ignore the prophecies of the Druids at their own peril.

The goddess Brigit is portrayed as learned in poetry and in divination and thus seems to become the patron-goddess of divination. The Irish myths and sagas are full of prophecy and divination. In some of the early hagiographies of her Christian namesake, we are told that a Druid foretold the greatness of St Brigit before she was born. Similarly, a Druid named Lughbran, at the court of Crimthann, prophesied the birth of St Ciaran of Clonmacnoise.

Eochaidh of Connacht consults a Druid to prophesy the best spot to build his new palace, while we have Cathbad the Druid of Conchobhar Mac Nessa making several prophecies, such as the birth and greatness of his own son, and the future of Deirdre, who would be the most beautiful woman in the world but who would cause the death of many heroes. Another Druid prophesied to Cumhail that if he married, his next battle would be his last. Cumhail married secretly but the prophecy was fulfilled. Biróg, the Druidess, tells Balor, on the birth of his daughter, that he would be killed by his own grandson. Balor locks his daughter, Ethlinn, in a crystal tower on Tory Island to prevent her from consorting with any man. But the prophecy is eventually fulfilled. Another story tells how a Druid told King Dara that he would have a son named Lugaidh who would succeed him to the throne. But Dara has five sons so the Druid advises the king to call them all by the name of Lugaidh to ensure the succession.

Druids also interpreted dreams. In AD 637 Domhnall Mac Aedh, the High King of Ireland, fought a battle with the king of Dàl Riada, Domhnall Breac, at Magh Rath (Moira) near Lisburn in Ulster. We hear that Domhnall of Ireland had a dream before the battle and it was interpreted by a Druid who advised him about its meaning, and the Irish king emerged victorious from the battle. This is particularly fascinating as we are well into the Christian period now and Domhnall's father Aedh was the king who presided over the synod of Druim Ceatt. Historical references to Druids interpreting dreams are confirmed by references in the myths – to Cesarn, for example, chief Druid to a Firbolg king, who interpreted his king's dream and was able to forewarn him about the approach of his enemies.

Druids as Astronomers and Astrologers

From the very beginning the human species has been perceptive of natural phenomena. Early societies noticed that the sun and moon together affected the tides, and that the sun regulated the seasons, giving light and heat which fructified the harvest. They also noticed that the motions of the moon could in some cases affect men and women and their mental attitudes. From these initial observations there developed a belief based on the premise that the motions of what was then thought of as 'stars' influenced individuals and events on the earth. Astrology was initially an integral part of astronomy. Indeed, Aristotle used the word 'astrology' rather than 'astronomy'. It was the same science. In fact, as late as the seventeenth century AD astronomical and astrological tracts were bound together or printed in the same book. It was not until the eighteenth century, during the 'Age of Reason', that what had been the one science was divided into two distinct forms. But even the founders of modern astronomy, Tycho Brahe (1546–1601) and Johannes Kepler (1571–1630) practised as astrologers as well.

Historians of astrology generally argue that it had its origins in ancient Babylonia and made its way into Europe via Greece. Not everyone in Greece accepted the new 'eastern' learning. Euxoxos of Cnidos (*c.*408 BC–*c.*388 BC) did not believe that the stars affected peoples' lives. Astrology did not begin to spread to Rome until the first century BC with the impact of Marcus Manilius' famous work *Astronomica*, dealing with astrology. Cicero was soon able to state: 'Nobody can deny to the heavenly bodies the possession of reason unless he himself is destitute of reason.' But the material society of Rome was in general more sceptical of astrology and its popularity there was not so widespread as among the Greeks.

By the late fourth century AD Augustine of Hippo had denied the validity of astrology and many Christians accepted his views. The interesting point here is that Augustine was well versed in astrology and in *De Doctrina Christiana* he had once argued that a knowledge of astrology was necessary for understanding the Scriptures as well as calendrical systems. When it came to *City of God* he derided astrology but with technical language which demonstrated his knowledge of it. Augustine's argument that salvation or damnation was preordained for human life did not go so far as accepting the view that such preordination could be read among the heavenly bodies, in spite of some arguments that Genesis clearly states that God set the stars in the firmament to *guide* mankind.

Augustine's arguments did not influence the entire Christian movement. But attacks on the belief certainly continued. In the twelfth century, Manuel Comnenus wrote his famous defence reconciling astrology with Christianity, while the Benedictine monk, Placidus de Titus (Placido Titi) (1603–1668) was recognized as one of the foremost astrologers of his day, along with the Abbé Jean-Baptiste Morin (1583–1659), who was astrologer to Cardinal Richelieu, prelate and chief statesman of France.

One thing that both pre-Christian Greek and Latin observers agreed upon, whether they were anti-Celtic or respectful of the Celts, and that is that the Druids were highly advanced in their study of astronomy and astrology. Caesar, of course using Poseidonios as his authority, says that the Druids had 'much knowledge of the stars and their motion, of the size of the world and of the earth, of natural philosophy.' While Cicero does not specifically state that the Druid Divitiacus, whom he knew, made auguries from the stars, he does write to his brother Quintus:

The system of divination is not even neglected among barbaric peoples, since in fact there are Druids in Gaul; I myself knew one of them, Divitiacus of the Aedui, your guest and euologist, who declared that he was acquainted with the system of nature which the Greeks call natural philosophy and he used to predict the future by both augury and inference.

Strabo, Caesar, Diodorus Siculus, Cicero, Pliny and Tacitus all pay tribute to Celtic knowledge in the field of astronomy. Pomponius Mela refers to the high regard in which the Druids were held for their 'speculation by the stars'. He says that the Druids knew 'the size and shape of the world, the movements of the heavens and of the stars'. And he goes on to offer explanations of the tides through the actions of the moon, as propounded by the Druids, and of the cause of the midnight sun. The earth is claimed to be the shape of a disc, a fairly common belief at this time.

Hippolytus is very specific, claiming that the Druids 'can foretell certain events by the Pythagorean reckoning and calculations'. Pliny states that the Druids watched the course of the moon until the time was auspicious for the cutting of mistletoe.

Jordanes, in *Getica*, quotes a lost work of Flavius Magnus Aurelius Cassiodorus (c.AD 490–583) which refers to the tribe of the Getae in the first century BC. According to Jordanes/Cassiodorus, the Getae were learned in natural and moral philosophy and knew the 'course of the twelve signs of the zodiac, and of the planets passing through them and of the whole of astronomy'. They are also reported to know the names of 365 stars. The reference goes on that the Getae were taught these things by a wise man named Dicenus whom Professor Piggott concedes might be the name of the Druidical teacher. Indeed, if we reassert the Celtic 'os' ending, Dicenos, the name is remarkably like the Brythonic name meaning 'wise', but which has come down in a varied form (*dicellos*, Welsh) meaning 'crafty'.

According to Jordanes, Dicenus 'trained novitiates of noblest birth and superior wisdom and taught them theology, bidding them worship certain divinities and holy places.'

We do have to mention that there is still some scholastic debate as to whether the Getae were a Celtic or German tribe, but their location, and time of that location, seems to place them within the Celtic sphere. It is Cassiodorus who also mentions Varro's text *De*

Astrologia but he is not referring to Publius Terentius Varro who was a Celt from Narbonese Gaul. Marcus Terentius Varro (116– 27 BC) was from Reate, in Sabine territory, although some authorities do put his birthplace further north-east in what would be Senones Celtic territory nearer to Ancona. The similarity of the names could be an argument for a connection between the Celt Publius and Marcus but Marcus' reputation as 'the most learned of Romans' does not seem to support a Celtic origin.

While Greeks and Latins praise the Celts for their learning in this field, do we have any evidence from the Celts themselves that they were competent in astronomy/astrology, in order to originate their own calendrical system?

The earliest surviving Celtic calendar is from Gaul and dated to the first century BC. This is the Coligny Calendar, in the Palais des Arts in Lyons. Produced before the Roman conquest of Gaul, this calendar is far more elaborate than the rudimentary Julian calendar and has a highly sophisticated five-year synchronisation of lunation with the solar year. It is a masterpiece of calendrical calculation and a practical demonstration of the proof of Cicero's claim as to the astronomical ability of the Druids. The language is Gaulish and against the months are subscribed the letters MAT and ANM. One doesn't need to be an expert linguist to see the equivalent of *Maith* (Irish) or *Mad* (Welsh), meaning good; ANM being the equivalent of *An Maith* (Irish) and *Anfad* (Welsh) meaning not good. The mid-winter month was Giamon and the mid-summer month Samon; both names can be recognized in the surviving Celtic languages.

The calendar itself consists of sixty-two consecutive months, divided into a period of twenty-nine nights or thirty nights each. In Celtic fashion, it reckons period by nights. As Caesar wrote at the time: 'They count periods of time not by the number of days but by the number of nights; and in reckoning birthdays and the new moon and the near year their unit of reckoning is the night followed by the day.'

Pliny ascribes a form of time-measurement to the Druids and says 'for it is by the moon that they measure their months and years and also their ages (*saeculi*) of thirty years'. This is in accord with the evidence of the Calendar of Coligny.

Dillon and Chadwick have observed:

The Calender of Coligny is evidence of a considerable degree of competence in astronomy, and may reflect the learning of the Druids. Moreover in the division of the month into a bright and a dark half, in the month of thirty days with a three year cycle, at the end of which an intercalary month was added, this Gaulish calendar resembles that of the Hindus.

John Rhŷs, in his *Origin and Growth of Religion as Illustrated by Celtic Heathendon*, argued that the Celts had a week comprising of nine nights. The number nine is often prominent in calculations of time and in the Laws of Hywel Dda the ninth day of the month often marked the end or the beginning of a period. The Rees brothers also observed this, pointing out that there was evidence in insular Celtic literature of nine being a significant unit of time. They point to the period of bright moonlight during the time of the harvest moon being called *y nawnos olau* (nine light nights) and in Irish the terms *nómad* and *noínden* are used as nine time spaces. They point to the fact that three weeks of nine nights would give a twenty-seven night month and twenty-seven is again highly significant in Celtic mythology and is related to the twenty-seven constellations of the lunar zodiac, as it is in Hindu mythology where the moon, Soma, has twenty-seven star wives.

We must now ask the question whether this acknowledged Celtic ability in the study of astronomy/astrology was native to the Celts or whether it was derived from the teachings of the Babylonians via Greece. As I have stated, the generally accepted view of those historians of astrology is that this was how the science entered Europe.

Hecataeus of Miletus, living around 500 BC, attributed a knowledge of calendrical computations to the Hyperboreans; moreover, he specifically places his Hyperboreans in the British Isles. Professor Piggott comments, however:

It is quite conceivable that some elements of Greek mathematics found their way into the Celtic world through the Massiliot contacts from *c*.BC 600, and these would support the statement of Hippolytus about 'Pythagorean' calculations, even if they were not literally these in fact. Indeed, it may be that any Pythagorean doctrine acquired by the Druids is less likely to have been concerned with the esoteric mysteries of transmigration of souls, than with such mundane affairs as the value of the square on the hypotenuse of a right-angled triangle.

However, one overlooks the great megaliths and stone circles, such as Stonehenge, which were constructed with highly advanced skill in astronomical observation. Now we cannot claim these constructions for the Celts for they date to a period well before we can safely identify the spread of a Celtic civilization. We are talking about a period of construction starting in the second millennium BC. Although, if we accept the views of Professor Christopher and Jacquetta Hawkes on proto-Celts, we may argue that they were constructed by the forebears of the Celts. As a parallel, the transformation of the Anglo-Saxon kingdoms into the English nation is cited to demonstrate the change from proto-Celts to Celts. But there are various other theories as to who built the megaliths. As we have discussed, some scholars believe the theory of a pre-Celtic people from North Africa, a non Indo-European culture, whom the Celts later dominated and absorbed, inheriting their knowledge.

It was Dr John Smith, the deviser of the smallpox inoculation, who published *Choir Gaur, the Grand Orrery of the Ancient Druids* in 1771, who first seemed to notice the astronomical alignments of Stonehenge. The 'Orrery' of his title was named for Charles Boyle, the earl of Orrery in Ireland in 1713, for whom a clockwork mechanism to show planetary motions around the sun was made. Dr Smith made several calculations and saw that the principal axis was aligned to midsummer sunrise. He claimed that the 'arch Druid standing in his stall, and looking down the right line of the Temple . . . sees the sun rise . . .' on midsummer's day. Henry Wansey was to report in 1796:

Stonehenge stands in the best situation possible for observing the heavenly bodies, as there is an horizon nearly three miles distant on all sides. But till we know the methods by which the ancient Druids calculated eclipses with so much accuracy, as Caesar mentions, we cannot explain the theoretical use of Stonehenge.

In 1943, Neven Henaff (1908–1983), a Breton chemical engineer, who had for many years studied both Stonehenge, in terms of the mathematics of its construction, and the Coligny Calendar, published his initial findings in *Zeitschrift für Celtishe Philologie*. He did further work following the publication of Professor R.J.C. Atkinson's work *Stonehenge* (1960), which appeared posthumously in *Carn* Nos 47–48. Henaff argued that the mathematics of the numbers of stones at Stonehenge and their groupings corresponded with the numbers indicated in the Coligny Calendar. 'So that, after all, popular tradition and "primitive" archaeologists, in persistently relating Stonehenge to the Druids, may well have been correct from the start.'

In 1963 Dr Gerald S. Hawkins, professor of astronomy at Boston University and research associate at Harvard Observatory, speculated that Stonehenge had been used as a huge astronomical instrument. His book *Stonehenge Decoded* (1966) demonstrated, using computer science, that a profound knowledge of astronomy and a mathematical skill was needed to align the stones and make an 'astronomical computer'. The ensuing controversy gave impetus to the new 'science' of archaeo-astronomy, the study of prehistoric astronomy, which was especially applied to the astronomical alignments of monuments sited in Celtic areas. After Stonehenge, studies of New Grange, Callinish, Carnac and other sites showed that their builders orientated their structures to specific positions of the sun, moon and stars. In 1967 the archaeologist Patrick Crampton, in *Stonehenge of the Kings*, became the first to overturn the popular idea that the British Celts had little idea of sophisticated building techniques before the coming of the Romans, by showing the excavations of Clickhimin as an example, and then pointing to a tradition of sophistication in building from the time of Stonehenge to the Roman Conquest, showing a continuum. But whether these great astronomical constructions were built by pre-Celts or proto-Celts, the evidence is that they became part of Celtic tradition and certainly the building knowledge was inherited by later Celtic culture.

Perhaps one of the greatest pieces of astronomical engineering is that of the three great tumuli of New Grange, Knowth and Dowth in the Boyne valley of Ireland. The radiocarbon dating of charcoal used by the builders of New Grange in the main chamber and passage gives, when calibrated, a date of around 3,200 BC. For example, on the winter solstice, 21 December, the first rays of the rising sun on that day pass through a deliberately contrived slit in the roof and illuminate the tomb chamber for seventeen minutes. Is the figure seventeen significant? It certainly is so in Irish mythology. Seventeen days, the seventeenth of the month, seventeen years occur in many contexts. Why did the Druid advise Maelduin to take only seventeen men with him on his fabulous voyage? Mil arrived in Ireland on the seventeenth of the moon and the battle of Tailtiu took place on the seventeenth of the moon. One's seventeenth birthday was the *aimsir togu*, the age of consent, when boys became men. Coincidentally, the Vedas say that the heavens were divided into seventeen regions. 'Prajapati is the year, so Prajapati is seventeen.' Additionally, the Irish reckoned that the seventeenth generation marked the limit to which kin could properly be reckoned to. The examples are too numerous to continue.

Whereas, of course, the megalith builders are far in advance of any society we can identify, with our current knowledge, as Celtic or even, with any degree of certainty, as proto-Celtic, there is an aspect to the Celtic ability in advanced mathematics which is so often overlooked. The Hungarian born, American mathematician, John von Neumann (1903–1957), in his study *The Theory of Games* (1943), developed a set of mathematical theories applying statistical logic to the choice of strategies in, particularly, board games such as chess, demonstrating that the development of such games required knowledge and skill in advanced mathematics. We know that in the Greek and Roman world games similar to draughts and back-gammon were played but chess, thought to have originated in India, did not reach Europe until after the 'Classical' period.

We also know, however, that the ancient Celts had developed several board games apart from games involving dice and counters, as these have been found in profusion by archaeologists in Britain and Ireland. A chieftain's burial from the first century BC, excavated at Welwyn Garden City, Hertfordshire, found not only a complete set of playing pieces but the remains of a gaming board. The wood had perished but its size could be reconstructed from its metal mounts. The gaming pieces consisted of twenty-four coloured glass playing pieces. It has been suggested that the game might have been similar to ludo (in Latin, 'I play'), an Indian-originated game which did not arrive in England until the late Victorian era. But ludo is played with dice and counters.

Several board games are known to us from both the Irish and Welsh myths. The first, *búanbach*, we know only by name and its identification as a board game. The name might well be connected

234

with the daughter of Danu, Búanann, 'The Ever-Lasting One', identified as a goddess of warriors, also known in Gaul as Buanu.

The second is 'wooden wisdom', called in Irish *fidchell* and in Welsh *gwyddbywyll*. It appears to be a form of chess in which a piece known as a king (*banán*) must escape to the side of a board and has to be prevented from doing so by the opponent's pieces (*fian/ gwerin*). It is played extensively in the sagas by the gods, kings and heroes and Lugh is said to have devised it. One famous *fidchell* game was played between the god Midir the Proud and King Eochaidh, over the possession of the beautiful Étain. In the Welsh tale 'The Dream of Rhonabwy' a famous game of *gwyddbwyll* is played by Arthur and Owain with gold pieces on a silver board. As they begin to play, strange events start happening and while Owain wishes to cease playing to attend to these supernatural occurrences, Arthur, oblivious to events around him, keeps telling him: 'Play the game!'

The third board game we know a little more about. This is black raven or *brandubh* in Irish and *tawlbwrdd* in Welsh. The find of a wooden board with sockets for movable pegs at Ballinderry, Co. Westmeath, has been claimed as an example of a *brandubh* board dating from the pre-Christian period. The board is divided into forty-nine squares (seven squares by seven squares) and significantly we are told that the High King's palace at Tara had 'seven views on every side'. A king piece is placed in the centre guarded by four defending pieces (the four provincial kings?). Eight opposing pieces are sited along the sides of the board. The idea of the game is confirmed by an ancient poem which pictures Ireland as 'a parti-coloured *brandubh* board', with Tara as the centre square and the surrounding squares the four provincial capitals of Cashel, Croghan, Naas and Oileach.

The games were not merely for amusement and Alwyn and Brinley Rees (*Celtic Heritage*, 1961) suggested that they also had a religious/ kingship symbolism as did such board games on the Indian continent where kings and even the Dalai Lama would enter these ritual games to establish or confirm their rôle. If we accept von Neumann's arguments, the development of such board games also confirms the status of the Celts as mathematical philosophers – and, according to the Rees brothers in their study, *brandubh*, or *tawlbwrdd* particularly, represents the cosmos or is a microcosmic symbol showing man's place in the world which is often opposed by a hostile Otherworld.

There is another corpus of evidence which is interesting. Dr Kevin Danaher, in his paper 'Irish Folk Tradition and the Celtic Calendar' (1981), has asserted: 'There has survived in Ireland from the remote into the recent past, and in many instances into the living present, a body of custom, usage and belief, which is so extensive and so cohesive as to constitute a folk calendar.' Dr Danaher, in listing festivals, observance of folk customs and other matters, demonstrates the occurrence of specific numbers of days between them. He adds:

> There is no reason to doubt the supposition that this calendar reckoning was determined and corrected, year by year, by observation of the heavenly bodies, sidereal or, more probably solar. It is probable that the duty of determining the dates of festivals was in the hands of some skilled or learned group or class of people, and it is not beyond the bounds of possibility that the association of bonfires with these festivals is a survival of a system of signal fires to announce to all the coming of the season day which was of such vital importance not merely as a festival but also as an indication to farmers that the time had come to begin some essential agricultural operation.

Dr Danaher points out: 'The few Classical references which we have to Celtic time reckoning indicate a lunar system'. Yet, he points out, 'the old Irish four season reckoning comes entirely from solar reckoning'. A new system appeared to have been adopted moving from lunar to solar calculations. Dr Danaher quotes the authority of Professor Patrick Wayman, of the School of Cosmic Physics, Dublin Institute for Advanced Studies, to state: 'Calculations have shown that this occurred in Ireland during the period AD 690–820.' Dr Danaher had earlier published *The Year In Ireland: Irish Calendar Custom* (Dublin, 1972) expounding his views on the matter.

Bearing such evidence in mind, I am inclined to accept the statement of Hecateus of Miletus that the ancient Celts possessed a native skill in calendrical and astronomical knowledge, linked to or incorporating what we call astrology. We can go further and argue that northern European or Celtic astronomy/astrology was not an 'imported' science from Babylonia via Greece but was, indeed, an evolution of native tradition.

Just what this native Celtic system of astrology was is not clear, nor indeed, can we tell exactly how the Celts viewed the zodiac. By the second century AD the British Celts, at least, knew the zodiac as we would recognise it today. There survives a sculptured representation of the zodiac dated to the mid-second century AD in Newcastle Museum with symbols which we can easily recognize and accept today.

Although evidence of the system is scanty, that which survives in Ireland indicates that astrology was practised in pre-Christian Ireland, and continued under Celtic Christianity, until the new Arabic system was introduced in the fourteenth century. Moreover, the surviving evidence shows that it was similar to Hindu astrology and was lunar-based. Certainly, as Heinrich Zimmer demonstrated in *Altindisches Leben* (1879), there are several parallels between the astronomy of the Calendar of Coligny and the Vedic or Hindu system of astronomy/astrology. This system, then, was an interpretive and predictive system whose ancient principles were first outlined in the Vedas and known as *jyotish* (Sanskrit for 'science of light').

A.H. Allcroft has argued, however:

It is odd that if Druidism was really so much concerned with astronomy, there should remain so little tradition of the fact ... there is nothing to show that Druidical star-study amounted to more than that very simple and very useful applied astronomy which meets us on every page of Hesiod's *Works and Days* and Vergil's *Georgics*, and with which every Greek and Latin farmer seems to have been conversant ... Apparently the modern belief that Druidism included astronomy or astrology, or both, is a growth of the last two centuries or so.

This is patently not so.

We must explain, however, that Hesiod wrote in the seventh century BC and is one of the earliest known Greek poets. *Works and Days* is a poem in 828 hexameters describing the activities of the farming year and including an almanac of the days of the month that are favourable or unfavourable. Allcroft overlooks one interesting point, that Virgil, Publicius Vergilius Maro (70–19 BC) was born in Cisalpine Gaul and it has been claimed that he was of a Celtic family. In *Eclogues*, Virgil was concerned about land appropriation,

reflecting the seizure of Celtic lands by the Roman conquerors following the conquest of Cisalpine Gaul. If he had been a Roman, and
therefore himself one of the 'land grabbers', one doubts whether
Virgil would have been so concerned about these appropriations.
More fascinating is the fact that *Georgics* (Husbandry), mentioned
by Allcroft, was a poem that was a parody of *Works and Days*. But
Virgil goes further to talk of men living in harmony with nature
within a divine scheme of things, and showing a deep sympathy for
all living things and insisting that mankind must cooperate with
nature. These concepts are all associated with Celtic religious perceptions rather than with the Roman religion of this period.

However, Lewis Spence argued: 'My own researches fully corroborate Mr Allcroft's findings'. Oddly, both Allcroft and Spence were
inclined to dismiss the evidence of the Calendar of Coligny, without
explanation, claiming it as not being of native Celtic learning. Spence
seemed to have denied his previous conclusion, perhaps made reluctantly, that 'Astrology seems to have formed an important feature
of later Cymric [Welsh] Mysticism'. He had made this assertion in
his *The Magic Arts in Celtic Britain* four years before agreeing with
Allcroft.

In support of the contention of Allcroft and Spence, others have
argued that if astronomy/astrology was so widely practised, then
why has some evidence of it not remained in the Celtic languages by
way of technical words? In Middle and Modern Irish, for example,
the astronomy 'jargon' consists mainly of loan words. *Astralaíocht*
for astrology and *stoidiaca* for zodiac, for example, are obviously
loan words from Greek. Even the popular astronomical term for
eclipse is borrowed into Irish as *éiclips*. Other observers have pointed
out, perhaps most damningly, that most of the planets in Irish have
no native names. By the eleventh century the Irish knew the planets
as Sathurn, Jóib, Mearchair, Mars and Véineas – names which are
all borrowed from Latin. If the Druids had studied the skies for
centuries before Greek and Latin culture influenced the Celtic voc-
abularies, where are the native names for the heavenly bodies?

Let us consider the arguments. The Druids, as has been observed
by Classical writers, revered the power of words. Words had vitality
and force. We have already discussed the Druidic religious proscription of knowledge being committed to writing in a Celtic language
and that it was not generally until Christianity broke this proscription

that such extensive native knowledge was finally set down in writing. Therefore, it can be argued that the native names by which the planets were known, the names which played so central a part in people's lives, continued to be the subject of proscription, a *geis*, so central to Celtic thought. People could only refer to them in general speech by euphemisms and so, when foreign words arrived, it was simple to use these non-prohibited terms. Can such a contention be proved? I believe so.

It is true that the Irish have lost all the native names for the planets but we can, in fact, recover the names of Mercury and Venus by looking at the sister Celtic tongue of Irish – Manx. Manx began to develop away from Irish in the fifth and sixth centuries AD. In Manx there are two names for Mercury – *Yn Curain* and *Yn Crean*, native Gaelic words. There are also two names for Venus – *Yn Vadlag* and *Yn Vaytnag*. The two different names, according to Dr Robert Thompson, the Manx expert, were no dialectal variations – for there is a north/south dialect in Manx – but were interchangeable words in both dialects.

The proscription on the use of the names of heavenly bodies can best be demonstrated in the Gaelic perception of the moon. There are several words for the moon in the Gaelic languages. It was the contention of Dr Tomás De Bhaldraithe, the compiler of the modern Irish/English dictionary, that the moon bore a proper name, the name of a god or, more likely, a goddess, which was made a taboo name by the Druids – never to be spoken by people nor written. William Camden noted, in the reign of Elizabeth, that the Irish would kneel facing a new moon and recite the Lord's Prayer, indicating a remnant of pre-Christian worship. Only euphemisms were allowed, however, to refer to the moon. Today, *gealach* (brightness) is the popularly used word to name the moon. As a comparison, in Greek, the moon goddess Selene was also named Phoebe (brightness). Other words exist as well – Old Irish contains *ésca* (*aesca*) and this word still survives in Manx as *eayst* but nowhere else. In an earlier chapter we have discussed that *éicse* was the word for wisdom, knowledge, poetry and divination. It is, perhaps, interesting that the word seems so close to *éisce*, another form of *ésca*, which doubles not only for moon but for water. Coincidentally (or perhaps not) the Hindu moon deity, Stoma, is also the name of the mystical drink of 'sovranty' of which we have spoken. Is this another water purification symbol?

Also intriguing is that the Old Irish word for a good aspect or auspice, used in the way of 'it is a good aspect/auspice to start the journey today', is *esclae*, a compound of the words for moon and day. This would imply that astrology is being consulted.

It is highly significant that Uisneach, the hill which was deemed 'the navel of Ireland', has, as its root, this same word *uis/esc*, easily recognizable in the modern Irish word for water – *uisce*. Uisneach (Ráthaconradh, Co. Westmeath) is where the first Druidic fires were lit and where the great 'Stone of Divisions' (Aill na Mirenn) marked the spot at which the five provinces of Ireland met. Here Tuathal Techtmhair built one of his four palaces and here one of the major festivals took place. Uisneach is identified in Irish tradition as the mystical Mount Killaraus where, according to Geoffrey of Monmouth, Merlin took the stones with which he is said to have built Stonehenge. In fairness, it should be pointed out that some Arthurian enthusiasts prefer to identify the site in Kildare by virtue of the similarity of the phonetics. Was Uisneach a place where one sought wisdom? A lunar observatory? Why was it chosen as the 'navel of Ireland' if not by astronomical observation?

Another Old Irish word for moon was *ré* and this, too, survives in Manx, used as a combined word with the word for light, *shollys* – giving *rehollys*, moonlight. And yet another Old Irish word *lùan* is now used as *An Lùan*, the name of the moon-day or Monday. This word is thought to be derived from the native Irish word for 'radiance' rather than being a loan word from Latin – *luna*. So there are four distinct Irish terms for the moon and all apparently euphemisms rather than a proper name.

To give an example of a Celtic taboo word in operation we can turn to Manx once again. When Manx fishermen set foot on ship it was taboo to speak of the moon as *eayst*. Until they returned to shore they would call the moon *ben-reine ny hoie* (queen of the night). There were similar practices among the fishermen of the Hebrides. And neither could Manx fishermen refer to the sun under the name *grian* but only as *gloyr na laa* (glory of the day). It is worth mentioning that in Irish there are several names for the sun, too. Not only do we have the modern word *grian*, which was also used in Old and Middle forms, but we have *ló-chrann* (head of the day) still used in Modern Irish for bright, brilliance, gleaming or guiding light and still in use in Scottish Gaelic. There is also *ré-an-lá* (light of the day) which is also used in Manx as *ree yn laa*. In addition, the word *Sol* is also used but philologists have been unable to decide whether this is a Latin borrowing or whether it is native, a word once shared by all Indo-European derived languages. In ancient Ireland a sundial was in use called a *solam* but, according to Dr Joyce, it was not derived from the Latin *solarium* but an obscure native word. The solar deity Grannos (Grannus in Latinized form) in ancient Gaul seems cognate with the Irish *grian*, although Dr Miranda Green disagrees. 'Attempts to link the name of Grannus philologically with an Irish word for the sun (*grían*) do not work.' But why this should be so is not stated. We have already mentioned that the Bretons of Morbihan used the euphemism of 'shoemaker' (*kere*, in Breton) for the sun and discussed the position of Lugh of the Long Arm as a solar deity found in other Indo-European traditions.

As to the technical jargon, we find that it is only from the seventeenth century that the Irish language adopted the word *stodiaca* (zodiac). In Old Irish we come across *reithes grían* (in the Maundeville Gaelic manuscript) as a term for zodiac. It means 'wheel of the sun'. It is practically the same linguistic concept by which the Sanskrit term for zodiac is known – *rasai chakra*, wheel of the constellation. The Irish term *roth* (*rhod* in Welsh) indicates a disc or sphere. Later, particularly into the Middle Irish period, the term for zodiac was *crois gréine*, 'the girdle of the sun'. Manx Gaelic also retains this form, *cryss greiney*, although A.W. Moore in *The Folklore of the Isle of Man* records an even older term – *Cassan-ny-greiney*, 'the footpath of the sun'. Scottish Gaelic uses the later form as *grianchrios*. There is an old native term for horoscope – *tuismeá* meaning beginning (*tuismed*), from the moment of being born. To cast a horoscope in Irish was *fios a bhaint as na réaltaí* – to gain knowledge from the stars. In Old Irish we also find the term *éolus leis an réltainn* – directing the course by the stars. A more poetic phrase for a horoscope is still found in Scottish Gaelic, *suidheadchadh nan reull aig àm bhreith* – laying the foundations from the stars.

So there were native terms. It was the loan words which were later adopted which had led Allcroft and Spence into stating that the traditions of astronomy and astrology were later cultural imports. *Astrolaice* and *astrolaic* (astrology and astrologer) were certainly borrowings. Several Middle Irish texts have *néladóir* as the word for an astrologer. The primary meaning of this word was 'cloud diviner' but in a medieval Irish text on Latin declensions, a gloss makes clear that the meaning of the word *néladóracht* was 'divination from the stars'. What is even more fascinating is that we have another medieval word for astrologer recorded – *eaystrolach*. This derives from *ésca*, one of the euphemisms for the moon, surviving in the Manx *easyt*. And returning to Manx there is another survival of an early native word for astrologer, *fysseree*, cognate with the Old Irish word *fisatóir*, an interpreter of visions. The same root was used as *fisicecht* to denote the art of natural science.

While Irish seems to have lost many of its native technical words connected with astronomy and astrology, judging from the glossary provided in *An Irish Corpus Astronomiae* (1912) by F. O'Connor and R.M. Henry, Manx and Scottish Gaelic retain some and provide the key to the original Irish words. To give a typical example, as mentioned before, *éiclips* is obviously from the Greek word *ekleipsis* (which originally meant 'failure') which was taken into Latin and hence to Irish. But Manx retains *doorey*, the darkening, while Scottish Gaelic has *dubaraich* and *dubharachd* as an eclipse. These words give us our clue to the native Irish word for eclipse. The word *dorchaigid* is used in many early Irish manuscripts, such as *Leabhar na Nuachonghbala*, to indicate an eclipse. In the *Leabhar Breac* (Speckled Book of Duniry) compiled in 1400, there is a transcription of the twelfth century 'Passions and Homilies' in which an eclipse of the sun is referred to as *co rosdorchaig grian*.

One can continue the exercise and find native words and concepts for astronomical terms such as the solstice, known as *grien tairisem* – the time of 'sun standing'. In modern Irish this has been made into *grianstad*, 'sun stopping'; while the equinox was *deiseabhair na grene*, the time of the sun facing south. Irish still uses *geiseabhan* as 'the sunny side' or *deiseach* as 'facing south'. Even names of constellations, or zodiacal signs, can be salvaged, such as *Med* for the constellation of Libra.

The point is that Allcroft and Spence were confused by a superficial glance at the modern vocabulary in which the original Celtic words and concepts pertaining to astrology and astronomy have been displaced so that it appears that there is no ancient tradition. The survival of so many technical native names is all the more surprising considering the extent of loan words in other European languages. In English, for example, of the 183 astronomical/astrological terms,

125 are Arabic, nine are Arabic-Latin, three are Persian, twenty-six are Greek and fourteen are Latin.

Using Irish as an example of a Celtic language which was less heavily influenced by Latin than, say, its Welsh cousin, we can see the survival of a lengthy native tradition. There are native words for zenith (*buaic*), for parallax (*saobhdhiall*), nebula (*néal*), penumbra (*leathscàil*), orb (*meall*) and so on. The Old Irish called the Pole Star *réalta eolais*, star of knowledge, a rather perceptive concept. A comet was *réalta na scuaibe*, a star with a brush or broom. Such terms underline the fact that the stars were well studied in the ancient Irish world.

That this tradition of astronomy/astrology passed from the Druids to the new Christian intellectuals is demonstrably clear. P.W. Joyce, in his *Social History of Ancient Ireland*, acknowledges the widespread use of astrology to forecast the most auspicious start to building a new house. This is actually confirmed in an eighth century AD manuscript, referred to in O'Curry's *Manners and Customs of the Ancient Irish*, in which the mythic architect Gobhan Saer symbolically seeks astrological advice before building. In fact, this electional method of astrology, that is, the seeking of divination by the stars to decide the most auspicious moments to begin projects, seems to have been used by early Church Fathers in Ireland. Whitley Stokes' study *Three Homilies* (p. 103) refers to Colmcille casting a horoscope to determine the best time for his foster son to commence his education as, indeed, a Druid had been consulted as to the best time when he was to have started his own education, with the Druid scanning the skies to make a decision.

Cúchulainn, sitting at a feast, suddenly wants to know the time and says to his charioteer, Loeg: 'Go out, observe the stars in the heavens, and ascertain when midnight comes.' More historically, in a story about Conn, the High King, we are told that he went to the ramparts of Tara with his Druids, Mael, Bloc and Blucine before sunrise and studied the heavens to see whether any hostile beings might descend on Ireland from the heavenly bodies. Even Lewis Spence has pointed out that this reference has 'assuredly an astrological significance'. As clearly marked on the Calendar of Coligny, lucky and unlucky days were observed. We have natal horoscopes being made by a Druid at Druim Dil (Drumdeel near Clonmel). Eoghan of Munster met the Druid who realized from the horoscope that the king would be slain in his next battle but if he conceived a son at that time he would become a great and powerful king. The Druid had a daughter named Moncha and he told her to sleep with Eoghan. She became pregnant and Eoghan was killed. Moncha, in order to prevent the birth occurring before the right planetary configuration, sat astride a rock in a stream. When the child was born, at the right time, his head had been flattened by Moncha's pressing against the stone which had prevented his birth and he was called Fiachu Muilleathan, or the Flathead. The horoscope was then fulfilled.

The Irish annals, such as the *Annals of Tighernach* (eleventh century), *Annals of Ulster* (fifteenth century) and the *Annals of Clonmacoise* (the original is lost but it survives in a seventeenth century English translation), all contain references to astronomical phenomena which confirm the abilities of native astronomers.

By the tenth century, the *Saltair na Rann* (Psalter of Quatrains) states very clearly that every educated person in Ireland should know the signs of the zodiac with their names in order and the correct month and day when the sun enters each sign. The *Saltair na Rann* stipulates that the sun remains thirty days and ten and a half hours in each sign. In other words, an Irish source confirms that every educated person in tenth century Ireland had to know the rudiments of astronomy/astrology.

The widespread knowledge of astrology in Ireland is confirmed by an earlier work written by Cormac Mac Cuileannain (AD 836–908), the famous *Sanas Chormaic* or *Cormac's Glossary*, which Kuno Meyer edited in Dublin in 1912. This states that all intelligent people could estimate the hour of the night throughout the year by studying the position of the moon and stars. With astronomy and astrology as twin sciences, the Irish had become the inheritors of many centuries of ancient Celtic traditions.

St Virgil of Salzburg, in reality, was an Irish monk named Fergal who had trained at Aghaboe, Co. Laois, in St Canice's famous monastery. Fergal's astronomical writings made him the subject of complaint to Pope Zacharias (AD 741–752). The complainant was none other than the Englishman St Boniface of Crediton who won a reputation as 'hammer of the Celtic Church' not only for his reforming zeal but also for his feud with Fergal, who had become abbot at Salzburg. Boniface objected to Fergal's writing and was scandalized that he was running his diocese according to Celtic Church customs.

St Virgil was assisted by Dubdáchrích (Dobdagrecus) who had been consecrated a bishop in Ireland and became abbot of a monastery in Chiemsee in Upper Bavaria.

Though it is recorded that Fergal's cosmographical speculations were considered shocking, nevertheless, the Pope dismissed the complaint. Unfortunately, the only text surviving concerning the speculations is the letter from the Pope to Boniface dated 1 May, AD 748 (?) in which the doctrine is 'that there are under the earth another world and other men or sun and moon'. This has been interpreted that Fergal was arguing that the world was spherical seven centuries before Columbus. He survived Boniface's attacks to become canonized by Pope Gregory IX in AD 1233.

Just after Fergal, came Dungal, from the famous monastery of Bangor, Co. Down. In the year AD 810 two solar eclipses had occurred. Dungal wrote a discourse at the request of Charlemagne explaining the phenomenon and he demonstrates that he knows the inclination of the plane of the moon's orbit to that of the ecliptic and he sets forth an astronomical principle for an eclipse of either sun or moon – that is that to occur it is necessary for the moon to be in the plane of the ecliptic. Dungal went on to establish a school which eventually became the university of Padua.

Yet another famous Irish astronomer, Diciul, was achieving fame among European scholars at this time, having written a geographical tract in AD 825. This is of considerable importance in that it contains a record of the discovery of Iceland and settlement by Irish monks at least sixty-five years before the Scandinavians arrived there. But Diciul's surviving astronomical work, *De Mensura Orbis Terrarum*, is a monument to Irish learning in the ninth century. The tract lay forgotten until identified by the German scholar Ernst Dümmler in 1879 in the library of Valenciennes in France. It was published in 1907 with an examination by Mario Esposito who claimed its importance for astronomy, astrology and medieval Latin studies. Esposito was surprised that it had never been published before and would probably be even more surprised that eight decades later Diciul's work is still largely ignored. Yet Diciul had much to say on the revolutions of the planets and their influences. He also made some fascinating speculations on the existence of a south polar star. Once more we are faced with evidence of Irish astronomers/astrologers taking a leading position in medieval Europe.

Further evidence of the knowledge of the ancient Irish in studying chronology and astronomical phenomena that determined the several cycles and dates also comes from the ninth century AD and was discovered by D'Arbois de Jubainville as glosses, or rough notes, on a leaf of an old manuscript in the library of Nancy.

As Arabic astronomy/astrology did not enter Ireland until the fourteenth century, it appears that the long native tradition was enhanced by Graeco-Roman influence with the introduction of Christianity.

By the fourteenth century, many Irish scholars were professors in the universities of Bologna, Padua and Montpellier and it was from these centres of learning that the concepts of Arabic medicine, philosophy and astrology were introduced to Europe and into Ireland. Together with the Irish medical books, to which we have already referred, we have a large number of tracts on astronomy, astrology, tables of zodiacal signs and discourses on the planets and their influences. By then, of course, we can no longer speak of native astrology for the forms are in the new Arabic learning.

In his paper 'Irish Medical Men and Philosophers', Professor Francis Shaw points out: 'Arabian medicine had for sisters Arabian philosophy and Arabian astrology . . . It is from these schools that the Irish medical tradition of the fourteenth, fifteenth and sixteenth centuries derives.' As already pointed out, Joseph O'Longan, in an unpublished work in the Royal Irish Academy, has demonstrated that astrology was then used as part of medical diagnoses and prognoses.

In Wales, in the sixteenth century *Hanes Taliesin*, there are allusions to *llyvfran serryddiaeth*, 'books of the stars' and Edward Davies, in his *Mythology and the Rites of the British Druids* (1809) refers to these although we have to take Davies with a large pinch of Druidical salt. Nevertheless, Gwydion the son of Don, Gwyn the son of Nudd and Idris the Giant all appear in Welsh myth as known for 'their skill in reading the stars'. Geoffrey of Monmouth in his famous *Historia regum Britanniae* talks of a college of two hundred astrologers at Caerleon-upon-Usk. Certainly, as Spence admits, 'throughout the Welsh mystical writings other allusions to astrology and star lore' are made. While the Welsh references are of a later period, there is, however, enough evidence prior to the fourteenth century to show that Allcroft and Spence were misled, and there is ample proof to verify the assertions of Classical writers as to the knowledge of the Celts, and particularly the Druids, in this field.

And is it coincidence that the old Manx term *fallogyssagh*, from *falsaght* and *loayr*, to speak, meant not only a philosopher but, very specifically, an astrologer?

This is not the place to talk about the philosophy of astrology. The ancient Celts, like most ancient societies, seemed to see astrology as just another natural influence or tool by which people could understand themselves and their place in the universe.

The Druids as Magicians

In native Celtic literature and tradition, Druids have come down to us most popularly as magicians, as wizards possessed of supernatural powers. Muirchú in his seventh century *Life of St Patrick* refers to Patrick's Druidic opponents at Tara as *magi* while Adomnán clearly calls Broichán, the Druid of Bruide Mac Maelchon, a magician. So by the time of the advent of Christianity in both Ireland and Britain, Druids were identified by the word *magus* and *magi*. Now, of course, the *magi* were the priestly caste of ancient Persia and *magian* priests were the exponents of Zoroastrianism. Their reputed power over supernatural entities gave us the word 'magic'. Thus, in their original form, they were probably no different to the Druids. Only by the degeneration of the term through Latin do the *magi* become what we perceive today by the term 'magician'. It is the *Book of Armagh* that applies this term, with its pejorative meaning, to the Druids. A poem in the *Book of Taliesin* uses the term *Derwyddon* for the Wise Men who visit the infant Jesus (Matthew 2), by which to translate the Graeco-Latin term 'Magi'.

Pliny clearly makes this connection when he refers to 'the Druids – as they (the Celts) call their *magi*'. But Hippolytus also classes the *magi* and Druids together. Pliny adds: 'Even today Britain is still spell bound by magic, and performs its rites with so much ritual that she might almost seem to be the source of Persian customs.'

There is certainly abundant evidence of magic in the myths and sagas of Ireland and Wales. Specifically, this is the art of influencing the course of events by compelling the agency of supernatural beings or controlling the principles of nature by sorcery. Again, in this there is no difference between the Celtic culture and that of Greece and Rome in which the practice of incantations, spells, charms, curses

and other rites came into being to influence and control the natural
course of human events. In historical times, in Greece and Rome, a
distinction came to be drawn between official religious practices and
the popular use of magic. While magic began to decline in Greece it
received considerable impetus under the Roman empire, perhaps as
a reaction to the materialism of society bred by the imperial ethics.
However, the rise of Christianity saw the energetic condemnation of
magic or, rather, any magic not in the service of Christianity.

Lewis Spence has observed: 'It is almost impossible to find a page
in early Irish literature which does not contain a reference to the
Druid in his character of a wielder of magic power . . .' The common
name for a magician in Ireland was *corrguinech* and his art, magic
or sorcery, was *corrguine*. In the story of the Battle of Magh Tuireadh
(Moytura) it is said that the *corrguinech* cast his spell standing on
one foot, with one arm outstretched and with one eye closed and
uttered the *glám dichenn* curse, to inflict injury on his enemies. Lugh
Lámhfada used this method before a battle and Cúchulainn also
inscribed his threatening Ogham message to Medb using the same
one foot, one hand, one eye ritual.

Druids in the old Irish sagas could cause a dense fog to envelop
the landscape or a storm to destroy or disperse their enemies. The
ability to harness the forces of nature is well evidenced. Muirchú
says the Druids of Laoghaire sent heavy snowfalls and darkness to
impede Patrick's approach to Tara. Broichán, the chief Druid of the
Pictish king Bruide, raised a terrific storm to stop Colmcille crossing
Loch Ness. Mathgen sent mountains to crush his enemies by falling
on them while Mug Ruith dried up all the wells, although he found
water for his own side by shooting an arrow into the air which then
caused a stream to form where it fell. Cathbad turned a plain into
'a great waved sea' to prevent the escape of Deirdre.

The *ceo druidechta*, the Druidical or magic fog, features in many
Irish tales. Fogs overtook Laoghaire the Victorious and Conall Cernach and when the Dé Danaans invaded Ireland they covered themselves in a magical fog. In the *Life of St Moling* we find Mothairén,
his friend, able to conjure up a fog to protect the Christian missionaries from their enemies. This is another example of Christians being
seen as taking over the powers of Druids.

As well as fogs, the Druids could produce a *dicheltair* or *fe-fiada*,
a cloak of invisibility to protect them from their enemies. In an Irish

version of the *Aeneid*, Venus puts such a cloak around the hero Ulysses to protect him on entering the city of the Phaeacians. The *fe-fiada* became synonymous for a mantle of protection. Significantly, St Patrick's hymn was called a *fe-fiada*. Many of the early Celtic Christians, in assuming some of the qualities of Druids – or, as I contend, many Druids in their transition to Christianity – took up magical powers. When the mother of St Finnchua was being pursued by a pagan king, she invoked the *celtchair dhichlethi*, a cloak or fog of darkness, so that she might escape.

Some texts refer to a Druidic wand, *slat an draoichta* (rod of the Druid) a branch on which little tinkling bells hung. This is similar to the branches carried by the bards. Mannanán Mac Lir carried a magic apple branch with silver bells. When Sencha, the chief bard of Ulster, waved his wand, the roar of battle hushed. Neidé carried such a wand in 'The Dialogue of the Two Sages'. W.Y. Evans Wenz in *The Fairy Faith in Celtic Countries* (1911) has much to say on Druidic magic and refers to the different wands reputedly used by Druids. This undoubtedly, as with bardic wands, was a symbol of their office.

Shape shifting was another gift ascribed to Druids. When Fer Fidail, a Druid, carried off a maiden, he did so by assuming the form of a woman. A Druidess, Badb, daughter of the Druid Calatín, deceived Cúchulainn by taking the form of Niamh, who was nursing the hero in his sickness, in order to encompass his death. Amairgen and Taliesin are said to have assumed many forms. Druids could change the identity of other people. Fer Doirche changed the beautiful Sibh into a deer when she rejected his love. The female Druid, Dalb, who changed three men and their wives into swine and Aoife, wife of Lir, who changed her step-children into swans, are further examples.

'Druidic sleeps' are referred to, suggestive of hypnotism, for Bodb, suspecting his daughter of lying, casts her into a Druidic sleep in which she reveals the truth. A 'drink of oblivion' is another tool of the Druids which makes people forget even their closest friends and loves.

J.A. MacCulloch comments:

The survival of the belief in spells among modern Celtic peoples is a convincing proof of their use in pagan times, and throws light upon their nature. In Brittany they are handed down in certain families, and are carefully guarded from the knowledge of others. The names of saints instead of the old gods are found in them, but in some cases diseases are addressed as personal beings. In the Highlands similar charms are found, and are often handed down from male to female, and from female to male. They are also in common use in Ireland. Besides healing diseases, such charms are supposed to cause fertility or bring good luck, or even to transfer the property of others to the reciter, or, in the case of darker magic, to cause death or disease. In Ireland, sorcerers could 'rhyme either a man or beast to death' and this recalls the power of satire in the mouth of the *filí* or Druid. It raised blotches on the face of the victim or even caused his death.

The early Celtic Christian writers, firmly believing in the magical powers of the Druids, put these same magical powers into the hands of the 'saints' of the Celtic church. Obviously, the 'saints' were possessed of greater magical power than the Druids so Patrick is able to dispel snow storms, darkness or destroy Druids by bringing down fire from heaven. The victory of Christian missionaries over the Druids is represented in native literature as basically a magical one. The *Lives* or hagiography of the early saints such as Fechin of Fore, Ciaran, Colmcille, Moling and others are full of saints controlling the elements, healing, causing invisibility, shape shifting and performing other forms of magic. But all their magical abilities are ascribed to Christ. Colmcille acclaims: 'Christ is my Druid'. The tradition went on even after the Reformation when Presbyterian ministers, according to William Walker's *Six Saints of the Covenant* (ed. by Dr Hay Fleming) could prophesy, heal, levitate, curse the ungodly and perform acts of magic. As MacCulloch says: 'The substratum of primitive belief survives all changes of creed, and the folk impartially attribute magical powers to pagan Druid, Celtic saints, old crones and witches, and Presbyterian ministers.'

[9]

Reviving the Druids

AFTER the spread of Christianity in the Celtic countries, the rôle of the Druids in Celtic society was altered and diminished. They eventually disappeared except as characters in the Celtic literatures. Indeed, as the Celtic peoples fell before new conquerors and those conquerors sought to destroy the Celtic languages and cultures, knowledge was even more confined to those who retained an understanding of the Celtic languages. Outside of the Celtic cultures the Druids were forgotten entirely.

This is the traditional interpretation of the demise of the Druids.

My contention, which I hope I have demonstrated, is that the term Druid, in pre-Christian Celtic society, referred to a social stratification, depicting the intellectual class. This division of social groups occurred in all Indo-European societies and is seen at its most obvious in modern times in the Hindu caste system. However, when Christianity established itself, the generic term Druid became corrupt, being connected with pagan society, and only applied to wizards, magicians, prophetic poets and bards.

The real Druid caste, like their Brahmin counterparts, did not 'disappear', but the generic term simply changed as the caste adapted to new religious and cultural values. There is evidence that the caste system was crumbling among the Celts anyway, as demonstrated in their law systems; indeed, as it was doing in other Indo-European societies. However, some remnants remain and so we see, especially in Irish society until the seventeenth century, some intellectual functions maintained by certain families in that we have hereditary doctors, judges, bards and so forth. To sum up: the intelligentsia remained but, after the rise of Christianity, were no longer called by the general term Druids.

Today, however, the Druids have become romantic figures of a 'never-never' world. How did this new perception come about?

From the mid-fourteenth century there occurred the Renaissance, a term which was not actually used until the nineteenth century. There came a rebirth of interest in the Greek and Latin writers of antiquity and a revival of the learning of what was now termed the 'Classical' world. The works of Caesar, Pliny and others were rediscovered. Caesar's *Commentarii de bello Gallico* (on his campaign in Gaul) and *Commentarii de bello civilis* (on the Roman civil war) were printed in Venice in AD 1511. It was in these works, now popularly available to scholars by the new printing methods, that the Druids were first rediscovered by the non-Celtic world.

In sixteenth century France the Druids, together with the ancient Celts, or rather the Gauls, first became respectable historical figures. Instead of the Franks recognizing themselves as Germanic conquerors of the Gauls, the Gauls now became honoured ancestors of the Franks. As Professor Piggott has observed: 'The pre-Roman past was seized on as the foundation of a national myth'.

Les Fleurs et Antiquitez des Gaules, où il est traités des Anciens Philosophes Gaulois appelez Druides was published in 1532 by Jean le Fèvre, significantly to coincide with the date of the Treaty of Union between Brittany and France on 18 September in that year. This was the date when Brittany was incorporated as an autonomous province within the French state. Brittany had finally succumbed to French military conquest after centuries of independence when, in 1488, its army was defeated by the French at Saint Aubin du Cormier. In the wake of this defeat the Bretons were forced to agree on a union of crowned heads of state. Soon afterwards, plans were formed to incorporate Brittany, a prosperous trading state until this time, into the French state, allowing it to retain its own parliament. The enthusiasm of French claims for a Celtic ancestry could clearly be viewed as a cynical political move to enforce the union with the philosophy: 'We are all Celts now!'

Many books on the ancient Gauls and the Druids began to appear in France. Most of the works used, as their source, a text attributed to Berossus which had been printed by Annius of Vitrebo in 1498. The work was actually a fake but Annius claimed it was a world history written by the Babylonian priest in the third century BC. Indeed, Berossus really existed and was known to have written a history of Babylon in Greek but only quotations have survived. Other works of Berossus are found in reference only, quoted in the writings of later writers. Berossus was said to have transmitted Babylonian astrology to the Greeks and set up a school of astrology on the island of Cos c.280 BC. But Annius' text of his world history is now seen as spurious. Annius, for we must now presume that he was the author himself, incorporated into his book some Greek and Roman references to the Druids but took names relating to Druids from several Greek and Latin texts, misinterpreting or changing them into real people such as Dryius, Bardus, Celtae and Samothes (the later name from *semnotheoi*).

The enthusiasm for these works carried into the seventeenth century. François Meinhard published a work in Latin in 1615 which translates as *The Mistletoe of the Druids as the Symbol of Jurisprudence*. In 1623 Doctor Jean Guenebault created an antiquarian 'stir' when he published *Le Réveil de L'Antique Tombeau de Chyndonax, Prince de Vacies, Druides, Celtiques, Dijonnois*. He maintained that in 1598, in his own vineyard at Poussat, near Dijon, a coffer with a glass cinerary urn was discovered, with an inscription in very questionable Greek which Guenebault translated as 'in this tomb in the sacred wood of the god Mithra is contained the body of the High Priest Chyndonax. May the gods guard my ashes from all harm'. Guenebault claimed he had discovered the remains of an ArchDruid. Here was the seed of the myth of the modern romantic Druidic imagery.

The Druids were even being claimed as ancestors of the Germans. In 1648 Elias Schedius argued the case in *De Dis Germanis*, subtitled 'The Religion of the Ancient Germans, Gauls, Britons and Vandals', which was published in Amsterdam. It presents a view of the Druids still in their gloomy oak groves with an oak-wreathed Druid, suitably robed, wielding a blood stained sacrificial knife while a sinister priestess stands by his side, a human skull hanging around her waist as she beats a drum with two massive human thigh bones. Schedius' work was followed in 1650 by a similar study from Esaias Pufendorf who published his *Dissertatio de Druidibus*. But Pufendorf also had dark Druidic oak groves awash with blood and decapitated human corpses.

By the end of the sixteenth century the Classical sources were being translated into English and becoming more generally available to English readers. Philemond Holland produced translations of Pliny and Ammianus Marcellinus while Clement Edwards translated Caesar. Gradually, the new romantic image of the Druid began emerging in English literature as well as French and German. The first known appearance was in a play entitled *Bonduca* (a corruption of Boudicca), written by John Fletcher, which appeared in 1618. Shortly afterwards, in 1624, Edmund Bolton credited 'Bonduca' (Boudicca) with building Stonehenge as her monument. Four years later the Druids entered English literature as respectable bards or poets in Michael Drayton's *Polyolbion* and started to appear in the works of John Milton and others.

In *Syntagama de Druidum moribus ac institutis* (1644), Thomas Smith believed that Abraham was the patriarch of the Druids. He was echoed by Edmund Dickinson in 1655 who exclaimed: 'Lo the Oak Priests! Lo the Patriarchs of the Druides! From these sprang the Sect of the Druides, which reached up at least, as high as Abraham's time.'

But many English of this period had difficulty with accrediting the Celts with any 'civilized' talents or capabilities. They were in the process of a savage 'ethnic cleansing' of the Irish in Ireland. As William Shakespeare expressed it in *Richard II* (Act II, Scene I):

> Now for our Irish wars:
> We must supplant those rough rug-head kerns,
> Which live like venom where no venom else
> But only they have privilege to live.

This was the time of Oliver Cromwell's 'final solution' for Ireland. His conquest of Ireland had wiped out just over one third of the population of the country. A further one hundred thousand Irishmen, women and children were in the process of being shipped off to the New World, particularly Barbados, as indentured labourers, their conditions worse than slaves, for the colonists had to buy slaves while the Irish 'indentured servants' were supplied free by the government, and there was a tendency to work such 'servants' to death. They could always be replaced but slaves cost money. English soldiers would surround Irish villages and ride down gathering up whoever they could find to put them on board ship for the colonies. There was no one left to protect the population for the remnants of the Irish army, some forty-thousand, having surrendered to Cromwell, had been allowed to take ship to Europe and serve in the armies of France, Spain or Austria.

The final step was the order that by 1 May 1654, all the Irish were to remove themselves into a 'reservation' west of the River Shannon, into the county of Clare and province of Connacht. Any Irish found east of the Shannon after that date were liable to immediate execution. Indeed, any English soldier bringing in the head of an Irish 'rebel' to his commanding officer would be rewarded with £5 and no one was too concerned with what constituted a 'rebel'.

Under such circumstances, it was not likely that English writers on Ireland would see anything culturally worthwhile in Irish culture whether ancient or modern. And they had long dismissed the Scots, Welsh and Cornish as racially inferior. After all, as conquerors, like the Romans, it would be imprudent of the English to attribute any 'civilizing qualities' to those that they had conquered or were in the process of conquering. As a demonstration of this prejudice, Inigo Jones (1573–1652) had made some notes about Stonehenge which his son-in-law, John Webb, published after his death as *The Most Remarkable Antiquity of Great Britain, vulgarly called Stone-Heng, Restored* (1655):

> Concerning the Druids . . . certainly, Stoneheng could not be builded by them, in regard, I find no mention, they were at any time either studious in architecture, (which in this subject is chiefly to be respected) or skillful in any thing else conducing thereunto. For, Academies of Design were unknown to them; publique Lectures in the Mathematiques not read amongst them: nothing of their Painting, not one word of the Sculpture is to be found, or scarce any Science (Philosophy and Astronomy excepted) proper to inform the judgment of an Architect . . .

The Celtic population of Britain, which had been conquered, massacred and forced to withdraw from the land then settled by the ancestors of the English, the Anglo-Saxons, were '. . . savage and barbarous people, knowing no use at all of garments . . . destitute of the knowledge . . . to erect stately structures, or such remarkable works as Stoneheng . . .'. He concludes: 'In a word therefore let it suffice, Stoneheng was no work of the Druids, or of the ancient Britons; the learning of the Druids consisting more in contemplation than practice, and the ancient Britons accounting their chiefest glory to be wholly ignorant in whatever Arts . . .' Inigo Jones' hilarious conclusion, to come to terms with the conundrum of his prejudice, was 'Stoneheng, in my judgment, was a work built by the Romans and they the sole Founders thereof . . .'

Jones' theory was not easily dismissed however and even in the next century Thomas Twining (1723) and Thomas Hearne (1729) enthusiastically supported it. The poet Samuel Bowden could observe (1733):

> Old Avebury's Relicks feed the curious Eye
> And great in Ruins Roman structures lie.

From Romans there came a swing to the Danes. A Viking claim to be the builders of Stonehenge was championed by Dr Walter Charleton in *Chorea Gigantum* (1663) and this was supported by several other scholars with the poet John Dryden giving his approval to the idea in a panegyric:

> . . . you may well give
> to Men new vigour, who make Stones to live.
> Through you, the Danes (their short Dominion Lost)
> A longer conquest than the Saxons boast.
> Stone-Heng, once thought a Temple, you have found
> A Throne, where Kings, our Earthly Gods, were crown'd . . .

Inigo Jones' son-in-law returned to the fray to give the Danes short shrift, reasserting once more the theory that the Romans built Stonehenge.

In 1649 John Aubrey had written a sketch of ancient Wiltshire. Aubrey made good use of Caesar and married it with reports of findings in the New World, so that, in his view, the ancient Celts emerged as a mixture of haughty barbarians and the 'noble savage' concept then associated with the American Indians. Later, Aubrey, studying Stonehenge, made a 'a humble submission to better judgments, offered a probability, that they (the stones) were Temples of the Druids . . .' He continued:

> My presumption is that the Druids, being the most eminent Priests, or Order of Priests, among the Britaines; 'tis odds, but that these

ancient monuments . . . were Temples of the Priests of the most eminent Order, viz. Druids and . . . are as ancient as those times. This Inquiry, I must confess, is a groping in the dark; but although I have not brought it into a clear light; yet I can affirm that I have brought it from an utter darkness to a thin mist, and have gone further in this Essay than any one before me . . .

Aubrey was certainly closer to the truth than Inigo Jones and his son-in-law, John Webb. And he had discussed his theories with Edward Lhuyd (1660–1709), the renowned Celtic scholar of the Ashmolean, Oxford, who was in agreement with him. 'I conjecture they were Places of Sacrifice and other religious Rites in the Times of Paganism, seeing the Druids were our antient heathen Priests,' Lhuyd wrote. Lhuyd's major scholastic work, *Archaeologia Britannica*, 1707, laid an important foundation to modern Celtic linguistic scholarship. This was only a first volume of the study, entitled the *Glossography*, but Lhuyd died before the completion of the next volume. *Archaeologia Britannica* contained the first studies on comparative Celtic philology.

Aubrey had also contacted James Garden, a professor at Aberdeen, in 1693, to ask him some advice on his new theory that all megaliths were Druidic temples. While Garden was attracted to the theory, he replied that there was 'nothing in the names of the monuments or in the tradition that goes about them, which doth particularly relate to the Druids'.

Aubrey was developing his theme into a book he proposed to call 'Templa Druidum', but which project eventually became relegated to a chapter in the *Monumenta Britannica*. When Aubrey died in 1697 only extracts of his entire thesis had been published in this work and in Edmund Gibson's edition of *Camden* in 1695. There was yet one more passing claim for the identity of the builders of Stonehenge, made by Georg Keyseler, a German scholar, who published *Antiquitates Selectae Septentrionales et Celticae* in 1720, in which he had the Saxons building it because of the resemblance to megalithic chambered tombs he had seen in Schleswig-Holstein, the European homeland of the Angles, Saxons and Jutes.

There was now great confusion about the identity of Stonehenge's builders. Walter Pope in 1676 had given a poetic shrug:

I will not forget these Stones that are set
In a round, on Salisbury Plains
Tho' who brought 'em there, 'tis hard to declare,
The Romans, or Merlin or Danes.

But during the seventeenth and eighteenth centuries the antiquarians were using the Poseidonian tradition of Caesar, Strabo and Laertius to paint their portraits of the Druids. The references to human sacrifices, and particularly the famous 'wicker man' burnings of victims, were repeated *ad nauseam*. Some writers added their own interpretations such as Aylett Sammes, in *Britannia Antiqua Illustrata*, 1676, in which the Druids take over from the Phoenician bards and philosophers whom Sammes has firmly in control in pre-Roman Britain. It was Sammes who included in his book the well-known engraving of 'the wicker man' which was to be used time and again by enthusiastic human sacrifice exponents. Indeed, Reverend Henry Rowlands, a vicar in Anglesey, in his *Mona Antiqua Restaurata*, 1723, dwelt exuberantly on human sacrifices. Rowlands, incidentally, was the first person to regard Abaris, whom we have already discussed, as a Druid.

Henry Rowlands was an important figure in the creation of the modern romantic image of the Druid. He has the Druids descending from Noah. He regarded them as 'being so near in descent to the Fountains of true Religion', having conveyed to Britain 'the Rites and Usages of that true Religion, pure and untainted'. The Druids, as portrayed by Rowlands, become patriarchal Old Testament figures, worshipping in the sacred oak groves with cairns and cromlechs identified as their altars. The human sacrifice aspect was not a matter of concern for the Druids were simply following the Old Testament traditions of sacrificing on stone altars to Jehovah.

The first serious work in English to be specifically confined to the Druids was John Toland's projected 'History of the Druids', contained in three letters addressed to his patron Lord Molesworth in 1726. Toland, in his youth, had talked to Aubrey about his work on the Druids and accepted his theory of their relation to stone circles. Toland's work was resurrected in 1740 when it was published as *Critical History of the Celtic Religion*. Later editions of the work were entitled *The History of the Druids*. So enthused was Toland about his subject that he even included physical descriptions of

Druids with hair cut short but long beards and white surplices over their habits.

Toland had certainly made some attempt to study the Irish literary sources and he includes a list of those he deemed as celebrated Irish Druids. His aberrate spellings of names can be easily identified.

The Druid Trosdan, who found an antidote against the poisoned arrows of certain British invaders. Cabadius, grandfather to the most celebrated champion Cuculand; Tagues, the father of Morna, mother to the no less famous Fin Mac Cuil; Dader, who was killed by Eogan, son to Olill Olom, King of Munster; which Eogan was married to Moinic, the daughter of the Druid Dill . . . Dubcomar, the chief Druid of King Fiacha; and Lugadius Mac-Con, the abdicated King of Ireland, was treacherously run thro' the body with a lance by the Druid Firchisus. Ida and Ono, Lords of Corcachlann, near Roscomon, were Druids; whereof Ono presented his fortress of Imleach-Ono to Patric, who converted it into the religious house of Elphin, since an episcopal see. From the very name of Lamderg, or Bloody-hand, we learn what sort of man the Druid was, who by the vulgar is thought to live enchanted in the mountain between Bunncranach and Fathen in the county of Dunegall. Nor must we forget, though out of order of time, King Niall of the Nine Hostage's Arch Druid, by name of Lagicinus Barchedius, who procured a most cruel war against Eocha, King of Munster for committing manslaughter on his son.

Toland's list displays some knowledge of Irish literary remains unusual in an Englishman of his time.

It was from the mid-eighteenth century that a change of attitude was seen. The Druid in his venerable nature-worshipping guise had emerged for better or worse in the poems of the forerunners of the romantic movement: John Thomson (1700–1748), William Collins (1721–1759) and Thomas Gray (1716–1771).

Professor Piggott comments:

From the middle of the eighteenth century it seems to have been increasingly felt by many that the rules of taste and the Age of Reason did not provide wholly adequate and inevitably satisfying standards for thought and emotion, and with the distrust of the ultimate validity of the doctrines of the Enlightenment, an alternative mood, emotive and romantic, seemed once more appropriate for the contemplation of the remote past. With this swing of mood, the accommodating Druids could change their character and take on a suitably romantic cast of countenance.

Outwardly the Celtic world was now 'at peace' with England. There had been no uprising in Cornwall since 1549. Ireland had been subdued during the Williamite Conquest of 1690–91. There had been no unrest in Wales since Tudor times and the Scottish Jacobite uprising had been firmly suppressed in 1746. So it was by the mideighteenth century that the English public were in a more receptive mood to believe in the romantic image of the Druids. Their association with the great stone circles, such as Stonehenge, seemed more acceptable.

Perhaps the most important figure in the creation of modern Druids was the Lincolnshire doctor, William Stukeley, born in 1689, who started a series of annual visits to Stonehenge between 1719 and 1724. Stukeley was a passionate antiquarian and helped to resurrect the Society of Antiquaries. He began to write a book which he originally called 'The History of the Temples of the Ancient Celts'. He later amended the title to *The History of the Religion and Temples of the Druids*. It was slow work. In 1729 he had changed his profession from medical doctor to minister of religion and was ordained in the Anglican church. Finally, in 1740, still an enthusiastic antiquarian, he published *Stonehenge, a temple restored to the British Druids*, in which he fully endorsed Aubrey's theories. In fact, Stukeley had seen a transcript of Aubrey's original manuscript of 'Templa Druidum' and made notes from it. And it was Stukeley, through Aubrey's original fieldwork, who brought the Druids both to Stonehenge and into modern folklore in a way which captured the public imagination and which still has repercussions to this day. Stukeley had an imaginative picture of the Druids worshipping a great serpent at Stonehenge which, he claimed, had been called 'Dracontia'. He traced a patriarchy priesthood from Abraham through 'the Phoenician colony into the Isle of Britain, about or soon after his time; hence the origin of the Druids . . .' He enthused: '. . . the Druids of Britain . . . advanced their inquiries, under all disadvantages, to such heights, as should make our moderns ashamed, to wink in the sunshine of learning and religion.'

In 1743 Stukeley added to his work with *Abury, a Temple of the British Druids, with Some Others Described*. This was a study of the Avebury megalith complex.

William Blake (1757–1827), himself the son of an Irish immigrant, was greatly intrigued by the Druids and by Stukeley's concepts. 'The Serpent Temple' is an engraving from the final page of *Jerusalem* in which he accepts the idea of Stonehenge and Avebury as being linked to the Druids worshipping a serpent. The subject of Blake's Irish parentage provides a necessary digression for those who view him as the arch-English poet and mystic of his day. The fact is that in early eighteenth century Dublin one John O'Neil found himself in debt and political difficulties. He escaped both by marrying Ellen Blake who kept a shebeen (illegal drinking house) in Rathmines, Dublin, and taking her name. His son James Blake migrated to England and married while another son went to Malaga and entered the wine trade, setting up a thriving business which was still functioning at the turn of the twentieth century when Dr Carter Blake of Malaga revealed some of the family history to the poet W.B. Yeats. James Blake became a hosier at 28 Broad Street, Golden Square, London, where, in 1757, his second son, William, was born.

Blake was a friend of the Welsh lexicographer William Owen Pughe, who helped Iolo Morganwg establish (or re-establish, depending on one's viewpoint) the Gorsedd of Bards of Britain in 1792. Blake conjures his Druids to his *Prophetic Books* with visions of Stonehenge and Avebury in his engravings. Blake came to believe that Britain was the original Holy Land and 'Jerusalem' was not far from Primrose Hill! 'All things Begin & End in Albion's Ancient Druid Rocky Shore' enthused Blake. Blake, totally confused about the ancestry of the Celts and Anglo-Saxons, claimed Druidism for England. 'Your Ancestors derived their origin from Abraham, Heber, Shem and Noah, who were Druids, as the Druid Temples (which are Patriarchal Pillars and Oak Groves) over the whole Earth witnesses to this day.' The Druids of 'England' had set out with missionary zeal in the mists of time to establish their sacred groves across the face of the world and create the one true religion, claimed Blake.

The influence of the literary and antiquarian arguments about the Druids is seen to its greatest effect in Blake's *Jerusalem, the*

Emanation of the Giant Albion, which he began to write in 1804 and which is considered his greatest poem. The theme is Man's (Albion's) recovery of his lost soul. In this Blake uses the Druids to symbolise deism but uses them in bloodthirsty guise with one of the hundred illustrations he made to illustrate his poem depicting Christ crucified to a 'sacred Druidic oak'.

> O ye Sons of the mighty Albion
> Planting these Oaken Groves, Erecting these Dragon Temples . . .
> Where Albion slept beneath the Fatal Tree
> And the Druid's golden knife
> Rioted in human gore
> In offerings of human life

Druidical elements occur in many of his illustrations, such as the famous 'wicker man'. It can certainly be argued that Blake's vision had nothing at all to do with the Druids and ancient Celts nor, indeed, anything but his own marvellous fantasies. Blake would agree for in the same poem we find the lines:

> I must Create a System or be enslav'd by another Man's.
> I will not Reason and Compare: my business is to Create.

The architect of Bath, John Wood, born in 1704, followed even more enthusiastically in Stukeley's footsteps and published a work in 1747 entitled *Choir Gaure, Vulgarly called Stonehenge, on Salisbury Plain, described, Restored and Explained.* The word *Gaure* came from the British Celtic *gwary* – a place to stage plays. It is recognizable in the medieval Cornish *plen-an-guaire.* A *plen-an-guaire,* a medieval amphitheatre, still stands in St Just, in Penwith, once used for the staging of the Cornish miracle plays.

Wood enthused:

Caesar! even Julius Caesar, the highest priest of Jupiter, and of Rome herself, undeniably proves the Brittanick Island to have been enriched with the great school of learning . . . wherein the Druids of the western world could perfect themselves in their profession . . . the venerable and stupendous work on Salisbury Plain, vulgarly ascribed to Merlin, the Prophet . . . appeared to me to

be the remains of a Druidical temple ... externally of the real
Monopterick kind ... neither could I avoid concluding that the
Britons and Hyperboreans were one and the same people.

Wood became obsessed by the Druids. When he was designing the
new buildings at Bath, he originated the Grand Circus which has
been called 'one of the most original concepts in European town
planning; wholly without precedent when designed by Wood'.
According to Professor Piggott: 'There seems to be the exciting possibility that the Circus owes something to the Druids as well ... The
Circus is planned as a true circle about 300 feet in diameter with
three symmetrically spaced entrances: an unusual lay-out with no
prototype in the Colosseum or in classical architecture at large.' Inigo
Jones, in his work on Stonehenge in 1655 and the reprint in 1725,
the year Wood designed the Circus, contains a plan of Stonehenge
with a geometrical circle of some 300 feet in diameter, with three
symmetrical gaps. According to Professor Piggott: 'In Wood's
delightfully confused archaeological enthusiasm, Druids, Stonehenge, the Circus Maximus and the Colosseum could well be blended
to produce the exquisite architectural conceit with which he
honoured the past of his beloved city.'

In case of any religious moral outrage about the re-emergence of
a pagan priesthood as a group worthy of respect, the Druids received
a Christian approval from William Cooke, the rector of Oldbury
and Didmarton in Gloucestershire, shortly after Wood published.
Cooke published a discourse in 1754 entitled *An Enquiry into the
Druidical and Patriarchal Religion*. He argued that although the
Druids erected Stonehenge before the birth of Christ, as the Druids
were so morally high-minded they were not ethically different from
Christians. In this he was actually repeating arguments first used by
Revd Henry Rowlands.

The usually highly cynical Dr Samuel Johnson (1709–1784) wrote
to Mrs Thrale on 9 October 1783 that he believed Stonehenge to be
'a Druidical monument of, at least, two thousand years; probably
the most ancient work of man upon the island'.

Against this antiquarian work, the imagination of poets, such as
Blake, was being fuelled. After the excesses of the Reformation, the
fractioneering or sectarianism of the early seventeenth century leading to more open debate on reforming the various sects, and out of

the hair-splitting and intolerance, the ideas of an ancient and true 'Nature Religion' appealed to many intellectuals, particularly writers and artists. Stukeley himself wrote a poem in 1758, unpublished, entitled 'The Druid', in which, significantly, he opens with a line quoted from Virgil whose Celtic background led to the introduction of some Celtic nature concepts into Latin poetry. Alexander Pope put forward the concept in 1733:

> Nor think in Nature's state they blindly trod;
> The State of Nature was the reign of God.

The Druids were now hailed as wise sages, sitting under the shade of great oaks, dispensing wisdom. Thomas Gray (1716–1771) produced his vision of the Druids in 'The Bard' (1757), turning them into prophetical poets. This was more in keeping with the Welsh tradition but whether Gray knew of this imagery in Welsh poetry one cannot be sure. The Druids had become the children and interpreters of nature – but not for everyone. George Richards published *The Aboriginal Britons* in 1791 in which he recalled the reports of human sacrifice with the lines:

> By rites thus dread the Druid Priests impress'd
> A sacred horror on the savage breast

Dr John Ogilvie of Aberdeen published anonymously *The Fane of the Druids* and enhanced the image of the ArchDruid:

> Though time with silver locks adorn'd his head
> Erect his gesture yet, and firm his tread . . .
> His seemly beard, to grace his form bestow'd
> Descending decent, on his bosom flow'd;
> His robe of purest white, though rudely join
> Yet showed an emblem of the purest mind

Throughout the nineteenth century speculation about the Druids and Stonehenge continued. In *An Illustration of Stonehenge and Abury* (Avebury), 1854, the author Henry Browne sneered 'Shall we attribute their (the stones) erection to Britons, to barbarians? – silly thought!' But even sillier was Browne's theory that the stones were erected in the days of Adam and knocked down by the Flood! In 1880, the famous Egyptologist, W.M. Flinders Petrie, produced a chart of Stonehenge, accurate to within an inch, and argued that it had been built before the Roman invasion. T.A. Wise in 1884 also maintained it was 'a high place of the Druids' but finally John Lubbock, afterwards Lord Avebury, succeeded in producing a more accurate date of building, at around 1500 BC. It was not until the mid-twentieth century that the archaeologist Jacquetta Hawkes pointed out, in *Early Britain* (1945), the advanced mathematics needed to build Stonehenge.

While all this was going on in England, or rather having its effect on the English-speaking areas of Britain, the Druids were being similarly reinvented in France. We have already discussed how, after the Union of Crowns of France and Celtic Brittany, the French were quick to claim the ancient Celtic Gauls as their ancestors and to reinstate the Celts and Druids as worthy of patriotic mythology.

In 1703 the Abbé Paul-Yves Perzon had published *L'Antiquité de la Nation et la Langue des Celtes*, which was translated into English three years later by David Jones as *The Antiquities of Nations, More Particularly of the Celtae or Gauls*. From this time on the word 'Celt' started to come into popular use again. In 1727 Jean Martin published *Religion des Gaulois*. Yet more influential was Simon Pelloutier's *Histoire des Celtes* (1740), which again equated the religion of the Germanic Franks and the Celts as one and the same thing. This work had obvious political motives, attempting to show no national differences between the French and Bretons. At that time French centralist policies were encroaching on Brittany's autonomous status, guaranteed under the Acts of Union. Not only was the Breton Parliament rejecting French legislation but several Breton leaders had been executed in Nantes for attempting to reassert Breton independence. Many Bretons sided with the colonists in British North America and when the American Revolutionary War broke out, some 300 Bretons became officers in the American Revolutionary army. Armand Tuffin de la Rouerie was appointed a general by George Washington. These Bretons took the creed of republicanism and 'The Rights of Man' back to Brittany and it was from Nantes and Rennes that the French Revolution started. Unfortunately the French republic, when it emerged, was as centralist as the former monarchy had been – perhaps more so. In 1790 the Breton Parliament was abolished in spite of protests from leading Breton republicans like the Marquis Lafayette, a member of the ruling family of Cornouaille, who spoke animatedly in the Breton parliament against its suppression, and Armand Kersaint.

While the Breton republicans, organized by the former American Revolutionary General Armand Tuffin de la Rouerie, were fighting a war of independence against French Republicans, and were also engaging French and Breton Royalists, La Tour d'Auvergne published his *Origines Gauloises* (1796) in which he claimed the megaliths to have been built by the Druids. His contribution was to introduce the Breton word *dolmen* (standing stone) into both French and English vocabulary as a technical archaeological term.

It was against this background that the image of the Druids and ancient Celts was developing in people's perceptions. Abbé de Tressan in 1806 decided to add a chapter on the Druids to his *History of the Heathen Mythology* painting a Gaulish Druidic paradise in an Ossianic shadow. James MacPherson (1736–1796), famous for his controversial work known collectively as *Ossian*, had discussed the Druids in his *History of Great Britain* in 1773, presenting them in the new romantic imagery.

It would seem from the foregoing that the Druids were being completely taken away from their origins and then severed from their direct cultural descendants. We may therefore ask, what was happening in the Celtic countries while the English and French made so free with their ancestors?

It was in Wales that the strongest Druidic traditions had survived into modern times but with the Druids represented as bards. We have seen how the earliest Welsh references to Druids had them as seers and poets. From the twelfth century bardic courts had survived, organizations for regulating performers and maintaining standards by competition and awards. At one time, when life was politically easier for the Celts, the eisteddfod, an assembly, had been proclaimed in the twelfth century in Ireland, Scotland, Wales and the other Celtic countries, so that bards and musicians could journey to Wales and participate in what was obviously seen as a pan-Celtic gathering. But as the English governments sought to suppress native Celtic culture, in particular, from the sixteenth century onwards, these gatherings became less prestigious and were driven almost underground. They were nevertheless difficult to suppress entirely. And, in 1568, Elizabeth's government granted a commission to some Welsh gentlemen to hold an eisteddfod in Caerwys, Clwyd, in order to grant licences to bards in order to distinguish them from the vagrant beggars. At taverns and local spots these bards continued to meet until the eighteenth century.

Scholarship and literary endeavour in Wales were at a high point during this period with Theophilus Evans (1693–1767) publishing *Gweledigaetheu y Bardd Cwsc* (Visions of the Sleeping Bard) in 1704 which became one of the major Welsh prose classics.

In 1764 the poet and cleric Evan Evans (1731–1788) published his *Specimens of the Poetry of the Antient Welsh Bards*, with translations and a Latin essay on medieval poets and their work. Evans was recognized as one of the foremost Welsh scholars of his day. He was known by the Welsh name Ieuan Fardd and sometimes as Ieuan Brydydd Hir, although he is usually known by the former name to differentiate him from the poet Ieuan Brydydd Hir Henaf who flourished in the fourteenth century. It was asserted, perhaps with too much enthusiasm, by Evan Evans, that a Druidic 'literature' had been discovered in Welsh poetry, obscure but discernible through the eyes of the faithful.

On the heels of this publication came Edward Jones' *Musical and Poetical Relics of the Welsh Bards and Druids*, 1784, and *The Bardic Museum of Primitive British Literature*, 1802, which actually formed a second volume to his first book. Jones styled himself 'bard to the Prince of Wales'. In this collection were included 'A Druidical Song' and 'Y Derwydd – The Druid'. Welsh scholastic endeavour during this period led to the foundation of a Cymmrodorion Society in London in 1751, for the publication of ancient Welsh texts, and this society still exists today.

In May 1789, a great eisteddfod was held in Corwen organized by a local enthusiast, Thomas Jones, with the backing of the Gwyneddigion, another leading London Welsh society, founded in 1771, but a more radical organization than the Cymmrodorion Society. The Gwyneddigion published *Y Cylch-grawn Cymraeg*, the first Welsh newspaper to discuss social and political matters. Later that year, another eisteddfod was held at Bala, also officially sponsored by the Gwyneddigion.

Among the members of the Gwyneddigion in London was Edward Williams (1747–1826), a stonemason from Glamorgan who was passionately interested in Welsh antiquities and literature. He adopted the writing pseudonym of Iolo Morganwg (Iolo of Glamorgan). His verse in Welsh and English was certainly radical and even republican in nature. Williams, like many literary and antiquarian men of his day, was deeply fascinated by the discussion on the Druids and the general interest in Nature Religion.

William Cooke's book of 1754 had been one of the inspirations for yet another new Druidic departure, for Cooke's arguments impressed a Welsh writer, a writer who would achieve notoriety as the author of one of the world's most scandalous books.

In 1749 the author John Cleland (1709–1778) was put into Newgate prison, London, for debt. While there, a publisher named Drybutter, of Fenton Griffiths, offered him twenty guineas to write a risque novel. He produced *Fanny Hill, or the Memoirs of a Woman of Pleasure* (1749) whose earnings secured his release. *Fanny Hill* became the subject of much controversy and as late as 1963, while published in the United States of America, it was still banned in England as an Obscene Publication. Cleland had found a vocation and followed up *Fanny Hill* with *Memoirs of a Coxcomb* (1751) and *Memoirs of the Celebrated Miss Maria Brown*: *the Life of a Courtesan* (1766).

Cleland, however, was a linguistic enthusiast and in 1766, influenced by William Cooke, he published *The Way to Things by Words and to Words by Things; being a sketch of an attempt at the retrieval of the antient Celtic to which is added a succinct account of Sanscrit or learned language of the Brahmins*. This was an impressive but misguided work in which he claimed that Celtic was the parent tongue of all European languages. This was long before German linguists tackled the matter and hypothesized the now accepted common Indo-European root. One could argue that Cleland was at least on the right path in observing the similarities of root words and was one of the first to spot the relationship of Celtic to Sanskrit. This was a short book with a seven-page introduction and only 123 pages of text. In it he depicted the Druids as preserving and transmitting the primeval wisdom of an ancient and united European society.

Cleland followed up his study with a more lengthy work entitled *Specimens of an Etimological Vocabulary or Essay by means of the analitic method to retrieve the antient Celtic*, published in London in 1768. This was twice as long as his earlier study but basically reiterated his earlier contentions about the Celtic languages and the Druids.

Cleland was inspired by William Cooke's work and he, in turn, influenced Rowland Jones, who claimed that the Children of Gomer were the original Druids, with Japhet as an ArchDruid. Rowland Jones produced a series of books between 1764 and 1771, the last being *The Circles of Gomer*. Rowland Jones influenced the lexicographer, William Owen Pughe and the radical poet Iolo Morganwg. Pughe was a friend of William Blake and became the compiler of an idiosyncratic two volume *Welsh and English Dictionary* (1803).

Taking the existence of a continuing bardic tradition in Wales as a foundation, Iolo Morganwg began to build on various suggestions from Welsh literature, and claimed that he could prove that the cult of the literary Druids had continued unbroken in Glamorgan. With his fertile literary imagination he created what he claimed to be a Druidic ritual and on 21 June 1792, on Primrose Hill, London, the Gorsedd Beirdd Ynys Prydain, Assembly of Bards of Britain, was held. It was attended by fellow enthusiasts including William Owen Pughe.

By 1819 Williams had persuaded the organizers of the major Carmarthen Eisteddfod, for there were now numerous *eisteddfodau* being held throughout Wales, to incorporate his Gorsedd as an integral part of the proceedings and so it has remained ever since. By 1858 at Llangollen, the Eisteddfod had become a major national institution for which a committee was formed to hold a National Eisteddfod annually. In 1880 a National Eisteddfod Association was formed. The Eisteddfod Genedlaethol Frehind Cymru is now held annually in August, alternately in north and south Wales.

The Gorsedd has three orders. Its Druids are clad in white robes, symbolizing recognition of a substantial contribution to Wales, bards are in blue robes, having passed the final Gorsedd examinations, and ovates, in green robes, showing that they have passed two Gorsedd exams or been honoured for services to Welsh culture. A tripod symbolizes the divine attributes of love, justice and truth. A six foot long great sword – *y cleddyf mawr* – is carried to the Gorsedd circle of bards, partly withdrawn from its sheath. It is never withdrawn entirely. The ArchDruid makes the ritual challenge to the assembly, *a oes heddwch?* (Is it peace?) The assembly shouts back, '*heddwch*!'

(It is peace!). Three times this is done. Then the ArchDruid receives the Fruits of the Earth, symbolically offered in the manner of a horn of wine and the *aberthged*, a sheaf of corn. Young girls, with flowers in their hair, dance barefoot.

With the great Celtic Revival sweeping the Celtic countries at the end of the nineteenth century, it was in 1901 that the Gorzez Gourenez Breiz Vihan (the Breton Gorsedd) was established, meeting in Guingamp under the patronage of the Union Régionaliste Bretonne. The principal founders were Yann Fustec, Taldir Jaffrennou, L. Le Berre, F. Vallée, E. Le Moal and Loeiz Herrieu. The same ritual as devised by Iolo Morganwg was adopted for the Bretons. The Bretons did not have the office of an ArchDruid, as in Wales, but the chief figure in their Gorsedd was a Grand Druid.

In Cornwall, too, where there was a revival of the Cornish language, which had ceased to be a generally used vehicle of communication by the turn of the nineteenth century, there were moves to set up a Gorsedd. Two Cornishmen and a Cornish woman had been honoured by the Welsh Gorsedd in 1899. In 1903 Henry Jenner, 'Father of the Cornish Language Revival', had been honoured by the Breton Gorsedd. In 1904 another Cornishman and woman were honoured by the Welsh Gorsedd. Early in 1928 eight more Cornish men and women were made bards of the Welsh Gorsedd. It was then in September 1928 that the Gorseth Kernow (Cornish Gorsedd) was inaugurated at Boscawen-Un. Unlike the other organizations, the Cornish have one order of membership only, that of the blue robed bards, and the head of the Gorseth Kernow is the Grand Bard. Henry Jenner became the first Grand Bard until his death in 1934.

It was in September 1971 that the three *gorseddau*, while recognizing the autonomy of each other in domestic affairs, accepted the supreme authority of the ArchDruid of the Gorsedd of Bards of the Isle of Britain in all matters of *gorseddau* constitution and practice.

Although, on a scholastic level, one can criticize Iolo Morganwg, as Professor Piggott has done, for his inventions, nevertheless, his inventions have now been given two hundred years of tradition and are an integral part of the Welsh, Breton and Cornish national life. Having created Druids from a 'never-never' world, the Gorsedd and its values, particularly its recognition of cultural endeavours of the Celtic communities, has taken on a serious and respected life of its own. Although not everyone approves of the ritual. For example, in

1971 an Anglican clergyman was fined £20 for giving a fake bomb warning having claimed that a bomb was planted under the Eisteddfod pavilion. The impassioned cleric denounced the Gorsedd to a local newspaper as 'a pagan institution'.

Professor Gwyn Williams has commented that 'the inventions of Iolo Morganwg ... helped to throw a mist of unreliable antiquarianism about the subject which scholarship has not the means completely to dispel.' Not only has the 'Druidism' of the Gorsedd spread to Brittany and Cornwall but, while the Goidelic Celts, the Irish, Scots and Manx have rejected the Brythonic Gorsedd and Druidic revival as applied to their own cultures, nevertheless, they have their own annual festivals of music, song and poetry on the lines of the Eisteddfod. In Scotland there is the *Mòd nan Alba*, in Ireland *An t-Oireachtas* and in the Isle of Man *Yn Chruinnaght*.

According to Professor Piggott: 'The influence of Iolo was not confined to the invention of the Gorsedd, for his Druidic fabrications were to poison the well of genuine scholarship in early Celtic literature for generations to come.' But it was not Iolo Morganwg who was totally responsible for 'scholastic' Druid mythology but Evan Evans. Evans, perhaps unintentionally, created the foundation of mythological Druidism to be utilized as a new 'Nature Religion'. In collecting and translating early Welsh poetry, he had made the claim that the poems attributed to the sixth century poet, Taliesin, contained a 'Druid's cabala', a secret traditional lore, theological, metaphysical and magical. Seizing on this, Iolo, in *Poems, Lyrical and Pastoral* (1794), repeated the claim that the poems of Taliesin 'exhibit a complete system of Druidism'. He also maintained, with, I believe, some degree of accuracy, that Celtic Christianity had inherited many Druidic concepts.

It would seem that Evans was the starting point of Iolo's theories. Where Iolo Morganwg departed from Evans was in going further than stating a belief and actually setting forth the 'Druid's Cabala' which, he claimed, was derived from information given in a sixteenth century manuscript in which twenty 'Druidic Ordnances' had been set out by one Noel Taillepied. The manuscript did not, of course, exist and, as Professor Piggott has pointed out, Iolo's 'Druids Cabala' was sheer literary forgery.

The idea that the rites and philosophies of the Druids were recoverable through translations of early Welsh poems was also enthusiastically taken up by Edward Davies in his *Celtic Researches* (1804) and *The Mythology and Rites of the British Druids* (1809). These works had a direct influence on *Costume of the Original Inhabitants of the British Islands*, by Samuel Rush Meyrick and Charles Hamilton Smith, published in 1815, in which colour aquatints purported to show ancient Druids in authentic costume. An ArchDruid, with white beard, was depicted in long white robes and wreathed in oak leaves and wearing a golden breastplate. The breastplate, in fact, was actually an authentic depiction of a Bronze Age gold forget from Glenishsheen, Co. Clare, now in the National Museum, Dublin. *The Patriarchal Religion of Britain* (1836) by David James expanded these notions even further. These works were even thought worthy of rebuttal by reputable academics such as Dr Algernon Herbert, Dean of Merton College, Oxford, in his *Neo-druidic Heresy in Britannia* (1838).

Romanticism about the Druids was certainly not confined to these islands and France. The Druids now translated to opera. The Italian composer Vincenzo Bellini (1801–35), who had a great impact outside Italy and especially influenced Chopin, composed the opera *Norma*. It was performed on 26 December 1831, at La Scala. The scene is Stonehenge and the main characters are Druids with Norma as the suffering daughter of the ArchDruid. It was an impressive piece demonstrating the virtuosic *bel canto* tradition of the eighteenth century and it was highly popular in England over the next two decades. In 1841 Angelo Catelani, a pupil of Gaetano Donizetti, had his opera *Carattaco* performed in Modena. It also had a Druidic theme. Druidry was becoming highly popular.

So popular were Druids in England, for example, that in this age of folly building, Druid Temples became all the rage. Field Marshal Henry Seymour Conway, a former Governor of Jersey, built his Druidic Circle in 1788. His 'folly' was set up at Temple Combe, Berkshire, which was based on an authentic megalith. The citizens of Jersey had given the Field Marshal a retirement present of a stone circle which stood at St Helier. The Field Marshal immediately had the circle unearthed, dispatched to his estate in Berkshire and reset there. It was enough to turn the hair of modern archaeologists and conservationists white overnight!

George Henry Law, bishop of Bath and Wells, decided to erect a semi-circular, roofed shelter, with five pointed arches, of pebblestone with a circular wooden table, and call it a Druidic Temple, in his gardens at Banwell, Avon, in around 1820. Inscribed there is a verse:

> Here where once Druids trod in times of yore
> And stain'd their altars with a victim's gore
> Here now the Christian ransomed from above
> Adores a God of mercy and of love.

Another polygonal hermitage called a Druidic Temple was erected at about the same time at Halswell Park, Goathurst, which has now vanished and which was part of a major folly group.

But perhaps the most spectacular Druidic Temple stands at Swinton Hall, Ilton, in North Yorkshire. William Danby (1752–1833), himself an egocentric writer of esoteric fashion, decided to recreate Stonehenge there. He built it together with a copy of the Cheesewring, from St Cleer in Cornwall, which is a stack of rocks piled one upon another by some freak of nature with the upper stone larger than the bottom ones. Dr William Borlase, in his *Antiquities of Cornwall* (1754) claimed it as a place of Druidic veneration, along with most all the pre-Christian remains in Cornwall. The Ilton Stonehenge and Cheesewring were built in 1820 and continue to stand today.

In 1781 English Druidic enthusiasts decided to establish an Ancient Order of Druids. The prime mover was a carpenter named Henry Hurle whose business was on Garlick Hill, in the City of London. Hurle had organized it on the lines of Freemasonry, to help impoverished members. But in 1833 those who adhered to the pseudo-theosophical ideas clashed with those who saw it primarily as a Friendly Society with Masonic rituals. They formed a breakaway movement. By 1839 the 'United' Ancient Order of Druids, renamed to distinguish it from its esoteric parent, had lodges in the United States and Australia and by 1872 there were even lodges in Germany. From 1841–1843 the United Ancient Order of Druids were publishing their own magazine, *The Druids' Journal and Monthly Gorsedd*. As a charitable society the United Ancient Order of Druids still flourishes as a widespread international organization today.

The esoteric enthusiasts clung to the original mystical theories of the Order. Curiously, it was into this latter sect that the newly appointed President of the Board of Trade, Winston Churchill (1874–1965) was inaugurated, joining the Albion Lodge of the

Ancient Order of Druids, at Blenheim Palace, where he hosted their meeting on 15 August 1908. The summer had been a busy one for Churchill. Following his appointment to Cabinet, under the then rules of the House of Commons, he had to defend his Manchester seat in a by-election. He lost. Asquith's Liberal Government immediately found him a safe Liberal seat in Dundee and on 11 May he had managed to get back into Parliament. The new Cabinet minister was obviously relieved as he joined the festive Druids at Blenheim. Some of the participants were wearing false beards and looking more like applicants for a job as Santa Claus than any self-respecting Druid. On 15 September, a month later Churchill was to marry Clementine Hozier.

No movement, however secret, would be complete without its own journal and *The Druids' Magazine: a compendium of Druidical Proceedings* was launched in London by one R.H. Hunt in 1830. He ran it until 1833 and then C. Letts took over from 1834 to 1839. A third new series of the magazine began from 1839. *An Ancient Order of Druids Introductory Book* had been published by Bros Coningham, London, in 1889. Then *The Druid*, as the official organ of the Ancient Order of Druids, was launched and ran from March 1907 to February 1912. It was revived in April 1936. It was relaunched as *The Druid* again in 1965. Even *The Order of Druids Directory* was compiled yearly from 1914–1938 by J.W. Shaw. It was compiled from 1939–1948 by H. Clayton and published in Manchester.

Mystic Druids continued to make annual appearances at Stonehenge but in 1900 visitors were causing a lot of damage to the monument. To offset this the owner, Sir Edward Antrobus, began charging entry. When the be-robed Druids arrived for their next solstice ceremony and refused to pay the entrance fee, the police summarily ejected them. In 1915 the monument was presented to the nation and by the end of the First World War (1918) there were five different sects of Druids vying to perform their 'sacred rites' there. The sects all seem to have been breakaway groups of the original Ancient Order of Druids. One of these called itself the Ancient Order of Druid Hermetists and launched their own magazine in 1938 entitled *The Pendragon*, subtitling it 'the official organ of Mount Nuada of the Ancient Order of Druid Hermetists'. By 1949 the five sects were reduced to two and from 1955 only one sect appeared claiming to be the sole survivor of Hurle's original Ancient Order of Druids. This was called The British Circle of the Universal Bond. The Bond not only claimed that they were the only descendants of Hurle's original movement but that they were the inheritors of an earlier movement founded by John Toland. They argued that Toland himself had, in fact, organized a meeting of Druids on Primrose Hill in 1717. There is no evidence for this. They also claimed that among their chief Druids were Stukeley, Lord Winchilsea and William Blake. From 1909 until 1946 they were led by George Watson MacGregor Reid, a friend of George Bernard Shaw. Reid had unsuccessfully stood for election in both the UK House of Commons and the USA Senate. In 1963 a further internal dispute gave birth to The Order of Bards, Ovates and Druids who decided that their rites should be performed at Tower Hill or Hunsbury hill fort near Northampton.

With the mis-named 'Celtic Renaissance' of the late nineteenth century, and the sudden outpouring of translations and tales from the various Celtic mythologies, the Druids became respectable subjects for literature. Aidan Lloyd Owen's *The Famous Druids; a survey of three centuries of English literature on the Druids* (1962) has been the only major study on the subject to date. Since 1962, however, there has been an even greater outpouring of fantasy literature in both the United Kingdom and United States with Druids appearing in all manner of guises. One of the most recent blockbusting novels in the field has been Morgan Llywelyn's *Druids* (1990). Druids, however they are presented, are with us in literary form for better or worse. It would, however, be impossible to attempt to encompass a survey of literary Druids in any meaningful form in this work.

Yet the search to discover the 'secret doctrines' of the Druids became a widespread passion.

Perhaps the most interesting attempt to discover the real philosophies of the Druids, and to revive and adapt them for use in the modern world, was made by the Breton Neven Henaff, whose work on the Coligny Calendar we have already discussed. Henaff was a chemical engineer by profession who, from 1932 to 1945, became leader of the militant wing of the Breton independence movement Gwenn ha Du (black and white, from the colours of the Breton flag). His simple, militant approach to Breton independence – that whoever was against France was a friend to Brittany – caused him to make grave political miscalculations. Sentenced to death *in absentia* by the French Courts, he escaped into exile. He was a religious man, a philosopher, whose study on the Coligny Calendar, its interpretation and links with Stonehenge astronomical construction, was first published in *Zeitschrift für Celtische Philologie* (1943). He came to reject Christianity and during the 1930s tried to organize a community who would live by a set of principles which he saw as Druidic. He spent the last forty years of his life in exile, mainly in Ireland, making further detailed examinations of native Celtic sources seeking to resurrect Druidical philosophy. To many who met him he was known as '*le Grand Druide*'.

Where Henaff's own creativity came into play was in evolving what he termed as the *Giam–Sam* philosophy, after the Celtic names for 'winter' and 'summer'. These terms he took from the Coligny Calendar, that is, in Gaulish, *Giamon* and *Samon* which, in Old Irish become *Gaim* and *Sam*. Henaff had spent some time in Japan and the *Giam–Sam* idea was based on the Chinese *Yin* and *Yang* concept of the negative and positive principles, for the words also meant 'shady' and 'sunny', so the Celtic terms were a close equivalent. *Yin* was female, massive, cold, negative, while *Yang* is male, active, hot, positive. *Yin* and *Yang* complement and grow out of each other, unlike European dualism where light is good and darkness bad. Associated with the theory is that concept that five elements or processes govern human events (wood, metal, fire, water and earth) and that events are changed even as these elements alternate. Henaff started to use the Celtic equivalent *Giam* and *Sam* in about 1970. At face value the idea seems merely an import of Chinese philosophy rather than Indo-European concepts. Unfortunately, Henaff published little during his lifetime although he did leave a considerable body of unpublished work in the hands of a literary executor, Louis Feutren. According to Feutren, 'all through his writings, be they scientific, philosophic, historic etc. . . . he classifies and qualifies every statement by a parenthesis (*giam*) or (*sam*)'. But 'nowhere does he write about it'. He apparently offered no explanation for his decision to identify the *Yin* and *Yang* concept in Celtic belief.

While Henaff was the only thinker who radically sought to resurrect Celtic paganism, the Breton artist, Raphael (Rafig) Tullou (1909–1990) was certainly an advocate of revising 'the Celtic religion' for modern day usage. Firstly involved in Celtic Christianity, it was in 1932 that Tullou, also a militant supporter of the Breton independence movement, moved to the pre-Christian ideas. He launched *Kad* (Struggle) and also *Nemeton* (Sanctuary) while running Koun Breizh (Breton Remembrance), an association for the defence of Brittany's national artistic heritage, which he had launched in 1934. Considered by some, like Henaff, to be a mere poseur when it came to paganism and too heavily influenced by Christian thinking, Tullou's movement was confined to the small group who subscribed to his magazines.

With the onset of the 1960s 'Hippies' and 'Alternative Religions', the Druids were fair game again. The Druids were called upon as the prototypes of many 'New Age' ideas and credos. It was almost inevitable that the Druids and ancient pre-Christian Celtic religion were waiting to be claimed by the new interest in 'witchcraft' which began to rise in the 1960s. One of the most popular media 'witches' was Sybyl Leek, whose books on 'witchcraft' together with Press and media interviews made her a bestselling author. In *The Complete Art of Witchcraft* (1975) she claimed to follow the Old Religion 'very closely allied to Celtic witchcraft'. Yes; 'Celtic witchcraft' had suddenly arrived out of all the mishmash and hocus-pocus of Druidism. 'Many covens in Germany and France follow the Celtic form of witchcraft,' Sybyl Leek assured her readers. In 1978 Gavin and Yvonne Frost produced *A Witch's Guide to Life* stating: 'we call our religion Celtic Witchcraft'. An explanation shows their scholarship deeply rooted in the sixteenth and seventeenth century balderdash with a mind-blowing reinterpretation of history; ie 'In 2000 BC or so, a great race of Celtic horsemen came out of the steppes of western China, flowing through northern Europe, conquering and civilising as they came. Later, they in their turn were driven northward by fresh conquerors. The remnants of these Celtic horsemen retreated to the hills, forests and lake villages of the far north, their last great stronghold, Glastonbury, being overrun in 52 BC by the invading Belgae.' One wonders who the authors thought the Belgae were, if not Celts, and what possible evidence they had for the idea of 'a last ditch stand' of the Celts in the vicinity of the site of Glastonbury in 52 BC (why 52 BC?); and why Glastonbury should be designated as the last stronghold of the Celts when Celtic nations and states have survived into modern times?

'Witchcraft' enthusiasts did not have the Druids all to themselves for very long. In 'The Celtic Spirit in the New Age', a Toronto based astrologer, Alexander Blair-Ewart, was among the first to conjure the Druids to 'New Age Christianity'. 'Because of its Druidic past, Celtic culture was, of all the cultural groups of early Europe, the most advanced spiritually and the best equipped in an inner sense for the encounter with Christianity,' he argued.

> In the twentieth century, in this dark age of technology and materialism, esoteric Christianity has become as elusive as it once was in a former dark age of dying empire and savagery. Esoteric Christianity is the undying Light of the world, the most exalted spiritual revelation, the deepest mystery of the ages. Ancient Celtic man turned to it in complete freedom from a spiritual tradition as rich and profound, though in a different way, as the ancient Judaic life through which Christianity entered the world. There has never been anything compulsive or mandatory about esoteric Christianity. It is the free choice of free individuals and this is part of the reason why it has a future as the spiritual path of emancipated humanity. A Celtic humanity still knows the meaning of love, the action of love in culture, which is compassion. A higher light shines in Celtic poetry, language, music, a richer mystical dimension.

Other writers began to invoke the Druids to a new form of Christianity, or rather a rebirth of old Celtic Christianity. Shirley Toulson's *The Celtic Alternative: A Study of the Christianity we have Lost* (1987) and *The Celtic Year* (1993) would wrest the Druids firmly back into the Christian camp. 'From their Druidic forebears the Celtic Christians also inherited a love of the land, and a feeling of the unity of all creation. In this aspect, the philosophy embedded in the Celtic church bore a strong resemblance to that of the Orthodox church today, which emphasises the sanctity of matter.' She sees the Druid's spirituality through its Celtic Christian offspring as having its nearest parallel in Buddhism and thinks Buddhism is actually the route to an understanding of the Celtic mind. 'Above all, we will come close to Celtic thinking as, inspired by the obvious threats to the survival of our planet, we learn to be constantly mindful of the part we have to play in the divinity of the universe.'

For a wild period, however, it seemed that whatever the subject, if it was esoteric, then all one needed to do was put the word 'Celtic' in front of it and people would sit up and take note. Witchcraft, esoteric Christianity and even the fad of the mysterious 'corn circles' of the late 1980s were given Celtic glosses. While Erich von Daniken, famous for his argument that the Earth has been visited by alien beings who constructed some of the ancient megaliths in *Chariots of the Gods* (1969) did not actually have Druids arriving in space ships, one had the impression that even this picture would be acceptable to the wilder 'Celtic esoterics'.

The current author once made a long journey to attend a talk by a well-known archaeologist whose title was 'The Celtic Zodiac'. As the talk unfolded the author sat bemused for the talk was mainly about the then mysterious appearances of 'corn circles', flattened circles in corn fields mainly in the west country of England. It had precious little to do with the Celts and nothing to do at all with a 'Celtic Zodiac'. In the interval, the author had the temerity to ask the lecturer why he had chosen his title which didn't relate to the talk. With disarming candour, the speaker admitted that by tagging the word 'Celtic' onto his title he was assured of getting a larger attendance than would normally turn out.

Less cynical enthusiasts conjuring Druids and their Celtic culture to 'New Age' philosophy continue to produce the most amazing plethora of works. Colin Murray, in a book completed after his death by his wife Liz, *The Celtic Tree Oracle: A System of Divination*, 1988, claimed 'the Druids also had a secretive hieratic alphabet, a special method of communicating with each other, limited to mnemonic learning by question and answer, and embodying special symbolic uses, by and large lost today. This was an early Irish alphabet in use from about 600 BC – the Ogham, or Beth Luis Nuin, alphabet.' At least Murray had more knowledge of Celtic culture than Gavin and Yvonne Frost. But to speculate about the ancient Celtic culture one can only do so from a basis of what is known and not from what one would wish to know. There is simply no evidence that Ogham was used prior to the third or fourth centuries AD as much as one would like to find Ogham records from 600 BC.

The current *guru* (or should that be *múintíd* or *athro*, to use the old Celtic equivalents?) in this new resurrection of Druidic 'teaching', conjuring them as Zen Masters of the Celtic World, is John Matthews whose books *The Celtic Shaman* (1991) and *Taliesin: Shamanism and the Bardic Mysteries in Britain and Ireland* (1991) display a deeper knowledge of Celtic sources than most work in this area. Matthews seems to be in the Evan Evans tradition in which he admits his work is 'undertaken in the full realisation that much of the material is speculative. Nevertheless, I am satisfied that a close scrutiny of extant Celtic records, together with the texts and later commentaries, shows beyond reasonable doubt that Celtic shamanism did exist, and that elements of it are still to be found in more recent folk-culture.'

Celtic and Druidic 'truths' of every description – from 'arcane knowledge', 'karmic destiny', 'the true path', to 'mystic awareness' – are solicited in the commercial deluge of New Age philosophies. The Druids and the Celts were there when our seventeenth and eighteenth century ancestors sought 'Romanticism' as a counter-balance to the 'Age of Reason' and industrialization. It is not surprising that they are still being reinvented at this time because, in our sad and sorry contemporary world, people still want a quick fix on spirituality; because people, in the quest for truth and meaning in life, which seems the perennial human drive, prefer simple answers. It is easier to accept the cosy pictures of non-existent romantic Celts and Druids rather than ponder the uncomfortable realities.

I have encountered many calling themselves 'New Age Celts', usually not Celtic by culture, preaching harmony with Nature, fighting to protect endangered species of animal and plant life, who have stared in incomprehension when it has been pointed out that the Celtic civilization itself is struggling in a last ditch attempt to survive in the modern world. Only two-and-a-half million people out of the sixteen millions living within the Celtic areas still speak a Celtic language. Language is the highest form of cultural expression. The decline of the Celtic languages has been the result of a carefully established policy of brutal persecution and suppression. If these Celtic languages and cultures die then it will be no natural phenomenon. It will be as the result of centuries of a careful policy of ethnocide. Once the languages disappear then Celtic civilization will cease to exist and the cultural continuum of three thousand years will come to an end. The world will be the poorer for one more lost culture. What price is 'spiritual awareness' with the ancient Celts when we have stood by and allowed their modern descendants to perish? This is the uncomfortable reality for those who would conjure Druids and ancient Celts to their new concepts of 'spiritual enlightenment' while ignoring the plight of the modern Celts.

I started this work by suggesting as a sub-title: 'An Introductory Argument'. During my argument I have posed some questions; I have endeavoured to make them the *right* questions, which is, as Lévi-Strauss implies, more important than simply attempting to find answers. There is, he says, no final truth. Hopefully, though, I have provided a few of the right answers as well; or, at least, pointed along the paths to where such truths might be found. When all is said and done, however, one is aware, along with Lévi-Strauss, of fallibility when dealing with a subject which has its roots at the dawn of civilization.

The German novelist and essayist, Thomas Mann (1875–1955), began *Die Geschichten Jaakobs* (1933, trs. The Tales of Jacob), the first novel in his famous tetralogy *Joseph und seine Brüder* (Joseph and his Brothers – 1933/43) with the observation: 'Very deep is the well of the past. Should we not call it bottomless? . . . The deeper we sound, the further down into the lower world of the past we probe and press, the more do we find that the earliest foundations of humanity, its history and culture, reveal themselves unfathomable.'

Select Bibliography

Because my purpose is to present a book for the general reader, I have, as in some of my previous works, dispensed with copious footnotes. Where sources obviously need crediting, I have made this clear within the body of the text. The following bibliography comprises 'secondary source' material. Primary sources, that is texts and translations of 'Classical works', such as those in Greek and Latin, as well as insular Celtic sources, in Irish and Welsh, have not been listed here. While the original sources are identified within the text, the choice of text and translations, for those who wish to consult them, is left to the reader from the many versions now available. Some excellent translations of Greek and Latin sources are currently to be found in the 'Penguin Classics' library.

Books

Ancient Laws of Ireland. 6 vols. Commissioners for Publishing the Ancient Laws and Institutions of Ireland, Dublin (1865–1879).

ALLCROFT, A.H. *The Circle and the Cross*, 2 vols., Macmillan, London, 1927.

ANDERSON, M.O. *Kings and Kingship in Early Scotland*, Scottish Academic Press, Edinburgh, 1980.

ANWYL, Edward. *Celtic Religion in Pre-Christian Times*, A. Constable, London, 1906.

BARTRUM, P.C. *Early Welsh Genealogical Tracts*, University of Wales Press, Cardiff, 1966.

BERGIN, O. *Irish Bardic Poetry*, Dublin Institute for Advanced Studies, Dublin, 1970.

BERTRAND, A. *Archéologie celtique et gauloise*, Paris, 1876.

BERTRAND, A. *Religion des gaulois*, Paris, 1897.

BLOOMFIELD, M.W. and DUNN, C.W. *The Role of the Poet in Early Societies*, D.S. Brewer, Cambridge, 1989.

BONWICK, James. *Irish Druids and Old Irish Religions*, Griffin Farran & Co, London, 1894.

BOWEN, E.G. *The Settlement of Celtic Saints in Wales*, University of Wales Press, Cardiff, 1956.

BROMWICH, Rachel. *Trioedd Ynys Prydein: The Welsh Triads*, University of Wales Press, Cardiff, 1961.

BRYANT, Sophie. *Liberty, Order and Law Under Native Irish Rule*, Harding & Moore Ltd., London, 1923.

BURTON, John Hill. *History of Scotland*, Edinburgh, 1853.

BURY, John B. *Conversion of the Kelts*, Cambridge Medieval History, vol. II, Cambridge, 1911–32.

BYRNE, Francis John. *Irish Kings and High Kings*, B.T. Batsford, London, 1973.

BRUNAUX, Jean Louis. *The Celtic Gauls: Gods, Rites and Sanctuaries*, Seaby, London, 1988.

CAMPBELL, John Francis. *The Celtic Dragon Myth* (introduction by George Henderson), John Grant, Edinburgh, 1911.

CAMPBELL, Joseph. *Transformation of Myth Through Time*, Harper & Row, New York, USA. 1990.

CARMICHAEL, Alexander. *Carmina Gadelica*, 2 vols., Norman MacLeod, Edinburgh, 1900 (revised, 5 vols., Oliver & Boyd, Edinburgh, 1928).

CHADWICK, H.M. *The Heroic Age*, Cambridge University Press, Cambridge, 1967.

CHADWICK, H.M. and Nora K. *The Growth of Literature*, 3 vols., Cambridge University Press, Cambridge, 1932–40.

CHADWICK, Nora K. *The Druids*, University of Wales Press, Cardiff, 1966.

CHADWICK, Nora K. *The Celts*, Pelican, London, 1970.

CHILDE, Vere Gordon. *The Dawn of European Civilization*, Kegan Paul, London, 1925.

CHILDE, Vere Gordon. *The Aryans: A Study of Indo-European Origins*, Kegan Paul, London, 1926.

CHILDE, Vere Gordon. *The Danube in Prehistory*, Clarendon Press, Oxford, 1929.

CONDREN, Mary. *The Serpent and the Goddess: Women, Religion and Power in Celtic Ireland*, T. & T. Clarke, Edinburgh, 1990.

CONNELLAN, O. ed. *The Proceedings of the Great Bardic Institution*, J. O'Daly, Dublin, 1860.

COOKE, William, *An Enquiry into the Druidical and Patriarchal Religion*, London, 1754.

CRAMPTON, Patrick. *Stonehenge of the Kings*, John Baker, London, 1967.

DALYELL, John Graham. *Darker Superstitions of Scotland*, Waugh Innes, Edinburgh, 1834.

DANIEL, Sir John. *The Philosophy of Ancient Britain*, Williams Norgate, London, 1927.

DAVIDSON, H. ed. *The Seer in Celtic and Other Traditions*, John Donald, Edinburgh, 1989.

DAVIDSON, Hilda Ellis. *The Lost Beliefs of Northern Europe*, Routledge, London, 1993.

DAVIES, Edward. *Celtic Researches*, London, 1804.

DAVIES, Edward. *The Mythology and Rites of the British Druids*, J. Booth, London, 1809.

DE JUBAINVILLE, Henri d'Arbois. *Les Druides*, Paris, 1906.

DE PAOR, Liam. *Saint Patrick's World: The Christian Culture of Ireland's Apostolic Age*, Four Courts Press, Dublin, 1993.

DE VRIES, *La Religion des Celtes*, Paris, 1963.

DILLON, Myles ed. *Early Irish Society*, Mercier Press, Cork, 1963.

DILLON, Myles and CHADWICK, Nora. *The Celtic Realms*, Weidenfeld & Nicolson, London, 1967.

DILLON, Myles. *Celt and Hindu*. The Osborn Bergin Memorial Lecture III, University College, Dublin, 1973.

DILLON, Myles. *Celts and Aryans*, Indian Institute of Advanced Studies, Simla, India, 1975.

DUVAL, P.M. *Les dieux de la Gaule*, Paris, 1976.

ELDER, Elisabeth Hill. *Celt, Druid and Culdee*, Covenant Publishing, London, 1962.

ELLIS, Peter Berresford. *Celtic Inheritance*, Muller, London, 1985.

ELLIS, Peter Berresford. *A Dictionary of Irish Mythology*, Constable, 1987.

ELLIS, Peter Berresford. *The Celtic Empire: The First Millennium of Celtic History 1000 BC–AD 51*, Constable, London, 1990.

ELLIS, Peter Berresford. *A Dictionary of Celtic Mythology*, Constable, London, 1992.

ELLIS, Peter Berresford. *Celt and Saxon: The Struggle for the Supremacy of Britain AD 410–937*, Constable, London, 1993.

ELLIS, T.P. *Welsh Tribal Law and Custom*, Oxford University Press, Oxford, 1926.

ELLIS, T.P. and LLOYD, John. *The Mabinogion*, Oxford University Press, Oxford, 1929.

EVANS, D. Ellis. *Gaulish Personal Names*, Oxford University Press, Oxford, 1967.

EVANS, Estyn. *Prehistoric and Early Christian Ireland*, Routledge, London, 1966.

EVANS, J. Gwenogfryn ed. *Facsimile and Text of the Book of Taliesin*, Llanbedrog, 1910.

FERGUSON, J. *Pelagius*, Cambridge University Press, Cambridge, 1956.

FILIP, Jan. *Celtic Civilization and its Heritage*, Publishing House of the Czechoslovak Academy of Sciences and ARTIA, Prague, 1960.

FRAZER, James George. *The Golden Bough; a study in comparative religion*, 2 vols. Macmillan & Co, London, 1890 (revised 3 vol, 1900).

FRICK, J.G. *Commentatio de Druidis*, Ulm, 1744.

GANTZ, Jeffrey. *The Mabinogion*, Penguin, London, 1976.

GANTZ, Jeffrey. *Early Irish Myths and Sagas*, Penguin, London, 1981.

GINNELL, Laurence *The Brehon Laws: A Legal Handbook*, T. Fisher Unwin, London, 1894.

GOMME, George Laurence. *Ethnology in Folklore*, Modern Science, London, 1891.

GOMME, George Laurence. *A Dictionary of British Folk Lore*, David Nutt, London, 1894.

GOUGAUD, Louis *Christianity in Celtic Lands*, Sheed & Ward, London, 1932.

GRAHAM Hugh. *The Early Irish Monastic Schools*, Talbot Press, Dublin, 1923.

GREEN, Miranda. *The Wheel as a Cult Symbol in the Romano-Celtic World*, Latoms, Brussels, 1984.

GREEN, Miranda. *The Gods of the Celts*, Alan Sutton, Gloucester, 1986.

GREEN, Miranda *Symbol & Image in Celtic religious Art*, Routledge, London, 1989.

GREEN, Miranda. *Animals in Celtic Life and Myth*, Routledge, London, 1992.

GREEN, Miranda, *Dictionary of Celtic Myth and Legend*, Thames & Hudson, London, 1992.

GREGORY, Lady Augusta. *Gods and Fighting Men: The Story of the Tuatha De Danaan and of the Fianna of Ireland*, London, 1904.

GUENEBAULT, J. *Le Réveil de l'antique tombeau de Chyndonax, Prince des Vacies, Druides, Celtiges*, Dijonnois, Paris, 1623.

GWYNN, E. *The Metrical Dindshenchas*, Royal Irish Academy, Dublin, 1913.

HARDINGE, Leslie. *The Celtic Church in Britain*, Church Historical Society, SPCK, London, 1972.

HASLEHURST, R.S.T. *The Works of Fastidius*, Society of SS Peter & Paul, Westminster, 1927.

HAWKINS, Gerald S. (with John B. White) *Stonehenge Decoded*, Souvenir Press, London, 1966.

HENDERSON, George. *Survivals in Belief among the Celts*, J. Maclehose, Glasgow, 1911.

HENDERSON, William. *Notes on the Folklore of the Northern Counties of England and the Borders*, London, 1866.

HERBERT, Algernon. *An Essay on the Neo Druidic Heresy in Britannia*, London, 1838.

HIGGINS, G. *The Celtic Druids*, London, 1829.

HOLMES, George. *Sketches of some of the Southern Counties of Ireland collected during a tour of 1797*, Longmans, London, 1801.

Howe, Dr E. Graham. *The Mind of the Druid*, Skoob Books Publishing, London, 1989.

Hubert, Henri. *The Rise of the Celts*, Kegan Paul, Trench and Trubner, London, 1934.

Hubert, Henri. *The Greatness and Decline of the Celts*, Kegan Paul, Trench and Trubner, London, 1934.

Hull, Eleanor. *Pagan Ireland*, (vol. 1 of *Epochs of Irish History*), Dublin, 1904.

Humphreys, Emyr. *The Taliesin Tradition*, Black Raven Press, 1983.

Hutton, R. *The Pagan Religions of the Ancient British Isles: Their Nature and Legacy*, Oxford University Press, Oxford, 1991.

Hyde, Douglas. *A Literary History of Ireland*, T. Fisher Unwin, London, 1899.

Jackson, Kenneth H. *A Celtic Miscellany*, Routledge & Kegan Paul, London, 1951.

Jackson, Kenneth H. *Language and History in Early Britain*, Edinburgh University Press, Edinburgh, 1953.

Jackson, Kenneth H. *The Oldest Tradition: A Window on the Iron Age*, Cambridge University Press, Cambridge, 1964.

James, David. *The Patriarchal Religion of Britain*, London, 1836.

Jamieson, John. *An Historical Account of the Ancient Culdees of Iona . . .*, J. Ballantyne, Edinburgh, 1811.

Jarman, A.O.H. and Jarman, G.R. *A History of Welsh Literature*, Christopher Davies, Llandybie, Wales, 1974.

Jenkins, Dafydd, and Owen, Morfydd E. *The Welsh Law of Women*, University of Wales Press, Cardiff, 1980.

Jones, Edward. *The Bardic Museum*, A. Strahan, London, 1802.

Jones, O. Williams, E. and Pughe, W.O. *The Myvyrian Archaeology of Wales*, 3 vols., London, 1801–1808.

Jones, T.G. *Welsh Folk-Lore and Folk-Custom*, Methuen, London, 1930.

Joyce, P.W. *A Social History of Ancient Ireland*, 2 vols., Longmans, Green & Co, London, 1903.

Jullian, Camille. *Recherches sur la religion gaulois*. Bibliotheque de l' Université du Midi, Bordeaux, 1903.

Jullian, Camille. *Histore de la Gaule*, Paris, 1908.

Kavuratna, Avinash Chandra. *Charaka-Samhita* (trs. into English) Calcutta, 1892–1914.

Kelly, Fergus. *A Guide to Early Irish Law*, Dublin Institute for Advanced Studies, Dublin, 1988.

Kendrick, Thomas Downing. *The Druids: A Study in Keltic Prehistory*, Methuen & Co, London, 1927.

Kinsella, Thomas. *The Táin*, Dolmen Press, Dublin, 1969.

LAING, Lloyd. *Celtic Britain*, Routledge & Kegan Paul, London, 1979.

LEJEUNE, Michel. *Lepontica*, Monographies Linguistiques, Société d'Édition, Paris, 1971.

LE ROUX, Françoise. *Les Druides*, (Mythes et religions, No. 41) Paris, 1961.

LOFMARK, C. *Bards and Heroes*, Llanerch Enterprises, Llanerch, 1898.

LOOMIS, R.S. *The Grail from Celtic Myth to Christian Symbol*, Columbia University Press, USA, 1963.

LOOMIS, R.S. *Celtic Myth and Arthurian Romance*, Columbia University Press, USA, 1926.

LOT, Ferdinand. *La Gaule: les fondements ethniques, sociaux et politiques de la nation francaise*, Paris, 1847.

MCBAIN, Alexander. *Celtic Mythology and Religion*, Eneas Mackay, Stirling, 1917.

MACCANA, Proinsias. *Celtic Mythology*, Hamlyn, London, 1970.

MACCULLOCH, John Arnott. *The Religion of the Ancient Celts*, T. & T. Clarke, Edinburgh, 1911.

MACCULLOCH, John Arnott. *Celtic Mythology*, Marshall Jones, Boston, USA, 1918.

MACCULLOCH, John Arnott. *The Celtic and Scandinavian Religions*, Hutchinson's University Library, London, 1948.

MACKINLAY, J.M. *Folklore of Scottish Lochs and Springs*, W. Hodge & Co, Glasgow, 1893.

MACNEILL, Eoin. *Phases of Irish History*, M.H. Gill, Dublin, 1919.

MACNEILL, Eoin. *Early Irish Laws and Institutions*, Burns Oates Washbourne, Dublin, 1935.

MCNEILL, F.M. *The Silver Bough*, Canongate, Edinburgh, 1989.

MANN, N.R. *The Celtic Power Symbols*, Triskele Press, Glastonbury, 1987.

MARKLE, Jean. *Women of the Celts*, Gordon Cremonesi, London, 1975.

MARTIN, Martin. *A Description of the Western Islands of Scotland*, A. Bell, London, 1703.

MATTHEWS, Catriona. *Mabon and the Mysteries of Britain*, Arkana, 1989.

MATTHEWS, John. *The Song of Taliesin*, Unwin Hyman, London, 1991.

MATTHEWS, John. *Taliesin: Shamanism and the Bardic Mysteries in Britain and Ireland*, The Aquarian Press, London, 1991.

MATTHEWS, John. *The Celtic Shaman*, Element Books Ltd, Dorset, 1991.

MEILLET, Paul Jules Antoine. *Les dialects Indo-Européens*, Société de la Linguiste, Paris, 1908 (trs. *The Indo European Dialects*, University of Alabama, USA, 1967).

MEYER, Kuno. *The Triads of Ireland*, vol. XIII, Todd Lecture Series, Royal Irish Academy, Dublin, 1906.

MILES, D. *The Royal National Eisteddfod of Wales*, Christopher Davies, Swansea, 1977.

MONCK MASON, Henry J. *Religion of the Ancient Irish Saints Before* AD *600*, Dublin, 1938.

MOORE, A.W. *Folklore of the Isle of Man*, David Nutt, London, 1891.

MORGANWG, Iolo. *The Triads of Britain*, Wildwood House, 1977.

MURPHY, Gerard. *Glimpses of Gaelic Ireland*, Dublin, 1948.

MURRAY, Liz and Colin, *The Celtic Tree Oracle*, Rider, London, 1988.

NASH, D.W. *Taliesin or the Bards and Druids of Britain*, J. Russell Smith, London, 1858.

NICHOLAS, R. *The Book of Druidry*, Aquarian Press, London, 1990.

NORRIS, John. *The Age of Arthur*, Weidenfeld & Nicholson, London, 1973.

O'BOYLE, S. *Ogam, the Poet's Secret*, Gilbert Dalton, Dublin, 1980.

O'CURRY, Eugene. *On the Manners and Customs of the Ancient Irish*, ed. W.K. Sullivan, 3 vols., Williams Norgate, Dublin, 1873.

O'CURRY, Eugene. *Lectures on the Manuscript Materials of Ancient Irish History*, Williams Norgate, Dublin, 1878.

O'DRISCOLL, Robert ed. *The Celtic Conciousness*, MacClelland Stewart, Toronto, 1981.

O'GRADY, Standish James. *Early Bardic Literature in Ireland*, Sampson Low, London, 1879.

O'GRADY, Standish Hayes. *Silva Gadelica*, 2 vols., Williams Norgate, Dublin, 1892.

Ó HÓGÁIN, Dáithí. *Myth, Legend and Romance: An Encyclopaedia of the Irish Folk Tradition*, Ryan Publishing, London, 1990.

OOSTEN, J.G. *The War of the Gods: The Social Code in Indo-European Mythology*, Routledge & Kegan Paul, 1985.

O'RAHILLY, Thomas F. *Early Irish History and Mythology*, Dublin Institute for Advanced Studies, Dublin, 1944.

OWEN, Aneurin, *Ancient Laws and Institutes of Wales*, English Records Commission, London, 1841.

OWEN, Aidan Lloyd. *The Famous Druids; a survey of three centuries of English literature on the Druids*, Oxford University Press, Oxford, 1962.

PARRY, Thomas trs. H. Idris Bell. *A History of Welsh Literature*, The Clarendon Press, Oxford, 1955.

PATCH, H.R. *The Otherworld*, Harvard University Press, Cambridge, Mass, USA, 1950.

PENNANT, Thomas. *A Tour in Scotland and a voyage to the Hebrides in 1769*, Chester, 1771.

PIGGOTT, Stuart. *The Druids*, Thames & Hudson, London, 1968.

PIGGOTT, Stuart. *Ancient Britons and the Antiquarian Imagination*, Thames & Hudson, 1989.

PIM, Herbert M. *A Short History of Celtic Philosophy*, Dundalk, 1920.

POWELL, T.G.E. *The Celts*, Thames & Hudson, 1958.

PROBERT, William. *The Ancient Laws of Cambria . . . to which are added the historical Triads of Britain translated from the Welsh*, London, 1823–28.

RAFERTY, Joseph ed. *The Celts*, Mercier Press, Cork, 1964.

RANKIN, H.D. *Celts and the Classical World*, Croom Helm, London, 1987.

RAOULT, Michael. *Les Druides: Les societés initiatiques Celtiques Contemporaines*, Editions du Rocher, Monaco, 1988.

REES, Alwyn and Brinley. *Celtic Heritage*, Thames & Hudson, London, 1961.

REINACH, Saloman. *Cultes, mythes et religions*, 4 vols., Paris, 1905–12. (trs. *Cults, Myths and Religions*, London, 1912).

RHŶS, John. *Lectures on Welsh Philology*, London, 1877.

RHŶS, John. *Lectures on the Origin and Growth of Religion as Illustrated by Celtic Heathendom*, Williams & Norgate, Dublin, 1888.

RHŶS, John *Celtic Folk-lore*, 2 vols., Oxford University Press, Oxford, 1901.

RHŶS. John. *Notes on the Coligny Calendar*, Henry Froude, London, 1910.

RICHARDS, Melville. *The Laws of Hywel Dda*, Liverpool University Press, Liverpool, 1954.

ROWLANDS, Henry *Mona Antiqua Restaurata*, London, 1723.

ROLLESTON, T.W. *Myths and Legends of the Celtic Race*, George G. Harrap, London, 1911.

ROSS, Anne. *Pagan Celtic Britain*, Routledge & Kegan Paul, London, 1967.

ROSS, Anne, and ROBINS, Don. *The Life and Death of a Druid Prince*, Rider, London, 1989.

RUSSELL, Bertrand. *A History of Western Philosophy*, George Allen & Unwin, London, 1946.

RUST, J. *Druidism Exhumed*, Edmonston & Douglas, Edinburgh, 1871.

RUTHERFORD, Ward. *The Druids and their Heritage*, Gordon Cremonesi, London, 1978.

SALMON, John. *The Ancient Irish Church*, Gill & Son, Dublin, 1897.

SEBBILOT, Paul Yves. *Traditions et superstitions de la Haute Bretagne*, 2 vols., Paris, 1882.

SEBBILOT, Paul Yves. *Le Folklore de France*, Paris, 1904–07.

SEYMOUR, St John Drelincourt. *Irish Witchcraft and Demonology*, Hodges Figgis, Dublin, 1913.

SHARKEY, John. *Celtic Mysteries*, Thames & Hudson, London, 1975.

SJOESTEDT Marie-Louise. (afterwards Sjoestedt-Jonval) *Gods and Heroes of the Celts*, (trs. by Myles Dillon) Methuen & Co, London, 1949.

SKENE, William Forbes. *The Chronicles of the Picts and Scots*, Edinburgh, 1867.

SKENE, William Forbes. *Celtic Scotland*, 3 vols., Edinburgh, 1876–80.

SMIDDY, Richard. *An Essay on the Druids, the Ancient Churches and the Round Towers of Ireland*, Dublin, 1871.

SMITH, Thomas. *Syntagama de Druidum moribus ac institutis*, London, 1644.

SPAAN, D.B. *The Otherworld in Early Irish Literature*, University of Michigan Press, Ann Arbor, USA, 1969.

SPENCE, Lewis. *The History and Origins of Druidism*, Rider & Co, London, 1949.

SPENCE, Lewis. *The Magic Arts in Celtic Britain*, Rider & Co. London, 1945.

SPOTTISWOOD, John. *History of the Church of Scotland*, London, 1655. (Revised edition, London, 1677.)

SQUIRE, Charles. *Celtic Myth and Legends*, Gresham Publishing, London, 1912.

STOKES, Whitley ed. *Three Middle Irish Homilies on the Lives of SS Patrick, Bridgit and Columba*, Calcutta, 1877.

STOKES, Whitley. *The Tripartite Life of Patrick*, 2 vols. (*Rerum Britannicarum medii aeri Scriptores*) London, 1887.

STUKELEY, William. *The History of the Religion and Temples of the Druids*, London, 1729.

STUKELEY, William. *Stonehenge, a temple restored to the British Druids*, London, 1740.

STUKELEY, William. *Abury, a Temple of the British Druids*, London, 1743.

TATLOCK, J.S.P. *The Legendary History of Britain*, Gordian Press, 1979.

THOMAS, Charles. *Celtic Britain*, Thames & Hudson, London, 1986.

THOMAS, Charles. *Christianity in Roman Britain to AD 500*, Batsford, London, 1981.

THURNEYSEN, R.; POWER, Nancy; DILLON, Myles; MULCHRONE, Kathleen; BINCHEY, D.; KNOCH, August; RYAN, John. *Studies in Early Irish Law*, Royal Irish Academy, Dublin, 1936.

TOLAND, John. *A critical History of the Celtic religion and learning containing an account of the Druids*, Lackington & Co, London, 1740 (?). Reprinted as *Toland's History of the Druids . . .*, notes by R. Huddleston, Montrose, 1814.

TOULSON, Shirley. *The Celtic Year*, Element, Dorset, 1993.

VENDRYES, Joseph. *La Religion des Celtes*, Paris, 1948.

WAITE, Arthur Edward. *The Hidden Church of the Holy Grail*, Rebman, London, 1909.

WARREN, F.E. *The Liturgy and Ritual of the Celtic Church*, Clarendon Press, Oxford, 1881.

WIESE, H. & FRICKE H. *Handbuch des Druiden Ordens*, Munich, 1931.

WISE, T.A. *History of Paganism in Caledonia*, London, 1887.

WILLIS, Roy, general editor, *World Mythology*, Duncan Baird Publishers, London, 1993.

WENTZ, W.Y. Evans. *The Fairy Faith in Celtic Countries*, Oxford University Press, Oxford, 1911.

WOOD-MARTIN, W.G. *Pagan Ireland*, London, 1895.

WOOD-MARTIN, W.G. *Traces of the Elder Faiths of Ireland*, 2 vols., London, 1902.

WRIGHT, Dudley. *Druidism: the ancient faith of Britain*, E.J. Burrow, London, 1924.

ZIMMER, Heinrich. *Altindisches Leben: Die Cultur Vedischen Arier nach den Samhitach*, Berlin, 1879.

ZIMMER, Heinrich. *Pelagius in Ireland*, Berlin, 1901.

ZIMMER, Heinrich. *The Celtic Church in Britain and Ireland*, trs. by A. Meye, David Nutt, London 1902.

Articles

BLAIR-EWART, Alexander. 'The Celtic Spirit in the New Age', *The Celtic Consciousness*, ed. Robert O'Driscoll, Toronto, 1981.

BOBER, J.J. 'Cernunnos: origin and transformation of a Celtic divinity', *American Journal of Archaeology*, No. 55.

BOUESSEL DU BOURG, Yann. 'Death of R. Tullou', *Carn* No. 70, Summer, 1990.

BOURNE, Harry. 'A View of the Origins of Druidism', *London Celt*, Winter, 1993

CAMPBELL, Joseph. 'Indian Reflections in the Castle of the Grail', in *The Celtic Consciousness*, ed. Robert O'Driscoll, Toronto, 1981.

DENNING, R. 'Druidism at Pontypridd', *Glamorgan Historian*, I. 1963, pp. 136–45.

DE WITT, N.J. 'The Druids and Romanization' *Transactions and Proceedings of the American Philological Association*, LXIX, 1938, pp. 319–321.

FEEHAN, Fanny. 'Suggested Links Between Eastern and Celtic Music', *The Celtic Consciousness*, ed. O'Driscoll, Toronto, 1981.

FUSTEL DE COULANGES, N.D. 'Comment le Druidisme a disparu', *Revue Celtique*, vol. IV, p. 44.

HENAFF, Neven. 'Le Calendrier Celtique', *Zeitschrift für Celtische Philologie*, vol. XXIII, No. 3 (1943).

HENAFF, Neven. 'The Stonehenge Druidic Calendar', *Carn* No. 45, Spring, 1985. pp. 18–19.

HENNESSY, W.M. 'The ancient Irish goddess of war', *Revue Celtique*, No. 1.

JOYNT, Maud. 'Airbacc Giunnae'. *Eriu*, No. X, 1928.

LAST, H. 'Rome and the Druids: A Note', *Journal Roman Studies*, XXXIX, 1949, pp. 1–5.

LEHMANN, R.P.M. 'Death and Vengeance in the Ulster Cycle', *Zeitschrift für Celtishe Philologie*, No. 43.

LEWIS, F.R. 'Gwerinn Ffristial a Thawlbwrdd', *Transactions of the Honourable Society of Cymmrodorion*, 1941.

MacCANA, Muiris. 'Astrology in Ancient Ireland' (unpublished paper given to the Irish Astrological Association, Dublin, 27 May 1991.

MacNEILL, E. 'On the Notation and Chronology of the Calender of Coligny', *Ériu* X 1926–28, pp. 1–67.

MacWHITE, E. 'Early Irish Board Games', *Éigse*, V (1945).

MOORE, Ramsey B. 'The Druids', *Proceedings IOMNHAS*, (Isle of Man Natural History and Archaeological Society), Douglas, 1956, p. 271f.

MORRIS-JONES, Sir John. 'Pre-Aryan Syntax in Insular Celtic', as an appendix to *The Welsh People* by J. Rhys and D. Brynmor-Jones.

PEATE, I.C. 'The Gorsedd of the Bards of Britain', *Antiquities*, XXXVIII, 1964. pp. 285–7.

POKORNY, Julius. 'The Origins of Druidism', *Celtic Review*, vol. V, No. 17 (1908/9). Also reprinted in the *Annual Report of the Smithsonian Institution*, 1910.

ROSS, Anne. 'The Human Head in Insular pagan Celtic Religion', *Proceedings of the Society of Antiquarians of Scotland*, No. 91.

TIERNEY, James J. 'The Celtic Ethnography of Posidonius', *Proceedings of the Royal Irish Academy*, Dublin, 1960.

TRAUBE, Ludwig. 'Quellen und Untersuchungen zur lateinischen Philologie' in *Sedulius Scottus*, Hellmann, Munich, 1906.

WAGNER, Heinrich. 'Origins of pagan Irish religion', *Zeitscrhift für Celtishe Philologie*, No. 38.

WAGNER, Heinrich. 'Near Eastern and African Connections with the Celtic World', in *The Celtic Consciousness*, ed. Robert O'Driscoll, Toronto, 1981.

Index